The Romanticism Handbook

Literature and Culture Handbooks

General Editor: Philip Tew, Brunel University, UK

Literature and Culture Handbooks are an innovative series of guides to major periods, topics and authors in British and American literature and culture. Designed to provide a comprehensive, one-stop resource for literature students, each handbook provides the essential information and guidance needed from the beginning of a course through to developing more advanced knowledge and skills.

The Eighteenth-Century Literature Handbook
Edited by Gary Day and Bridge Keegan

The Medieval British Literature Handbook
Edited by Daniel T. Kline

The Modernism Handbook
Edited by Philip Tew and Alex Murray

The Post-War British Literature Handbook
Edited by Katharine Cockin and Jago Morrison

The Renaissance Literature Handbook
Edited by Susan Bruce and Rebecca Steinberger

The Seventeenth-Century Literature Handbook
Edited by Robert C. Evans and Eric J. Sterling

The Shakespeare Handbook
Edited by Andrew Hiscock and Stephen Longstaffe

The Victorian Literature Handbook
Edited by Alexandra Warwick and Martin Willis

The Romanticism Handbook

Edited by

Sue Chaplin

and

Joel Faflak

continuum

Continuum International Publishing Group

The Tower Building 80 Maiden Lane, Suite 704
11 York Road New York
London SE1 7NX NY 10038

www.continuumbooks.com

British Library Cataloguing-in-Publication Data
A catalogue record for this book is available from the British Library.

ISBN: 978-1-4411-6402-5 (hardback)
　　　978-1-4411-9002-4 (paperback)

Library of Congress Cataloguing-in-Publication Data
A catalog record for this book is available from the Library of Congress.

Typeset by Fakenham Photosetting Ltd, Fakenham, Norfolk

Contents

Contents

Detailed Table of Contents

General Editor's Introduction

The Continuum *Literature and Culture Handbooks* series aims to support both students new to an area of study and those at a more advanced stage, offering guidance with regard to the major periods, topics and authors relevant to the study of various aspects of British and American literature and culture. The series is designed with an international audience in mind, based on research into today's students in a global educational setting. Each volume is concerned with either a particular historical phase or an even more specific context, such as a major author study. All of the chosen areas represent established subject matter for literary study in schools, colleges and universities, all are both widely taught and the subject of on-going research and scholarship. Each handbook provides a comprehensive, one-stop resource for literature students, offering essential information and guidance needed at the beginning of a course through to more advanced knowledge and skills for the student more familiar with the particular topic. These volumes reflect current academic research and scholarship, teaching methods and strategies, and also provide an outline of essential historical contexts. Written in clear language by leading internationally acknowledged academics, each book provides the following:

- Introduction to authors, texts, historical and cultural contexts
- Guides to key critics, concepts and topics
- Introduction to critical approaches, changes in the canon and new conceptual and theoretical issues, such as gender and ethnicity
- Case studies in reading literary and theoretical and critical texts
- Annotated bibliography (including websites), timeline, glossary of critical terms.

This student-friendly series as a whole has drawn its inspiration and structure largely from the latest principles of textbook design employed in other disciplines and subjects, creating an unusual and distinctive approach for the undergraduate arts and humanities field. This structure is designed to be user-friendly and it is intended that the layout can be easily navigated, with various points of cross-reference. Such clarity and straightforward approach should help students understand the material and in so doing guide them through the increasing academic difficulty of complex critical and theoretical approaches to Literary Studies. These handbooks serve as gateways to the particular field that is explored.

All volumes make use of a 'progressive learning strategy', rather than the traditional chronological approach to the subject under discussion so that they might relate more closely to the learning process of the student. This means that the particular volume offers material that will aid the student to approach the period or topic confidently in the classroom for the very first time (for example, glossaries, historical context, key topics and critics), as well as material that helps the student develop more advanced skills (learning how to respond actively to selected primary texts and analyze and engage with modern critical arguments in relation to such texts). Each volume includes a specially commissioned new critical essay by a leading authority in the field discussing current debates and contexts. The progression in the contents mirrors the progress of the undergraduate student from beginner to a more advanced level. Each volume is aimed primarily at undergraduate students, intending to offer itself as both a guide and a reference text that will reflect the advances in academic studies in its subject matter, useful to both students and staff (the latter may find the appendix on pedagogy particularly helpful).

We realise that students in the twenty first-century are faced with numerous challenges and demands; it is our intention that the Handbook series should empower its readers to become effective and efficient in their studies.

Philip Tew

Introduction: Defining Romanticism

Sue Chaplin and Joel Faflak

Students approaching the Romantic period for the first time (and under-graduate students of literature are certain to encounter the field in their first or second year) are likely to be presented with a difficulty that reflects wider tensions, contradictions and disputes within the discipline of Romanticism studies: how does one define the object of study? What exactly is 'Romanticism'? First of all (and this reflects difficulties of periodization generally within literary studies), the Romantic era lacks any firm historical definition. It does not begin and end with the coronation and death of a monarch, for example; nor does it derive its historical identity exclusively from some defining event, such as the Restoration or the English Civil War. Indeed, attempts to fix the historical time-frame of the Romantic period invar-iably reveal something of the literary and historical priorities of the critic or historian. For instance, the Romantic era is sometimes bounded by the dates 1770–1850. Not only is this a lengthy period, running in fact into the first two decades of the Victorian era, it also perhaps reveals something of what Jerome McGann has termed the 'ideology' of Romanticism: the fact that the difficulties of defining the period are symptomatic of the history of debates over *how* to define the period, both of which issues we shall take up below and in subsequent chapters (see Chapters Six and Seven especially). One reading of this symptom is the fact that we have come to define Romanticism historically, in terms of the lifespan of the poet traditionally regarded as one of the foremost writers of the movement – William Wordsworth. Another popular timeframe for this period is defined by the revolutionary movements of the late eighteenth century (the American Revolution of 1776 and the French Revolution of 1789) and the reform movements of the mid-nineteenth century, beginning with the passing of the first Reform Act in 1832.

Even more recently, because of arguments that Romanticism marks a clear development out of rather than a radical break from Enlightenment ideas, we have begun to speak of a Romantic century that runs from 1750 to 1850. Consequently there has also been some debate about Romanticism vs. romanticism, Romantic vs. romantic. One of the things that the lower case indicates is a shift away from privileging historical or literary designations and towards critiquing the ideological implications that come with deploying such designations. Despite these ambiguities, most critics and historians still tend to agree that the British Romantic movement is in its early stages at least by the time of the storming of the Bastille in July 1789, and that it is relatively over by the publication of Tennyson's *Poems, Chiefly Lyrical* in 1830, by the 1832 Reform Act, or at the latest by the accession of Victoria in 1837, Wordsworth's 1850 death marking a symbolic coda to this trajectory. These are the parameters we shall follow for this Handbook, although we have extended the historical timeline at the end of this chapter back to 1776 to give our reader some sense of the historical, literary, and cultural framework from which British Romanticism emerges.

If Romanticism can be difficult to periodize, it can also be difficult to conceptualize. This is not to say that Romanticism lacks defining character-istics or that we cannot apply these characteristics with some certainty to the period's various literary achievements. But it *is* to say that one of these defining features is the fact that these features frequently contradict one another, and so paint the picture of a period often distinctly at odds with itself and its own desires, potentials and aims. The same could be said of any literary period, but seems distinctly apt when speaking of Romanticism and the idea of the Romantic. We need to ask, beginning with Romantic writers themselves, what factors were at stake when they set about self-fashioning their identities for their own and future audiences. One of the first usages of the word to define both an aesthetic practice and cultural movement is by the German philosopher and literary critic Friedrich Schlegel, leading figure of a group of intellectuals and artists who opposed both French politics and French thought. In his early writings Schlegel embraced the *ancient*, which was characterized by a kind of authentic striving towards the ideal, against the *modern*, about which there was something limited and strained (another German writer and philosopher, Friedrich Schiller, makes a similar distinction between the 'naive' and the 'sentimental'). Yet gradually Schlegel embraced the Romantic as deeply expressive of something authentic about the time's own nature. The word 'Romantic' had emerged by the early nineteenth century as a way of taking the pulse of the times, what the critic William Hazlitt in 1825 would call 'the spirit of the age'. But the word indicated more the experience of the period than any clear-cut self-definition, more the period's mood than its identity. As the editors of the Norton Anthology of the Romantic Period point out in their introduction: 'Writers working in the period 1785–1830 did not think of themselves as "Romantic"; the word was not applied until half a century later, by English historians' (p. 6). Indeed, as McGann, Anne Mellor and many other critics have observed, 'Romanticism' is in many ways the construction of critics and historians writing in the early to mid-twentieth century and seeking coherently to categorize and theorize about a diverse body of work according to certain carefully defined cultural and aesthetic reference points. This is not to deny that there are certain principles, movements and aspirations that broadly unite the writers and texts of the late eighteenth and early nineteenth centuries, but rather to acknowledge that traditional conceptualizations of Romanticism have tended to over-simplify, neglect or even deny the diverse contexts of the period.

From the beginning of this Romantic Literature Handbook, then, we need to be wary of the fact that when we engage in the definition or summarizing of what a literary period means, we also need to be aware of the fact that this meaning will inevitably be altered by our own perceptions about this period. These perceptions have been affected now by over two centuries of historical and critical interpretation, so that Romanticism itself – its actual historical occurrence and dramatic range of poems, novels, plays, essays and other texts written in the wake of this history – is like a palimpsest, to borrow Thomas De Quincey's famous metaphor, written over by layers of historical, cultural and critical expression, each successive layer inevitably obscuring, displacing or disfiguring the previous one. By using such metaphors, however, the period indicated a kind of self-consciousness about its own historical and cultural process that helps us in turn to understand how such metaphors are necessary, and necessarily at once hinder and help us in the task of re-collecting and re-interpreting what the period meant. It will be our task in this Handbook to try to read the layers with some precision, even if ultimately to present a picture of the period that is necessarily partial, yet hopefully with an awareness that such limitations are part and parcel of any critical anthologizing effort. Accordingly, the first chapter of this handbook seeks historically to situate the emergence and development of what became known as 'Romanticism' with reference to its complex political, social and economic contexts. The second chapter complements the first in introducing students to the diverse literary and cultural movements, authors and genres of the period.

In terms of the conceptualization and contextualization of Romanticism, one vital point of reference has to be the notion of 'revolution' in its widest sense. The seismic political and social shifts of the late eighteenth century gave the Romantic literary movement its shape and defining features. The early Romantics were engaged in producing complex and often ambivalent responses to the revolution in France and its aftermath. The abolitionist movement provides another significant context for the emergence and devel-opment of early Romanticism; the anti-slavery campaign found considerable support among writers of the 1790s and early nineteenth century, often across party political lines, and various discourses of liberation and emanci-pation began to find expression through the literature of Romanticism. These emancipationist discourses often had an explicit social and political aspect (anti-slavery, rights for women, justice for the poor, criminal law reform, suffrage reform and so on), but often Romantic writing reveals a more abstract, conceptual, intellectual commitment to liberation and innovation.

Often this commitment took a reactionary turn. Early Romantics like Coleridge, Godwin, Southey, Williams, Wollstonecraft or Wordsworth were deeply sympathetic to the revolutionary cause. But in the face of British reaction against French influence early in the 1790s, and certainly in the light of the Napoleonic Wars that plagued the balance of power in Europe at least until Napoleon's final defeat at Waterloo and the Congress of Vienna in 1815, this sympathy gave way to careful and cautious revision in these writers' later work (especially Wordsworth, Coleridge, Southey, and Godwin). Political reaction and reformation determine the period just as much as revolution, radicalism and progress, so that conservative and liberal, Tory and Whig, are not so much clearly delineated positions as shifting markers of a frequently malleable cultural temperament, the desires of a protean body politic. Other factors were economic and industrial. The growth of Britain's military and economic power around the globe, fuelled by a burgeoning industrialism at home, helped draw the map of an imperial expansion in the eighteenth century that the Victorians, with evangelical fervour, were to make their mission to take British civilization to all quarters of the globe. Still other factors were cultural and social. A rising industrial and mercantile class clashed with a tradition-bound ruling class, a spectre of revolution across the Channel in France that continued to haunt Britain well before and well into the nineteenth century. Both fomenting and articulating these tensions fell to a burgeoning print culture that, coupled with advances in print technology and fuelled by a continuing rise in and demand for literacy, access to education, and political representation, mediated the complex negotiation of literary, political, and cultural identities that defined the Romantic period. The developing cultural negotiation between the middle and working classes characterizes an expanding public sphere increasingly hungry for information.

Rather than seeing Romanticism as a falling off from or radical break from the past precedent of Enlightenment or neo-Classical ideals, then, one can read the Romantic as transforming this precedence, a way of marking the revolutionary ferment of the time as breaking through to something new in the history of human expression, and thus risking clarity of thought for the triumph of the novel. The latter was marked by the time's aesthetic experimentation, symptomatic of a post-Enlightenment political fervour that strove to challenge the bounds of tradition and power in the name of a more democratic social franchise. Insofar as revolution means a turning back as well as a movement forward, a tying together as much as a breaking apart, Romanticism thus also suggests a rather less decisive, more inchoate trajectory of turns and re-turns, a restless re-negotiation of history that is typical of much Romantic thought and writing. As we noted above, Romanticism is often understood as a reaction against Enlightenment thinking that has its origin in the mid-eighteenth century and is sometimes associated with the spirit of reason, proportion, and scientific objectivity, typified by the French *philosophes* and the rational skepticism of David Hume or Adam Smith and thus of the Scottish Enlightenment. But this is implicitly to denigrate Romanticism as a capitulation to the waywardness of feeling against the Enlightenment's steadier ballast of reason, reducing both to a singular identity. Long before 1789 we can trace what we would call a Romantic concern with the bodily sensorium, signified in science and aesthetics: the rise of empirical psychology and the mind sciences; writings about the beautiful, the sublime; explorations of the pleasures and terrors of imagination. In the mid-eighteenth century this concern saw the rise of the 'cult of Sensibility', typified in the work of the French philosopher Jean-Jacques Rousseau, English sentimental novelists such as Samuel Richardson, and the 'graveyard poets' such as Thomas Gray. Here we see a privileging of feeling, of spontaneous emotion, coupled with an interest in confessional writing and interiority that feeds into the Romantic emphasis upon passion, individuality and untrammelled creativity. Wordsworth, in his preface to the second edition of the *Lyrical Ballads* in 1800, gave the best-known Romantic definition of poetry as 'the spontaneous overflow of powerful feeling'. As Margaret Drabble observes in the *Oxford Companion to English Literature,* Imagination becomes the watchword of Romanticism as writers seek liberation from Enlightenment neo-classical rules of literary composition, as in the exquisite aesthetic balance of Alexander Pope's heroic couplets.

The liberation of the imagination is coupled with an increased emphasis upon the role of the poet as an individual who is, as Wordsworth puts it in his preface of 1800, a 'man speaking to men' in the language of the 'common man'. Poetry is therefore to an extent democratized and there is an emerging sense in this period of the poet as an agent of social change: as Percy Shelley contended in his 1821 essay 'The Defence of Poetry', the poet is 'the unacknowledged legislator of the world'. What is evident here is an elevation of the cultural status of the poet and of poetry; the poet is increasingly posited as a uniquely gifted individual whose creativity is the expression of an original genius that has transformative power. The democratization of the role of the poet thus exists in tension with what might be regarded as a rather elitist conceptualization of poetry as the ultimate expression of a Romantic aesthetic that emerges in and through the work of a small number of especially gifted men. This assumption undoubtedly influenced the formation of the Romantic canon from the late nineteenth century onwards: Romanticism has been defined almost exclusively in terms of the work of a handful of poets writing over a period of some sixty years.

It can therefore be said that in spite of the ambiguity pertaining to Romanticism's *historical* identity, there has (until fairly recently) been an exceptionally precise and narrow understanding of what constitutes the Romantic canon. From the late nineteenth to the late twentieth century, the Romantic canon has been largely understood as comprising the work of the poets who have become known as the 'Big Six' of Romanticism: William Wordsworth, Samuel Taylor Coleridge, John Keats, Percy Shelley, Lord Byron, William Blake. It is still most unlikely that any undergraduate module taking 'Romanticism' as its focus would omit to cover the major works of these six poets, and it is only since the final decades of the twentieth century that university curricula in this area have really opened up to include the work of 'minor' poets, novelists and dramatists. This handbook reflects recent developments in the re-conceptualization of Romanticism and the consequent broadening of Romanticism curricula at undergraduate level. Whilst we do give coverage here of the work of the 'Big Six', our contributors seek first to re-position canonical work in terms of some of the wider and (until recently) rather neglected contexts of Romanticism (imperialism and nationhood, slavery, class, gender, diverse print cultures and so on), and secondly to challenge the very definition of Romanticism in terms of a narrow, fixed canon comprised of the work of six male poets. As new theories and practices of criticism have emerged in the last few decades (feminism, deconstruction and New Historicism, for instance), critics have increasingly emphasized the extent to which this construction of Romanticism has effaced the work of numerous prolific and influential writers of the period.

This work therefore introduces students to a wide range of primary material and to the diverse critical methodologies that have developed within the field of Romanticism studies, especially over the last thirty years. Each chapter is arranged with a particular aim in view. The first and the final five chapters are presented broadly in an essay format, with subheadings and cross references where appropriate. The second and third chapters provide students with reference material arranged alphabetically: chapter two covers authors, movements and genres of the period, and chapter three considers key concepts, topics and critical approaches within the discipline. Chapters four and five offer case studies in the reading of Romanticism: chapter three considers certain core primary texts of the period and offers students examples of particular critical readings of those works, whilst chapter four analyzes the work of six influential critics and theorists whose work has helped shape the discipline of Romanticism studies over recent decades. Chapter six complements chapter four in covering more broadly the key shifts in critical approaches to Romanticism since the 1960s, and chapter seven gives a specific critical analysis of the problematics of canonicity within Romanticism and more generally within English literary studies (and this chapter ends with an opportunity for students to formulate their own judgement as to the potential canonical 'worth' of a little-known and rather provocative text). Chapters eight and nine take as their topics gender, sexuality, and ethnicity in the period; these chapters encourage students to engage critically with a diverse range of primary texts and to extend their understanding of the different political, social and cultural configurations of Romanticism at a national and global level. Finally, Peter Kitson's 'key note' chapter reflects upon the location of the field at present and considers new directions that promise to open up fresh possibilities for the study of Romanticism.

HISTORICAL TIMELINE

1776 American War of Independence (1775–83)
Transportation Act

1778 France declares war on Britain
Papists Act, first Catholic relief bill

1779 Spain declares war on Britain
Penitentiary Act creates state prisons for the first time

1780 Gordon Riots, anti-Catholic uprising against 1778 Papists Act

1781 Battle of Yorktown, American with French armies fight decisive battle against Lord Cornwallis, leader of British forces

1782 Frederick North, Lord North, resigns as Prime Minister after vote of no confidence

1783 Stamp Duties Act to raise money to pay for American War of Independence
Treaty of Paris ends war between Britain and United States
William Pitt becomes PM (1783–1801, 1804–06)

1784 Commutation Act reduces tax on tea, stimulates trade with China
India Act brings East India Company under control of British government

1785 Pitt introduces into Parliament a bill to reform rotten boroughs, which fails
Governor-General of India, Warren Hastings, charged with maladministration of East India Company

1786 British Cabinet approves penal colony in Botany Bay
Impeachment of Hastings
Eden Treaty, commercial agreement with France

1787 Russo-Turkish War (1787–92)
Austro-Turkish War (1787–91)
Society for Effecting the Abolition of the Slave Trade established
American Constitution adopted by Constitutional Convention in
Philadelphia

1788 Hastings trial begins (1788–1795)
Triple Alliance between Britain, Prussia, and Dutch Republic to curtail
French power
First Regency Crisis, George III temporarily insane (1788–89)

1789 Pitt introduces Regency Bill for Prince of Wales to serve as Regent
while George III is mentally ill, but George recovers
Washington elected first US President
William Wilberforce's first motion to abolish slave trade
Christian Fletcher leads mutiny against William Bligh, captain of the
Bounty
Tennis Court Oath taken by first meeting of French National Assembly,
vowing to establish constitution
Fall of the Bastille
Declaration of Rights of Man and the Citizen in France

1790 Henry James Pye becomes Poet Laureate
General election gives Pitt increased majority
Louis XVI accepts constitutional monarchy
Treason Act modifies penalty against females convicted of treason

1791 Roman Catholic Relief Act extends reforms of 1778 Papists Act
William Wilberforce introduces bill in Parliament to abolish slave
trade; bill defeated
Constitutional Act splits province of Quebec into Lower and Upper
Canada
Priestley Riots in Birmingham against dissenters

1792 Libel Act of 1792, securing trial by jury for accused, seen through
Parliament by Fox
Pitt's attack on slave trade
London Corresponding Society founded
Massacres in Paris; Thomas Paine flees to France after being indicted
for treason
Trial of Thomas Paine begins

1793 Aliens Act regulates immigration to Britain
France declares war on Britain
Execution of Louis XVI
The Reign of Terror
Execution of Marie Antoinette

1794 Execution of Lavoisier in France
Habeas Corpus suspended; suspension lifted June 1795
Robespierre arrested

1795 Treasonable Practices Act, after George III is stoned en route to
Parliament
Seditious Meetings Act restricts size of public meetings to 50
Hastings acquitted
New Zealand first settled

1796 War between Spain and Britain

1798 Habeas Corpus suspended; expires February 1799
Newspaper Publication Act restricts printing and circulation of
newspapers to reduce slander

1799 Napoleon named First Consul
First of two Combination Acts (also 1800) prohibits trades unions and
collective bargaining
Habeas Corpus Suspension Act of 1799

1800 Thomas Jefferson elected President of United States
Act of Union joining England and Ireland
Treason Act of 1800 equates imagining of the King's death or misprision
of treason with murder

1801 First Census (pop. 9,168,000)
General Enclosure Act limits access to public lands
Henry Addington, 1st Viscount Sidmouth elected PM (1801–04)

1802 Peace of Amiens temporarily ends conflict between France and Britain
Health and Morals of Apprentices Act regulates factory conditions,
especially for child workers

1803 War with France resumes

1804 Napoleon crowned emperor

1805 French fleet defeated by British at Battle of Trafalgar

1807 Slave Trade Act abolishing slave trade in Britain

1808 Convention of Cintra signed, allowing defeated French army to evacuate from Portugal
Peninsular War on Iberian Peninsula between France and allied powers of Britain, Portugal and Spain (1808–14)

1811 George III declared insane; Prince of Wales becomes Regent
Shelley expelled from Oxford
Luddite Riots begin (1811–12, 1814, 1816), protesting changes from Industrial Revolution

1812 War between Britain and United States (1812–15)
French army retreats from Moscow
Robert Jenkinson, 2nd Earl of Liverpool elected PM (until 1827)

1813 Robert Southey becomes Poet Laureate

1814 Napoleon abdicates, exiled to Elba
First Treaty of Paris between Allies and France
Congress of Vienna (November to June 1815) of European states to settle conflict from French Revolutionary and Napoleonic Wars and dissolution of Holy Roman Empire

1815 Napoleon defeated at Battle of Waterloo
Importation Act (Corn Law) to protect corn prices against foreign imports

1816 Spa Fields Riots, mass meetings to protest against British government

1817 Death of Princess Charlotte
Habeas Corpus suspended

1819 Peterloo Massacre at St. Peter's Field, Manchester, against protesters for parliamentary reform

1820 Death of George III
Accession of George IV

1821 Death of Keats in Rome
Death of Napoleon
London Co-operative Society founded

1822 Death of Percy Shelley in the Bay of Spezia, Italy

1823 Gaols Act institutes prison reforms
First Burmese War (1823–26)
First Anglo-Ashanti War (1823–31)

1824 1799 and 1800 Combination Laws repealed
Death of Byron in Missolonghi

1825 Commercial crisis in England
Cotton Mills Regulation Act
Combination Act allows trade union, but restricts activities

1826 Anti-Power Loom Riots, Lancashire protest against increased mechanization of textiles industry

1827 George Canning PM (April – August)
Frederick Robinson, 1ˢᵗ Viscount Goderich PM (August – January 1828)

1828 Arthur Wellesley, 1ˢᵗ Duke of Wellington PM

1829 Catholic Relief Act allows Catholics to sit in Parliament

1830 Death of George IV; accession of William IV
Revolution in Paris; election of Louis Philippe as King of France; liberal revolts in Italy, Belgium, Germany and Poland
Wellington elected PM
Swing Riots, uprising of rural works against industrial effects on agrarian livelihood
Wellington resigns, succeeded by Earl Grey

1831 First Parliamentary Reform Bill passes Commons, defeated in Committee
Merthyr Rising, South Wales
General Election, Whig reformers victorious
Second Reform Bill defeated in Lords
Third Reform Bill introduced

1832 Cholera outbreak in London
Third Reform Bill passes Lords
Reform Bill approved; rotten and pocket boroughs abolished, constituencies created in new towns, franchise extended to selected property owners

1833 Factory Act abolishes work for children under nine, limits working day to nine hours for under-13s, inspectors appointed
Slavery Abolition Act abolishes slavery throughout British Empire

1834 William Lamb, 2ⁿᵈ Viscount Melbourne PM (to November)
Poor Law Amendment Act sets up workhouses
Duke of Wellington PM (to December)
Robert Peel PM (to April 1835)

1835 William Lamb, 2nd Viscount Melbourne PM (to August 1840)

1837 London Working Men's Association founded
Death of William IV, accession of Victoria

LITERARY TIMELINE

1774 J. W. von Goethe, *The Sorrows of Young Werther*

1776 Thomas Paine, *Common Sense*
Richard Price, *Observations on Civil Liberty*
Adam Smith, *The Wealth of Nations*
Edward Gibbon, *The History of the Decline and Fall of the Roman Empire* (1776–89)

1777 Richard Brinsley Sheridan, *School for Scandal*

1778 Frances Burney, *Evelina*

1779 Samuel Johnson, *Lives of the English Poets* (1779–81)
Jean-Jacques Rousseau, *Confessions*
Friedrich Schiller, *The Robbers*

1781 Immanuel Kant, *Critique of Pure Reason*

1783 Sophie Lee, *The Recess* (1783–85)

1784 Charlotte Smith, *Elegiac Sonnets*
William Cowper, *Poems*
Ann Yearsley, *Poems on Several Occasions*
James Boswell, *Journal of a Tour of The Hebrides*
Death of Samuel Johnson

1785 William Cowper, *The Task*
Clara Reeve, *The Progress of Romance*
Thomas Reid, *Essays on the Intellectual Powers of Man*

1786 William Beckford, *Vathek*
Robert Burns, *Poems, Chiefly in the Scottish Dialect*
Richard Payne Knight, *Discourse on the Worship of Priapus*
Helen Maria Williams, *Poems*

1787 Mary Wollstonecraft, *Thoughts on the Education of Daughters*

1788 Hanna More, *Slavery: A Poem*
Charlotte Smith, *Emmeline*
Mary Wollstonecraft, *Original Stories form Real Life*

1789   Jeremy Bentham, *Principles of Morals and Legislation*
       William Blake, *Songs of Innocence*
       Olaudah Equiano, *The Interesting Narrative of the Life of Olaudah Equiano
       or Gustavus Vasa the African*
       Elizabeth Hands, *The Death of Amnon*

1790   Joanna Baillie, *Poems*
       Edmund Burke, *Reflections on the Revolution in France*
       William Blake, *Marriage of Heaven and Hell*
       Anne Radcliffe, *The Romance of the Forest*
       Helen Maria Williams, *Letters Written in France* [*Letters from France*
       (1790–96)]

1791   Jeremy Bentham, *Panopticon*
       James Boswell, *Life of Johnson*
       Robert Burns, *Tam o' Shanter*
       Anna Barbauld, *Epistle to William Wilberforce*
       Erasmus Darwin, The Botanic Garden (*Loves of the plants* and *The
       Economy of Vegetation*)
       William Gilpin, *Observations on the River Wye*
       Elizabeth Inchbald, *A Simple Story*
       Thomas Paine, *Rights of Man*
       C. F. Volney, *The Ruins, or a Survey of the Revolutions of Empires*

1792   Jane Austen, *Love and Friendship*
       Robert Burns, *Songs*
       Samuel Rogers, *The Pleasures of Memory*
       Mary Wollestonecraft, *A Vindication of the Rights of Woman*

1793   George Dyer, *The Complaints of the Poor People of England*
       William Godwin, *Political Justice*
       Thomas Paine, *The Age of Reason*
       John Thelwall, *The Peripatetic*

1794   William Blake, *Songs of Experience*
       Erasmus Darwin, *Zoonomia* (1794–96)
       William Godwin, *Caleb Williams*
       Anne Radcliffe, *Mysteries of Udolpho*
       Robert Southey, *Poems*

1795   Maria Edgeworth, *Letters for Literary Ladies*
       Eliza Fenwick, *Secrecy, Or, The Ruin of the Rock*
       J. W. von Goethe, *Wilhelm Meister's Apprenticeship*

1796   Matthew Gregory Lewis, *The Monk*

Elizabeth Hamilton, *Letters of a Hindoo Rajah*
Mary Hays, *Memoirs of Emma Courtney*
William Wordsworth, *The Borderers*
Ann Yearsley, *The Rural Lyre*
Mary Wollstonecraft, *Letters Written … Sweden, Norway, and Denmark*

1797   Samuel Taylor Coleridge, *The Ancient Mariner*
Friedrich Hölderlin, *Hyperion* (second part, 1799)

1798   Joanna Baillie, *Plays on the Passions*, Volume 1
Jeremy Bentham, *Political Economy*
Thomas Malthus, *An Essay on the Principle of Population*
Walter Savage Landor, *Gebir*
William Wordsworth and Samuel Taylor Coleridge, *Lyrical Ballads*

1799   Mary Hays, *The Victim of Prejudice*
Hannah More, *Strictures on the Modern System of Female Education*

1800   Maria Edgeworth, *Castle Rackrent*
Elizabeth Hamilton, *Memoirs of Modern Philosophers*
Mary Robinson, *Lyrical Tales*
William Wordsworth and Samuel Taylor Coleridge, *Lyrical Ballads* (second edition)
Dorothy Wordsworth keeps her Grasmere Journal (1800–3)

1801   Maria Edgeworth, *Belinda*
Amelia Opie, *The Father and Daughter; Memoirs of Mary Robinson*
Joanna Southcott, *The Strange Effects of Faith*

1802   Joanna Baillie, *Plays on the Passions*, Vol. 2

1803   Mme. De Staël, *Delphine*
Mary Hays, *Female Biography*

1804   Joanna Baillie, *Miscellaneous Plays*
Matilda Betham, *Biographical Dictionary of Celebrated Women*
William Blake, *Milton; Jerusalem*
Amelia Opie, *Adeline Mowbray, or The Mother and the Daughter*

1805   Walter Scott, *Lay of the Last Minstrel*
Jane and Ann Taylor, *Original Poems for Infant Minds*
Mary Tighe, *Psyche, or The Legend of Love*
William Wordsworth completes *The Prelude* (published 1850)

1806   Lord Byron, *Fugitive Pieces*
Charlotte Richardson, *Poems Written on Different Occasions*
Charlotte Smith, *Beachy Head and Other Poems*

Sydney Owensen, *The Wild Irish Girl: A National Tale*

1807 Lord Byron, *Hours of Idleness*
Mme. De Staël, *Corinne*
Georg Wilhelm Friedrich Hegel, *Phenomenology of Spirit*
Charles and Mary Lamb, *Tales from Shakespeare*
Thomas Moore, *Irish Melodies* (1807–34)
William Wordsworth, *Poems in Two Volumes*

1808 Anne Grant, *The Highlanders*
J. W. von Goethe, *Faust*, Part 1
Felicia Hemans, *Poems*
Amelia Opie, *The Warrior's Return*

1809 Charles and Mary Lamb, *Poetry for Children*

1810 Alexander Chalmers, *English Poets*
Samuel Taylor Coleridge lectures on Shakespeare
George Crabbe, *The Borough, A Poem in Twenty-Four Letters*
Anna Seward, *Poetical Works*

1811 Jane Austen, *Sense and Sensibility*
Sir Walter Scott, *The Lady of the Lake*
Percy Shelley, *The Necessity of Atheism*

1812 Joanna Baillie, *Plays on the Passions*, Vol. 3
Lord Byron, *Childe Harold's Pilgrimage*, Cantos 1 and 2
Maria Edgeworth, *The Absentee*
Felicia Hemans, *The Domestic Affections*

1813 Jane Austen, *Pride and Prejudice*
Lord Byron, *The Bride of Abydos*
Percy Shelley, *Queen Mab*

1814 Jane Austen, *Mansfield Park*
Frances Burney, *The Wanderer*
Lord Byron, *The Corsair*
Sir Walter Scott, *Waverley*
William Wordsworth, *The Excursion*

1816 Jane Austen, *Emma*
Lord Byron, *Poems on His Domestic Circumstances; Childe Harold*, Cantos
3 and 4
Samuel Taylor Coleridge, *Christabel, Kubla Khan, Pains of Sleep*
Percy Shelley, *Alastor and Other Poems*
Jane Taylor, *Essays in Rhyme on Morals and Manners*

1817 Lord Byron, *Manfred*
Samuel Taylor Coleridge, *Biographia Literaria* and *Sybilline Leaves*
William Godwin, *Mandeville*
William Hazlitt, *The Round Table*
John Keats, *Poems*
Mary and Percy Shelley, *History of a Six Weeks' Tour*

1818 Jane Austen, *Northanger Abbey; Persuasion*
John Keats, *Endymion*
Thomas Love Peacock, *Nightmare Abbey; Persuasion*
Arthur Schopenhauer, *The World as Will and Representation* (1818–19)
Mary Shelley, *Frankenstein*

1819 Lord Byron, *Don Juan*, Cantos 1 and 2
William Hazlitt, *Political Essays*
William Hone, *The Political House that Jack Built*
John Polidori, *The Vampyre*
David Ricardo, *Principles of Political Economy and Taxation*
Sir Walter Scott, *The Heart of Midlothian*
Mary Shelley, *Matilda*
Percy Shelley, *The Cenci*

1820 Anna Barbauld, *The British Novelists*
John Clare, *Poems Descriptive of Rural Life*
John Keats, *Lamia, Isabella, The Eve of St. Agnes, and Other Poems*
Charles Maturin, *Melmoth the Wanderer*
Thomas Love Peacock, *Four Ages of Poetry*
Percy Shelley, *Prometheus Unbound*
Robert Southey, *Vision of Judgement*
William Wordsworth, *The River Duddon, a Series of Sonnets*

1821 Joanna Baillie, *Metrical Legends*
John Clare, *The Village Minstrel*
Thomas De Quincey, *Confessions of an English Opium-Eater*
Letitia Landon, *The Fate of Adelaide*
James Mill, *Elements of Political Economy*
Percy Shelley, *Adonais; Epipsychidion*

1822 Lord Byron, *The Vision of Judgement*
Percy Shelley, *Hellas*
William Wordsworth, *Ecclesiastical Sketches*

1823 William Hazlitt, *Libor Amoris*
Felicia Hemans, *The Siege of Valencia*
Charles Lamb, *Essays of Elia*

Percy Shelley, *Poetical Pieces*
Helen Maria Williams, *Poems on Various Subjects*

1824   James Hogg, *The Private Memoirs and Confessions of a Justified Sinner*
Letitia Landon, *The Improvisatrice*
M. R. Mitford, *Our Village*
Thomas Moore, *Memoirs of Captain Rock*
Percy Shelley, *Posthumous Poems* (ed. Mary Shelley)

1825   Anna Barbauld, *Poems*
William Hazlitt, *The Spirit of the Age*
Felicia Hemans, *The Forest Sanctuary*
Letitia Landon, *The Troubador*

1826   Elizabeth Barrett (Browning), *An Essay on Mind with Other Poems*
Mary Shelley, *The Last Man*

1827   John Clare, *The Shepherd's Calendar*
Letitia Landon, *The Golden Violet*
John Keble, *The Christian Year*

1828   Thomas Carlyle, *Essay on Burns*
Felicia Hemans, *Records of Woman*

1829   Letitia Landon, *The Venetian Bracelet*
James Mill, *Analysis of the Human Mind*

1830   William Cobbett, *Rural Rides*
Felicia Hemans, *Songs of the Affections*
Charles Lyell, *Principles of Geology* (1830–33)
Mary Shelley, *Perkin Warbeck*
Alfred Tennyson, *Poems, Chiefly Lyrical*

1831   Thomas Love Peacock, *Crotchet Castle*
Alfred Tennyson, *Poems*

1833   Robert Browning, *Pauline*
Thomas Carlyle, *Sartor Resartus*
Edward Bulwer-Lytton, *Last Days of Pompeii*
John Henry Newman, *Tracts for Times*

1834   Thomas De Quincey, *Recollections of the Lakes and Lake Poets* (1834–39)

1835   Robert Browning, *Paracelsus*
William Wordsworth, *Yarrow Revisited*

1836   Charles Dickens, *Sketches by Boz*; begins *Pickwick Papers*
Frederick Marryat, *Mr Midshipman Easy*

1837 Thomas Carlyle, *French Revolution*
Charles Dickens, *Oliver Twist*
Benjamin Disraeli, *Venetia*

CULTURAL

1777 Second edition of *Encyclopaedia Britannica*
John Howard, *Prison Report on the State of the Prisons in England and Wales*

1778 Sir Joshua Reynolds, *Discourses*

1779 Spinning mule, invented by Samuel Crompton

1780 John Brown, *Elementae Medicinae*

1781 William Herschel discovers Uranus
Iron Bridge completed across Severn River in Shropshire
Henry Fuseli exhibits *The Nightmare* at the Royal Academy

1784 First mail coach between Bristol and London
John Wesley charters Methodist Church
First hydrogen balloon ascent
Orientalist Sir William Jones founds Asiatic Society of Bengal
Jacques-Louis David, *Oath of the Horatii*

1785 Edmund Cartwright patents the power loom
First balloon crossing of English Channel
The Daily Universal Register, later *The Times*, first published
Thomas Gainsborough, *The Morning Walk*
Sarah Siddons performs Lady Macbeth at Drury Lane

1786 Mozart's *The Marriage of Figaro* premieres in Vienna

1787 First performance of Mozart's *Don Giovanni* in Prague

1788 *The Times* first published

1789 Andrew Philip, *The Voyage of Governor Philip to Botany Bay*
First cotton textiles factory in Manchester
Thames-Severn canal opened

1791 Publication of *The Observer*, first Sunday newspaper

1792 Coal gas lighting introduced
James Gillray engraves 'Sin, Death and the Devil', satire on the King and Queen

1793 David, *The Death of Marat*

1794 Theatre Royal, Drury Lane opens
Eli Whitney granted patent for cotton gin

1796 Royal Technical College founded (Glasgow)

1797 *Journal of Natural Philosophy, Chemistry and Other Arts* founded
Friedrich Wilhelm Joseph Schelling publishes *Ideen zu einer Philosophie der Natur*

1798 Edward Jenner, *Inquiry into the Causes and Effects of Variolae Vaccinae*
Athenaeum founded by August Wilhelm and Friedrich Schlegel (1798–1800)
First performance of Haydn's *The Creation* (1796–98), partly based on Milton's *Paradise Lost*, in Vienna
J. M. W. Turner, *Buttermere Lake*

1799 Religious Tract Society founded
Sir Humphry Davy, *Researches, Chemical and Philosophical*

1800 Royal Institution of Science founded

1801 David, *Napoleon at the Saint Bernard Pass*

1802 *Edinburgh Review* founded
William Cobbett establishes *The Political Register*

1803 Dalton's atomic theory
Turner, *Calais Pier*

1804 Thomas Telford, construction of Caledonian Canal

1805 London Docks opened
First gas-lit factory in Manchester
Turner, *Shipwreck*
Sir William Drummond, *Academical Questions*

1806 East India docks opened in London
Benjamin Haydon, *The Flight into Egypt*

1807 Air pumps for mines introduced
Davy lectures on electricity and chemistry at the Royal Society

1808 Ludwig van Beethoven, *Symphonies 5 and 6*
Leigh Hunt founds *Examiner*

1809 *Quarterly Review* founded

1810 J. W. von Goethe, *Theory of Colours*

1811   John Nash designs Regent's Park and Regent Street (1811–26)

1812   Elgin Marbles brought to England
John Common invents reaping machine
Turner, *Snow Storm: Hannibal and His Army Crossing the Alps*

1814   Cylinder press printing invented
Edmund Kean performs Shylock in *The Merchant of Venice* at Drury
    Lane theatre
Turner, *The Frosty Morning*

1815   George Stephenson patents steam engine
John Nash redesigns the Royal Pavilion at Brighton (1815–26)
John Constable, *Boat Building*

1816   Robert Owen opens school in cotton mill
Mungo Park, *Travels in the Interior Districts of Africa*

1817   *Blackwood's Edinburgh Magazine* founded
Waterloo Bridge opened
Encyclopaedia Metropolitana, 30 vols. (1817–1845)
John Constable, *Flatford Mill*
Benjamin West, *Death on the Pale Horse*

1818   First iron passenger ship
Institute of Civil Engineers founded
Théodore Géricault, *The Raft of the Medusa* (1818–19)

1819   First Macadam roads laid
George Cruikshank illustrations: *A Radical Reformer; Massacre at St
    Peter's*

1820   Royal Astronomical Society and Royal Society of Literature founded
Regent's Canal opened in London

1821   Michael Faraday establishes principle of the electric motor
The Manchester Guardian founded
Constable, *The Hay Wain*
John Martin, *Belshazzar's Feast*

1822   Franz Schubert, *Unfinished Symphony*
Royal Academy of Music founded
Charles Babbage proposes 'difference machine', forerunner of modern
    computer, to Royal Astronomical Society

1823   Birkbeck College founded
King's Library gifted to the British Museum

1824 National Gallery established

1825 First passenger train in Britain (Stockton-Darlington)

1826 University of London founded
Carl Maria von Weber's *Oberon* premiers at Covent Garden

1827 Martin publishes illustrations for Milton's *Paradise Lost*
Eugène Delacroix, *Death of Sardanapalus*

1828 London Zoo opens
John Martin, *Belshazzar's Feast*

1829 Metropolitan Police Service established
King's College London founded
Turner, *Ulysses deriding Polymphemus: Homer's Odyssey*

1830 Royal Geographical Society founded
Liverpool and Manchester Railway opens
Delacroix, *Liberty Leading the People*

1831 Charles Darwin embarks on first *H.M.S. Beagle* voyage
New London Bridge opened
Violin virtuoso, Niccolo Paganini arrives in London

1834 Charles Babbage's analytical engine
Hansom cab
Houses of Parliament destroyed by fire

1836 University of London founded
London Bridge to Deptford railways opens

1837 National Gallery opens
Morse code and electric telegraph used
Euston Station opens

1 Historical Context

Joel Faflak

Chapter Overview

This chapter traces the historical context of social, political and economic factors from which literature of the British Romantic period emerges. Although Romantic literature can be and has been read separately from its historical context, our understanding of Romantic literature is ultimately enriched by looking at the various circumstances that shape its writing and production, or to see how Romantic literature shapes history in turn. This statement is true of any literary period, of course, but is especially true of the Romantic period, when our current ideas of literature and literary criticism emerge as distinct objects of study. This is not to say they emerged as homogeneous fields, and the Romantics debated fiercely the aesthetic and social significance of fictional vs non-fictional writing, all in the name of defining the category 'Literature'. Indeed, with this Handbook in front of you, we can say that the battles have not ended. In our current time of political, economic, techno-logical and climatic change, when the necessity of thinking about the material conditions of our lived existence has become especially crucial, we frequently wonder if literature matters. What concrete solutions can it provide for urgent problems? For the on-going struggle to answer this question we can thank the Romantics, who used literature to respond to tumultuous historical change, but also wondered if such responses were making a difference. For it is this shifting ground between texts and contexts that articulates the ground of

Romantic history itself. At the end of each section in this chapter you will find cross-references to subsequent chapters in which relevant authors, works and issues related to the history outlined in this chapter are discussed in further detail. You can also refer to the historical timeline in the Introduction.

The Romantic Period

The period from 1789 to 1837 was a time of great economic, social, political and cultural ferment. For one thing, from 1793 to 1815, with the exception of 1801 to 1803, Britain was at war with France. Even after the 1815 Congress of Vienna realigned the balance of power in Europe upset by Napoleon, things did not go smoothly. The social climate in Britain post-1789 veered between idealism and paranoia. The war only partly distracted the nation from internal pressures created by a burgeoning industrial economy. By the time the 1832 Reform Bill began redistributing political power away from the ruling elites, the expanding middle and industrial classes had created a more stratified public sphere. Britain was establishing itself as the world's manufacturing powerhouse and its population went from just under 10 million at the time of the first census in 1801 to nearly 25 million by the time Victoria took the throne. The largest growth was in industrial centres like Birmingham, Bristol, Leeds, Liverpool and Manchester, as well as London, nerve centre for the growing Empire. Add to this the colonies Britain ruled over for most of the nineteenth century and this number nearly triples.

The progress from an agrarian to an urban industrial society did not always yield benefits. Many of England's working class had been displaced from the countryside, where manufacturing had created widespread unemployment in the farming community. Social conditions in increasingly overcrowded cities, as the social critic Friedrich Engels describes in the mid-nineteenth century, were dire. Besides being the world's factory, Britain was also the world's dominant colonial power, which tied industry at home to wars and markets abroad, exerting an often volatile influence on Britain's domestic economy. A cultural revolution of shifting and divergent tastes and ideas was ushering in the modern age. The intellectual and political enlightenment begun in the seventeenth century, advocating the rights and imagination of the individual in a civil society, was materialized in the French Revolution, which exerted an enormous influence on British thought and literature thereafter. The impact of scientific and technological advances, coupled with social, political and cultural revolution, marked the period as what Richard Holmes calls The Age of Wonder.

One fact about the less than smooth progress from 1789 to 1837 is undeniable: the time did not stand still, and indeed seemed to its inhabitants to be moving forward with increasing speed and uncertainty. As the poet

Percy Shelley noted in 1820, information was expanding at such a fast pace that the world was losing its capacity to make sense of this exploding body of knowledge. Humanity having supposedly liberated itself above its natural surroundings, it was re-enslaved by its own power of enlightenment. We can thus read the history of the Romantic period less as a forward trajectory than as a movement of starts and stops, advances and retreats, revolution and reaction, progress and decline. Of the passing nature of its own time Romanticism seemed distinctly self-aware in a way that previous periods had not been. It seemed, that is, especially sensitive to the fact that it was not always sure *where* it was going, a period of what Tilottama Rajan calls restless self-examination.

Pre-Romanticism

Great Britain was forged by the 1707 Act of Union joining England and Scotland. Henry VIII's creation of the Church of England in the sixteenth century had pitted Protestants against Catholics in subsequent battles over royal succession. These bitter struggles came to a head in the Glorious Revolution of 1688, which deposed James II (James VII of Scotland) in favour of the Protestant William I. Subsequent Jacobite uprisings threatened Britain for the first half of the eighteenth century after James exiled himself to France, one of Britain's main enemies during the Seven Years' War (1756–1763). The war realigned both the European and colonial balances of power, effectively ending French domination in North America. The year 1707 was thus also key to the consolidation of what is called the First British Empire. Elizabeth I had begun the push for exploration and trade in competition with Spain, France and the Netherlands for control of North America, Africa and central and far Asia. This expansion was not without its hazards. The 1711 founding of the South Sea Company to oversee trade with Spain's South American colonies resulted in the 1720 South Sea Bubble, which nearly bankrupted the British economy. On the far side of the world, rampant mismanagement by the East India Company, a private mercantile conglomerate given exclusive control over trade with Asia via a 1600 royal charter, resulted in the 1784 impeachment of Warren Hastings, the first Governor General of India. Hastings' 1795 acquittal came only after his trial made a public spectacle of Britain's imperial ambition, necessitating the 1784 East India Act, which brought the Company's *laissez faire* administration under government control.

If the end of the First Empire comes with the United States winning the War of Independence in 1783, however, Britain triumphed in other ways. In the second half of the eighteenth century the joint Pacific expeditions of explorer, cartographer and navigator James Cook and naturalist and botanist Joseph Banks epitomized Enlightenment expansion: the expression of man's capacity, in the name of scientific advancement, to know, classify and understand the world with unprecedented comprehension. In print culture this comprehensiveness was symbolized by the first publication of the *Encyclopaedia Britannica* between 1768 and 1771 (this paralleled the French publication of the *Encyclopédie* between 1751 and 1772). The *Encyclopaedia* originated in Edinburgh, which in the mid-eighteenth century emerged as a centre of learning that profoundly influenced British thought thereafter. Indeed, many of our modern notions of medicine, political economy and psychology can be said to emerge during what is known as the Scottish Enlightenment.

Compendiums like the *Encyclopaedia* reflected dramatically improving literacy rates, expanding a previously small class of learned readers among the ruling elites to include the professional, middle and working classes. This diversification created an ever-growing demand for information, a curiosity fed by a variety of print forms, from the rise of the novel to the growth of journals, newspapers and other serial publications in the late eighteenth and early nineteenth centuries. These networks of communication helped to make sense of the increasingly complex world of Britain's domestic and foreign affairs, the politics of which were often ugly. England's and later Britain's colonial expansion was fuelled by slave trade in West Africa and the Caribbean, resulting in the 1787 establishment of the Society for the Abolition of the Slave Trade. Human trafficking of British citizens was also a matter of some concern. The 1779 Penitentiary Act created state prisons at home, and abroad Australia's Botany Bay, where Cook's *HMS Endeavour* first landed in 1770, became the site of a penal colony in 1786, which solved the problem of where to ship Britain's convicts after it lost the American colonies.

The 1790s and the King's Madness

Despite the above upheavals, Britain entered a period of relative peace, prosperity, and reform in the second half of the eighteenth century. Changes in favour of parliamentary governance since the Glorious Revolution had made the balance of power between the British state and people, if not equal, at least more equitable than in France, which is why the events of 1789 in Paris galvanized British politics and culture. The French *ancien regime* was epitomized by the extravagant monarchy of Louis XIV, 'The Sun King', and held power in conjunction with the Catholic church. These two Estates exerted autocratic influence over the third Estate – the rest of French society. Economic crisis due to a number of factors brought this oppression to account in 1789 with the formation of the First National Assembly in June, followed by the storming of the Bastille prison, symbol of royal authority, on July 14, and the Declaration of the Rights of Man and the Citizen in August. Writers like Thomas Paine, William Godwin and Mary Wollstonecraft saw the Declaration as the fulfilment of Enlightenment ideals of liberty and progress. Others, like Edmund Burke, saw the Revolution as an unleashed political force that, by turning its back on history and tradition, would wreak havoc on social order. Still others, like Wordsworth and Coleridge, despite an early flirtation with libertarian principles in the 1790s, ended up more Burkean in their later writings, as time (and the subsequent pillorying of Paine, Godwin, and Wollstonecraft in British cultural life) came to temper their initial enthusiasm for the French republican cause.

It did not help that Burke's prediction came true. By 1793, the French government had executed Louis XVI and Marie Antoinette and instituted a Reign of Terror against perceived dissidents within the new republic. Of more immediate consequence to British life was the fact that in the same year France declared war on Britain, fomenting a period of patriotism and paranoia that labelled anyone in favour of reform as French or Jacobin sympathizers and thus traitors. Government fears of dissidence resulted in a series of legislations (known collectively as The Gagging Acts) and various suspensions of *habeas corpus* from the 1790s well into the 1810s. These were meant to curtail threats, whether real or perceived, against the British body politic, particularly against the body of the King. The 1795 treason trials of John Thelwall, Horne Tooke and others, or the stoning of George III en route to the opening of parliament, were flashpoints for this reactionary fervour, which also attempted to curb the enthusiasm of calls for political reform at home. This reformism was mirrored in an evangelical movement that emerged in the 1780s as a reaction to the British religious establishment. This movement began in rural areas but spread to towns and cities. Evangelical groups were often divided amongst themselves but advocated similar aims: freedom of private and personal religious belief and practice. Evangelicism thus also called for 'proper' moral conduct as a reproach to a moral laxity and social corruption associated with 'High Church' Anglicanism and its conservative, reactionary nature. The broad appeal for stricter modes of social behaviour, corresponding with the rise of the modern temperance movement, was thus meant to counteract a perceived corrupt climate of gambling, drinking, and sexual permissiveness in late-eighteenth and early nineteenth-century public life.

One potent symbol of a nation 'out of control' was the King's madness. George III was on the throne for most of the Romantic period, from 1760 to 1820, nearly as long as Victoria. But he suffered from what is now thought to be porphyria, a neurological disorder resulting in often severe physiological and mental disturbances. He was momentarily declared insane in 1788–89, and recovered again after a second bout in 1798, during which time his son George, Prince of Wales, served as Regent. Finally, in 1811 George III was deemed unfit to rule, and the younger George became Prince Regent until his father's death in 1820, when he took the throne as George IV. These Regency Crises reflect the political turbulence of George III's reign, beginning with losing his grip on North America in 1783, a definitive challenge to the Old World's governance of the New World that foreshadows the decline of the British Empire in the later nineteenth century. If Victoria sometimes lost touch with her time – after Prince Albert's death, she entered a prolonged period of mourning – she nonetheless came to symbolize a singular dedication to her age, whereas her grandfather's mental illness suggests a different 'commitment'. George III's sixty-year reign seems long more by dint of sheer endurance, and his madness is a fit reminder of the Romantic period's often tempestuous history, which fuelled its hugely creative, at times apocalyptic temperament, and of reformist and reactionary attempts to come to terms with this volatility.

Post-1800: The Napoleonic Wars

The constitution of Great Britain changed again in 1800. In 1798 the Society of United Irishmen, uniting dissenting Presbyterians and Catholics in common cause against British rule, and soliciting French help, attempted to form an independent Irish republic. This rebellion was squashed by both the Irish and British governments and resulted in the 1800 Act of Union, joining Britain and Ireland to form the United Kingdom of Great Britain and Ireland. If the marriage between Scotland and England had been uneasy, coming at a time of increasingly perceived threats to British autonomy, this second Union signified a rather more ruthless 'home rule', resulting in a divisive relationship between the two countries throughout the nineteenth and twentieth centuries. Britain had partly secured the cooperation of the Irish government over the Act of Union through bribes and the guarantee of peerages to various Irish supporters from the ruling elite. This situation was not helped by the fact that Britain promoted its own economic concerns at the expense of Irish social development, which was troubled by a series of famines that threatened the country's agricultural self-sufficiency, the most devastating of these being the 1840s famine that decimated the Irish population.

Treatment of the Irish was partly fomented by the fact that by 1800 British patriotism was needed more than ever, so that the ability (and necessity) of London to subjugate a population so close to home came to symbolize an imposed sense of British unity against a foreign threat equally close to home. The previous year Napoleon was named First Consul of France, and by 1804, after a brief peace between Britain and France, he had crowned himself emperor and proceeded with a program of imperial conquest that embroiled Europe in war for the next decade. Having lost North America to the British, the French seemed driven to gain global supremacy. Napoleon's dreams of domination by sea ended with the British 1805 defeat of the battle of Trafalgar, though Napoleon continued his land campaigns. The 1808 Convention of Cintra allowed the defeated French army to evacuate from Portugal, precipitating the Peninsular War between France and the allied powers of Britain, Portugal and Spain (1808–14). Only with Napoleon's catastrophic retreat from Moscow in 1812, followed by his 1814 exile to Elba, and subsequent return and final defeat at the 1815 Battle of Waterloo, were the Napoleonic wars brought to an end.

That Napoleon's ambition re-ignited 1790s' fears of a French invasion also redounded on Britain's responses to its domestic troubles. The first British census in 1801 made real the nation's productivity, but also resulted in increased anxiety about how to care for and control its rapidly expanding population both at home and abroad. The 1807 Slave Trade Act abolished one of Britain's more egregious colonial practices, though it did not outlaw slavery itself. Closer to home, the 1802 Health and Morals of Apprentices Act, addressing the treatment of child labourers, was among the first of several reforms of working conditions among the industrial class. But such reforms were an indication of the compounding effects of industrialization and urbanization. The 1801 General Enclosure Act, consolidating previous acts, further restricted public access to arable common lands. Depending on one's perspective, this process either made agriculture more efficient and productive to support a growing economy, or privatized farming and hastened the transformation of the rural class into waged labour. Either way, the Enclosure Act came to symbolize the time's growing utilitarianism which, while its intent was to ensure social well-being for the largest number of people, also signified the managerial spirit of an intent to impose effective social controls over a growing and increasingly diverse population.

The evangelical movement noted above was a moral response and corrective to the often degrading social effects of such economic transformations. The often apocalyptic nature of evangelicism turned pragmatically dour in the first decade of the nineteenth century. Thomas Trotter's *An Essay, Medical, Philosophical, and Chemical, on Drunkenness* (1803), an earlier treatise expounding temperance, or his *A View of the Nervous Temperament* (1807), a nervous malady that resulted from too much luxury and refinement, warned against the enervating effects of an increasingly industrialized society. Such prognostications came in the light of Napoleon's rise to power, which at once fed the Romantic myth of the individual's capacity to overcome all adversity and posed a cautionary tale about man's reach exceeding his grasp. Napoleon flew in the face of nature and divine law, an excessive Promethean ambition that demanded to be reined in. Indeed, Napoleon's example was a self-admonishment to Britain for its own dreams of expansion and for Romantic ideals of self-fulfilment, a self-restraining corrective to individual desire that became the model for Victorian notions of moral hygiene.

Even more dire was Thomas Malthus' *An Essay on the Principle of Population*, which went through six successive editions from 1798 to 1826. Malthus' theory that famine, disease and mortality were nature's curb against unbridled population growth ran in the face of an earlier Romantic idealism, like that of Godwin's *Enquiry Concerning Political Justice* (1793), which advocated the rational expression of each individual's will as the means to improving and perfecting society, thus ending all institutional oppression. Malthus, an Anglican cleric, saw nature's check on endless human empowerment as God's object lesson in the necessity of hard work and virtuous action. But his views also implied an incipient notion of evolutionary development that was already creeping into Romantic natural history, as reflected in the work of Charles Darwin's grandfather, Erasmus Darwin. Obsessed with finding the animating principle of life itself, Romantic science in the first decades of the nineteenth century was torn between respecting earlier preformationist models of the planet's life as working by divine plan and advocating proto-evolutionary ideas that saw nature as self-propagating and thus capable of its own mutations. Such emergent notions flew sufficiently in the face of religious notions of divine ordination to fuel debates between religion and science that raged well into the nineteenth century.

Post-Napoleon: The Regency

Napoleon's 1815 defeat at the Battle of Waterloo and final exile to St Helena ended Britain's war with France. The Congress of Vienna in the same year redrew the political landscape of Europe and meant that Britain's considerable economic and military investment in winning the war with France could be diverted elsewhere. The opening of the first passenger railway, the Stockton-Darlington line, in 1825, followed by the opening of the Liverpool and Manchester Railway in 1830, were a symbol that the Industrial Revolution was now in full swing and life in British society – and in the world in general – was moving with increasing speed towards its technological, automated future. But peace brought famine and unemployment along with prosperity and progress. Partly in response to the post-war economic crisis, the government passed the Importation Act in 1815, the first of a series of Corn Laws (eventually repealed in 1846) imposing tariffs against corn imports. For some, the Laws hindered free trade and the expansion of the British economy. For others, they ultimately benefited landowners and further justified the necessity of reform, resulting in a period of increased political and social insurgency. Mass rallies like the 1816 Spa Fields Riots in Islington were among the first organized protests against the British government.

Anti-government sentiment reached a crisis point three years later in 1819, when a gathering of thousands in St Peter's Field, Manchester to demand parliamentary reform, specifically to extend suffrage in the industrial cities of northern England, ended in local magistrates firing on the crowd, killing fifteen and wounding hundreds. Known as the Peterloo Massacre, a deadly comment on the British triumph over Napoleon at Waterloo, the tragedy galvanized radicals like Percy Shelley, who viewed the British political climate post-1789 as conservative and reactionary. Government response to Peterloo was swift, resulting in yet another series of gagging legislations known as the Six Acts: The Training Prevention Act, The Seizure of Arms Act, The Misdemeanours Act, The Seditious Meetings Prevention Act, The Blasphemous and Seditious Libels Act, and The Newspaper and Stamp Duties Act. All were designed to cripple the reform movement by labelling any form of perceived activism as a radical and treasonable conspiracy against the government.

There was a continued effort to alleviate various social pressures. The Gaols Act of 1823, though it did little to address systemic problems within the British penal establishment, at least began the push towards future prison reform. Though it did not at first address the lack of political representation among the industrial class, in 1824 the government repealed the 1799 and 1800 Combination Laws prohibiting collective bargaining and trade unions. The Cotton Mills Regulation Act of 1825 restricted the working day of children under sixteen to twelve hours, another step towards improving dire working conditions in England's factories. Such changes seem paltry to us today, but we need to remember the slow pace of reform in Great Britain throughout the nineteenth century. There was a further commercial crisis in 1825, and the 1826 Anti-Power Loom Riots in Lancashire protested against increased mechanization of the textiles industry, which had resulted in unemployment, low wages and starvation. A new Combination Act in 1825 permitted trade unions, though it restricted their activity, driving radical organizations further underground and resulting in the Chartist Movement of 1838–1850, named after the People's Charter of 1838, penned by the emerging labour movement as its call for sweeping reform of the political and economic establishment. In education, the founding of what was later called Birkbeck College in 1826 (at that time, 'London Mechanics Institute') pioneered the concept of adult and part-time education. The founding of the University College London (later the University of London) in 1826 marked a shift away from the privilege and discrimination that had governed Britain's elite upper schools (Oxford, Cambridge) by admitting students regardless of religious background and according to accessibility and merit. And in a move whose significance has become especially relevant to us in the early twenty-first century, the government passed the first animal rights bill in 1822, in this case to prevent the cruel treatment of cattle (1822). This was followed by the formation of the Society for the Prevention of Cruelty to Animals in 1824, the world's first animal welfare organization, of which William Wilberforce, lead instigator of the anti-slavery movement, was a key figure. Such changes indicated a post-Enlightenment, proto-evolutionary sense that 'man', otherwise responsible for the world's development and proud of his ability to dominate the world, was not the only player on the field.

The tense post-1815 negotiation between radicalism, reform and reaction in Britain typifies what is generally called the Regency, though the term covers a variety of designations. In the broadest sense the Regency defines the period between the Georgian period, which covers the reigns of the Kings of the House of Hanover (George I to George IV), and the Victorian period. It has also been used to designate the crises around the King's madness, beginning in 1788–89, resulting in the Prince of Wales becoming Prince Regent once George III was declared insane for a final time in 1811. The Regency thus also corresponds both to 1811–1820 and to George IV's reign (1820–1830) after his father's death, and signifies this period's distinctive fashion and taste, exemplified by the architect John Nash's design of George IV's summer pavilion in Brighton, or his transformation of London during the same period (Trafalgar Square, Regent's Park and surrounding Terraces, Regent Street, the Royal Mews and Marble Arch, the remodelling of Buckingham House as the current Buckingham Palace). Arts, science and culture flourished under George IV's patronage, which supported the founding of the Royal Society for Literature (1820), the Royal Society of Music (1822), the National Gallery (1823), and the Royal Geographical Society (1830), as well as the donation of the King's Library to the British Museum (1823).

Played out against the backdrop of political upheavals, class disparities, and economic deprivations, the spectacle of Regency society also seemed flagrantly insensitive, increasingly superfluous, and generally out of touch with Britain's changing population. Long before 1811 the Prince of Wales' debts and extravagant lifestyle (in contrast to his father's austerity) had been the focus of much scorn in the public press and necessitated parliamentary intervention on several occasions. Given royal prerogative to make a public spectacle of his private excesses after 1811, George was very much a foolish and profligate figure to most of his subjects. By the time he took the throne he was alcoholic and obese, and spent much of his reign in seclusion in Windsor Castle. In 1820 he entreated parliament for the Pains and Penalties Bill to annul his marriage to his wife Charlotte (from whom he had lived apart since 1795) and strip her of the title of Queen. Charlotte being the object of much sympathy with the British public, the move was immensely unpopular, though George prevented her attending his coronation, which was itself an extravagant affair. Other interventions, like his opposition to the Catholic emancipation from political disability that resulted in the Catholic Relief Act of 1823, did little to endear him to a reform-minded public. Insofar as the monarch had effective political power, George's meddling, like his mismanagement of political tensions between the British government's two parties, liberal Whigs and conservative Tories, only further exacerbated social tensions that were to result in the First Reform Bill of 1832. By the time of his death in 1830, George was roundly vilified. His obituary in *The Times* famously wrote, 'There never was an individual less regretted by his fellow-creatures than this deceased king'. In general the Regency is thought of as a period of both cultural refinement and ostentatious display, enlightened progress and retrogressive politics. In short, the Regency, like the 1790s, defines the ambivalence of Romantic history *par excellence*. If George IV is remembered as a cultural patron of considerable vision, his death also marked the time for a change.

Coda: Empire

The time from George III's loss of the American colonies in 1783 to the Congress of Vienna witnesses the rise of what is thought of as the Second British Empire, also called Britain's imperial century, which ends definitively with the beginning of World War I in 1914. The 1815 treaty ceded significant lands around the globe to Britain and left it free to pursue global expansion, mostly unchallenged on the international stage. Either directly because of the colonies it controlled or indirectly because of its pre-eminence in world trade, Britain became the world's business partner and manager. Under what was later called the Pax Britannica, it also assumed the role of the world's police force, dedicating itself to stabilizing instabilities in far-flung regions of the globe. Although the influence of the East India Company began to wane in the early nineteenth century, it had done its work as a central mechanism through which the government could exert its political and military rule abroad. By the time Victoria took the throne in 1837, Britain's project of colonial rule had taken on a life of its own in the form of the Empire's self-appointed civilizing mission around the globe, a supremacy that eventually came under fire mid-century via Chinese and especially Indian resistance to British rule.

George IV leaving no surviving heirs, his brother William IV took the throne. More restrained than his brother in his desire to make a spectacle of the royal household and lifestyle, though domestically and politically nearly as volatile (he had nine illegitimate children), William did his best to endear the monarchy once again to the British people. This restraint was a sign of the times, for by 1830 liberal revolts across Europe were ushering in a spirit of reform that would transform profoundly the social climate of the nineteenth century. In many ways the polestar of this movement were the events of the early 1830s in Britain. The new elections called when William took the throne brought to power a Whig government, which pushed against Tory opposition to introduce the First Reform Bill in 1831. The Bill's primary aim was the overhaul of political representation across Britain: rapidly expanding industrial cities like Manchester, for instance, elected no representatives to parliament, whereas older or 'rotten' boroughs like Old Sarum, with a population of under ten, sent two. The House of Commons defeated the bill, forcing the dissolution of parliament, the re-election of a Whig government, and a state of political crisis. When the Upper House defeated a Second Reform Bill later in 1831, a series of reform riots ensued. The Whig ministry of Lord Grey refused to accept the defeat, resulting in the House of Lords agreeing to a much-amended bill that then resulted in the ministry's resignation, the King attempting to restore the Duke of Wellington to office. At this point the public turned decidedly against the monarchy, forcing the restoration of Grey's ministry and the formal passing of the Reform Bill in 1832.

The Bill's success came just in time, although the victory further divided Tory traditionalists and reactionaries from Whig reformers. William spent the rest of his reign attempting to resolve the schism, and the blatant failure of his meddling essentially ended royal precedent in directly guiding affairs of state, such as making and dissolving governments. The role of the Prime Minister had assumed increasing political authority since the late eighteenth century, but emerged as the de facto leader of state by this time. The following year the Factory Act abolished work for children under nine and limited the working day to nine hours for children under thirteen, and appointed inspectors to ensure the Act's enforcement. The same year the Slavery Abolition Act eliminated slavery throughout the British Empire. In 1832 a Royal Commission into the Operation of the Poor Laws was established partly in response to the Swing Riots by rural workers in southern and eastern England. Implicitly reflecting the increasing spirit of Benthamite utilitarianism in British society (which touted the general notion of the greatest good for the greatest number), the resulting 1834 Poor Law Amendment Act centralized smaller parishes formerly responsible for dealing with the poor into Poor Law Unions and established workhouses for relief of the poor.

With the ascension of Victoria in 1837 we can risk the general statement that the British Romantic period comes to a definitive end. Though the harnessing of turbulent social, economic and cultural forces that defines the history of Great Britain post-1789 up to the reigns of George IV and William IV by no means ends with the start of Victoria's reign, we can say with some certainty that a new spirit of sobriety, utilitarianism and what was to soon to be known as moral hygiene – the idea that subjects are self-empowered to overcome their own internal desires and so become happy and well-functioning citizens in the name of nation and Empire – emerges to distinguish the Victorian from the Romantic. The change in the social, political and cultural landscape of Great Britain from the 1790s to the 1830s – the change in the physical landscape itself from the effects of industrialism – was profound. This is not to signify any death of Romanticism, although several of the major Romantic writers were dead by the early 1820s (Byron, Keats, Shelley) or later 1830s (Coleridge). And certainly it is only by the 1820s, when writers like William Hazlitt start to speak of the 'spirit of the age', by which time the age of which he was speaking was, at least in historical terms, largely over, is there any concerted effort to say what the period itself meant.

This is not to say that the period had gone without any consciousness of itself, however, for history tells a rather different story of the time racing to catch up to its own progress, and thus to its own passing. The roots of reform can be traced back to 1789 and even further to Enlightenment ideals of civil, moral, economic, and social progress. The history of the Romantic period comes to signify the turbulent negotiation of these ideals within the pulse of the everyday in the public sphere of government, commerce and print culture. If Romanticism itself is characterized by its own idealisms, it is also a time for testing these ideals. To say that Romanticism marks the general transition between the first and second British Empires, however, is not to diminish the power of its transitional status. On the contrary, if Romanticism marks Great Britain as an Empire in search of itself, and Romantic history as the restless search to consolidate this identity, the Romantic period also submits this identity to both productive and often violent scrutiny. One can debate whether the United Kingdom Britain of 1832 or 1837 was more progressive than in the 1790s when, despite a strong backlash against political radicalism, in many ways the time was more open to the idealism of reform. What remains relatively certain is the fact that the period was never quite sure about itself, and as much as that uncertainty translated into a society polarized between Tories and Whigs, reaction and reform, standing still and moving forward, it also indicates a society aware of the uncertainty of history. If anything, the period reminds us of the extent to which history and historical designations are always in transition, which is what makes the history of the Romantic period such a potent reminder of our own times.

See also: Literary and Cultural Contexts; Key Concepts and Topics

2 Literary and Cultural Contexts: Key Figures, Contexts, Genres and Movements

Sue Chaplin

Chapter Overview

Key Figures

Jane Austen (1775–1817)

Major Works: *Northanger Abbey* (1818); *Sense and Sensibility* (1811); *Pride and Prejudice* (1813); *Mansfield Park* (1814); *Emma* (1816); *Persuasion* (1818)

See also: *Prose fiction*

Although not especially prolific (she published six novels in adulthood and wrote a novella, *Love and Friendship*, aged 15), Austen has been credited with bringing the English novel to maturity. Her novels are concerned with middle class provincial life and her detailed observation of the nuances of class, her irony and sharp dialogue provide for vivid and often satirical social commentary on the manners and mores of polite society in Regency England. Her first work, *Northanger Abbey* (published posthumously in 1818, but begun in the 1790s), was a satire on the Gothic romances so popular in the 1790s. *Sense and Sensibility* and *Pride and Prejudice* were also started in the 1790s although unpublished until 1811 and 1813 respectively. *Sense and Sensibility* reveals in particular Austen's concerns regarding the debilitating influence of excessive sensibility upon the mind and body, and suggests the need for feeling to be balanced by sound judgement. This concern is reflected elsewhere in Austen's work in terms of style and content: her narrative voice is cool and detached; the characters that thrive are those who feel deeply, but who possess or develop the capacity to judge dispassionately between competing claims and interests. Austen's novels also privilege the self-development of young women (Emma in *Emma*, Fanny Price in *Mansfield Park*, Anne Elliot in *Persuasion*), and although Austen was not politically radical as such, her work does expose the tensions, contradictions and injustices suffered by women whose security depended upon making a good marriage. Indeed, though her novels might be said ultimately to condone the values of the property-owning middle and upper classes, they also often challenge the notion that a 'good marriage' is to be understood solely in terms of financial gain and social enhancement: *Pride and Prejudice* is a prime example. Austen herself remained unmarried and was well aware of the limitations facing the single female; in a letter of 1816 she observed that 'single women have a dreadful propensity for being poor, which is one very strong argument in favour of matrimony'.

Joanna Baillie (1762–1851)

Major Works: *Poems: Wherein it is attempted to Describe Certain Views of Nature and of Rustic Manners* (1790); *Plays on the Passions* (1798); *De Montfort* (1798) *Constantine Paleologus: the Last of the Caesars* (1805); *Orra* (1812)

See also: *Drama*

Joanna Baillie was a Scottish-born writer whose life and career span the whole of the Romantic period and who was, at various times, part of diverse intellectual circles that included Robert Southey, William Wordsworth, Anna Laetitia Barbauld, actress Sarah Siddons and ex-slave Olaudah Equiano (whose memoirs Baillie sponsored). She is best known as a prolific and highly influential playwright of the period whose first dramatic work *Plays on the Passions* was a very well received, sparking considerable interest in the identity of the author (it was published anonymously). Baillie achieved considerable literary success, was well known in Europe as well as England,

and was acclaimed by Sir Walter Scott and Lord Byron as one of the best (if not the best) dramatists of her generation. She had innovative ideas regarding drama and poetry and the preface to *Plays on the Passions*, entitled 'Introductory Discourse', anticipates later Romantic aesthetic thinking in significant ways. Baillie contends that a writer ought to be concerned with the lower and middle classes of society for it is amongst these classes that key aspects of human nature can be most clearly observed; she argues that a writer ought also to speak in the language of plain, ordinary people as far as possible. Baillie thus anticipates Wordsworth's similar observations in the preface to the *Lyrical Ballads* by two years.

Anna Laetitia Barbauld (1743–1825)
Major Works: Poems (1792), including 'Epistle to William Wilberforce'; Works (1825), including 'The Rights of Woman'; 'Eighteen Hundred and Eleven' (1811)

Barbauld's father, John Aikin, was part of the community of radicals and dissenters based at the Warrington Academy in the mid-to-late eighteenth century. Anna Barbauld was a teacher at the Academy, and there in the 1770s she met Joseph Priestley who encouraged her to begin to write. Her first volume of poetry was published in 1773 and by the 1790s Barbauld was a respected and productive writer well known to the leading literary figures of the day. Much of her later work reflects her radicalism: see the powerful anti-slavery poem 'Epistle to William Wilberforce', 'The Rights of Woman' and possibly her most famous poem, 'Eighteen Hundred and Eleven'.

Barbauld was also highly influential in the development of literature for children in the Romantic period. The notion of writing especially for children in a style that they could readily understand (Barbauld, for instance, used large print and well-spaced text to ensure children could read her stories easily) was relatively new and Barbauld was key to the establishment and popularization of this genre and its conventions.

William Blake (1757–1827)
Major Works: *Book of Thell* (1789); *Visions of the Daughters of Albion* (1793); *Songs of Innocence and Experience* (1794); *The Book of Urizen* (1794); *The Song of Los* (1795); *The Four Zoas* (1797); *There is No Natural Religion* (1788)

See also: *Religion*

Although Blake is now one of the best known poets of the Romantic era, his work was not widely acknowledged during his lifetime, nor was he a part of the social and intellectual circles that embraced Wordsworth, Coleridge and other key Romantic writers. Blake was never financially prosperous and he worked for most of his adult life as an engraver. Indeed, the engravings that accompany Blake's poetry (and that often utilized highly innovative production methods) form a significant component of Blake's art.

Blake was a deeply and unconventionally religious artist who was influenced early on in his career by his father's adherence to the doctrines of Swedish philosopher, Emanuel Swedenborg. The mystical and mythic vision that characterizes his later work is evident early on in the 1789 *Book of Thell* and the collection published in 1794 under the title *Songs of Innocence and Experience Shewing the Contrary States of the Human Soul*. Blake's long poems go on to develop an entire Blakean mythology, expressing a vivid sense of the necessity of spiritual and social struggle, and the possibilities of redemption through rebellion against oppressive moral and religious codes. *The Visions of the Daughters of Albion* (1793) introduces the psychological and spiritual forces that comprise the key components of this mythology: the oppressive force of conventional religion and morality, represented by the figure of Urizen, and the embodiment of emancipatory rebellion, Orc. *Visions of the Daughters of Albion* was quickly followed by works which developed these thematic and symbolic elements and which posed a significant and sustained assault upon the traditional Christian notion of a benevolent God and a sinful, fallen humanity: see *The Book of Urizen* (1794); *The Song of Los* (1795); *The Four Zoas* (1797). This religious radicalism was accompanied by a pro-revolutionary political commitment influenced by the writing of Thomas Paine and William Godwin in the early 1790s. Blake was extremely hostile to institutions of authority, including monarchy and the established church (see *There is No Natural Religion* and *All Religions are One*, 1788, and 'The French Revolution: A Poem', 1791). Blake was also one of a growing number of writers in the period to support the abolitionist movement and the poem 'America: A Prophecy' uses the mythic symbolism developed elsewhere to oppose the institution of slavery.

Edmund Burke (1729–1797)
Major Works: *A Philosophical Enquiry into the Origin of our Ideas of the Sublime and the Beautiful* (1757); *Reflections on the Revolution in France* (1790)

Burke was an influential Anglo-Irish political thinker and Whig parliamentarian in the late eighteenth century. He is remembered especially for his condemnation of the French revolution, which prompted a number of radical refutations of his arguments (Thomas Paine's *The Rights of Man* and Mary Wollstonecraft's *Vindication of the Rights of Man*, for instance). Burke was prompted to write *Reflections on the Revolution in France* after reading in January 1790 a pro-revolutionary sermon that had been delivered by the

Reverend Richard Price to the Revolution Society two months earlier. Burke immediately set to work composing a repudiation of Price's position and *Reflections on the Revolution in France* was published in November 1790. The work argued that the evolution over centuries of the British constitution rendered it especially suited to the governance of the British people; Burke was deeply hostile to revolutionary change based upon, as he saw it, abstract principles that had no practical application to government and that would destroy the security and stability guaranteed by ancient systems of monarchical rule. Burke praised the French monarchy and came under particular attack on account of what radicals regarded as his emotional and irrational defence of Marie Antoinette (see Wollstonecraft's *Vindication*).

Burke's aesthetic philosophy was also an important component of his thinking; set out in *A Philosophical Enquiry into the Origin of our Ideas of the Sublime and the Beautiful* in 1757, his ideas had a great influence upon Romantic aesthetic theory. Burke defines beauty not in terms of aesthetic perfection, but in terms of feelings of pleasure and affection inspired by certain objects; beauty, for Burke, has an important social purpose in generating affection towards certain individuals, objects and social goals. His reasoning here is evident later, in the *Reflections*, where he insists that social institutions ought to be beautiful in order to inspire the affection, trust and loyalty of the people. The sublime, on the other hand, is related to experiences of pain that produce terror in a subject confronted by a seemingly overwhelming manifestation of 'Power' (the power of God, or of the violent forces of nature, for example). Burke's theory of the sublime was especially influential upon later conceptualizations of the Romantic sublime in Britain and Europe.

Robert Burns (1759–1796)
Major Works: 'To a Mouse' (1785); 'Auld Lang Syne' (1788); 'Tam O'Shanter' (1790); 'Highland Mary' (1792); 'A Red, Red Rose' (1794)

Burns was born into a poor farming family in Ayrshire and received no formal education. When his poetry began to be published in the late 1780s, however, it received some critical acclaim and Burns came to be celebrated as an unschooled rural poet, a 'heaven taught ploughman' in the words of Scottish novelist Henry Mackenzie. Burns wrote many songs and poems in the Scottish vernacular that became widely known, including 'Auld Lang Syne', 'Tam O'Shanter', 'To a Mouse', 'A Red, Red Rose' and 'Highland Mary'. Burns had sympathy with the American and French revolutions and some of his poems express antipathy towards religion, especially the Calvinist faith of his family: see 'The Two Herds' and 'Holy Willie's Prayer'. Burns' politics and his personal life (he had several affairs before finally marrying) caused him to be regarded with some suspicion by the church, though Burns did have a lifelong active association with freemasonry which helped spread his fame: he was named poet laureate of the Edinburgh lodge in 1784.

Burns' literary success (his output was prolific in his early career) allowed him some financial security and he was able to take a lease on a farm holding at Ellisland with his wife, Jean Armour. Financial difficulties remained, however, and the family was forced to move from the farm in 1791. A period of poor health followed and a longstanding heart condition resulted in Burns' premature death at the age of 37. Burns' reputation grew considerably after his death and he has achieved the status of Scotland's national poet: 'Burns Night' is celebrated in Scotland on 25th January, Burns' birthday.

Lord Byron, George Gordon (1788–1824)

Major Works: 'Childe Harold's Pilgrimage' (1812); 'Don Juan' (1818); *The Prisoner of Chillon and Other Poems* (1816); 'Manfred' (1816–7); *Poems* (1816) *Hebrew Melodies* (1815)

See also: *Poetry and the poet*

Possibly the most colourful and controversial of the Romantic poets, Lord Byron gave his name to the Romantic archetype: the 'Byronic hero'. Byron's poetry is diverse and often difficult to reconcile with the emerging Romantic aesthetic of the period. Indeed, Byron at times set himself deliberately apart from the movement associated with the first-generation Romantics: Wordsworth and Coleridge. Byron privileged the neo-classical aesthetic of the early eighteenth century against what he described in a letter of 1811 as the 'wrong revolutionary poetic system' of some of his peers. This aesthetic position informed Byron's satirical poem, 'Don Juan', in which Byron scathingly attacks the sensibility of the 'lake poets'. In spite of his aesthetic distance, in certain respects, from Romanticism, and in spite of the notoriety of his personal life, Byron was nevertheless one of the best-selling poets of the moment and the semi-autobiographical poem 'Childe Harold's Pilgrimage' sold out in three days following the publication in 1812 of the first two cantos. His greatest work, 'Don Juan', as well as satirizing the style and sensibility of the early Romantics, also outraged public opinion on account of its amorality and a profanity verging on blasphemy. The poem is comic, but bleak in its appraisal of human nature and it reflects a dark strain in Byron's work that finds fuller expression in poems with a distinct 'Gothic' quality: 'The Giaour' and 'Manfred', for instance.

Like his close friend Percy Bysshe Shelley, Byron was politically radical (which provided him with a further bone of contention in relation to poets such as Wordsworth and Southey) and delivered a rousing speech in support of the Nottingham weavers in 1812. He had an aversion to institutionalized authority, especially the authority of the established church, and this found expression in Byron's poetry as it did in Shelley's. After Shelley's death in 1822, Byron devoted himself to the cause of Greek independence, joining the forces fighting the Turks and supporting the cause financially until his death of a fever in Greece in 1824.

John Clare (1793–1894)

Major Works: *Poems Descriptive of Rural Life and Scenery* (1820); *The Village Minstrel* (1821) *The Shepherd's Calendar* (1827);

See also: *Changing Landscape*

Clare was born into difficult circumstances. His father was an agricultural labourer dependent on poor relief and Clare received no formal education. His first published work, *Poems Descriptive of Rural Life and Scenery* (influenced by the eighteenth century poets Oliver Goldsmith and James Thompson) was well received and offered Clare a brief respite from poverty and a degree of literary fame as he became acquainted with Coleridge, William Hazlitt and Charles Lamb. His next two publications, *The Village Minstrel* and *The Shepherd's Calendar*, were less successful and Clare had to continue working as a labourer to support his growing family. He suffered bouts of severe mental and physical ill health and was committed to the Northampton asylum in 1841.

Clare is best known for his close connection to the landscape of his childhood, the village of Helpstone in Northamptonshire. This region was transformed by the Enclosure Acts of the late eighteenth and early nineteenth centuries and much of Clare's poetry addresses and laments the changed landscape in terms that reflect a distinctly Romantic sense of mourning and loss; his works are nostalgic, often intensely personal and infused with a powerful political awareness of the devastating impact of Enclosure upon the land and working people of rural England: see the group of poems known as the *Enclosure Elegies* which include 'The Mores', 'Remembrances', 'Lament of Swordy Well' and 'To a Fallen Elm'.

Contributing to Clare's mental ill health was his sense of literary failure. His poetic style was deemed so unconventional by his publisher John Taylor that Taylor was in the habit of significantly reworking Clare's poetry and Clare felt unable to develop a poetic voice capable of expressing his poetic sensibility. Indeed, Clare was barely read following his death in 1864 and it was only in the late twentieth century that Clare's work began to be significantly re-appraised and the extent of his achievement acknowledged.

Samuel Taylor Coleridge (1772–1834)

Major Works: 'Frost at Midnight' (1798); 'This Lime Tree Bower my Prison' (1797); 'Christabel' (1798–1801); Kubla Khan (1797); 'The Rime of the Ancient Mariner' (1817); *Biographia Literaria* (1817)

See also: *Literary Criticism; Poetry and the Poet; Religion*

Coleridge is one of the first-generation Romantic poets and one of the 'Big Six' of the Romantic canon along with Wordsworth, Blake, Keats, Shelley and Byron. Like many other writers of the early Romantic period, including his close friends William Wordsworth and Robert Southey, Coleridge was politically radical in the immediate years after the French revolution and, inspired by the philosophy of William Godwin, he devised a scheme with Robert Southey to establish a commune in New England based upon what Coleridge called 'Pantisocracy'. The scheme did not materialise, but Coleridge retained his radicalism throughout the 1790s before becoming, like Wordsworth, increasingly conservative and disillusioned with the revolution.

Coleridge's literary career began in earnest with his 1797–9 collaboration with Wordsworth on the *Lyrical Ballads*. His early poems share Wordsworth's developing belief in the transformative power of Nature and Imagination, a belief reflected also in Coleridge's long, critical and philosophical essay, *Biographia Literaria* (1817). This period of collaboration with Wordsworth was one of intense creativity for Coleridge and some of the poems published in *Lyrical Ballads* are amongst his most important work ('The Ancient Mariner',' Kubla Khan', 'This Lime Tree Bower My Prison',' Frost at Midnight'). Coleridge's work often offers a darker poetic vision than Wordsworth's; it tends at times towards the fantastical, the supernatural and can be almost Gothic in its treatment of sin, damnation and redemption. Wordsworth was not always comfortable with Coleridge's darker Romantic vision and left the long poem 'Christabel' (in which a vampiric female, Geraldine, seduces the virginal Christabel) out of the 1798 edition of *Lyrical Ballads*.

Coleridge's middle years were characterized by opium addiction, self-doubt and depression (exacerbated by his addiction and factors in his personal life – notably the failure of his marriage, his infatuation with Wordsworth's sister-in-law, Sarah Hutchinson, and the deterioration of his relationship with Wordsworth). Coleridge's poetic powers also declined as he lost the radicalism and creative drive of his youth. As a critic, philosopher and social commentator, however, Coleridge continued to thrive: see the *Lay Sermons* (1816–17); *Aids to Reflection* (1824); *On the Constitution of the Church and State* (1829). In the *Statesman's Manual* of 1816, Coleridge established a distinction between Symbol and Allegory that became fundamental to later understandings of Romanticism. Through his lectures on Shakespeare, he exerted great influence upon later Shakespeare criticism, and the *Biographia Literaria* of 1817 is one of the key texts of the British Romantic movement, asserting as central to the Romantic aesthetic the unifying, transformative power of Imagination.

William Godwin (1756–1827)
Major Works: *Enquiry Concerning Political Justice* (1791); *Caleb Williams* (1794)

Godwin was a philosopher and novelist whose pro-revolutionary writings in the 1790s influenced key Romantic figures including Wordsworth and Southey in their early careers, and, later, Hazlitt, Byron and Shelley (who married Mary, Godwin's daughter with Mary Wollstonecraft). Godwin was part of the radical circle in the post-revolutionary decade that included Richard Price, whose sermon on the revolution Godwin attended in 1789. In 1794, Godwin came to the aid of fellow radicals charged with treason under the draconian sedition laws of the period. He wrote *Cursory Strictures on the Charge Delivered by Lord Chief Justice Eyre to the Grand Jury, 1794*, which helped secure the acquittal of the defendants. His best known works of this time are *Enquiry Concerning Political Justice* (1791) and the political novel *Caleb Williams* (1794). The *Enquiry* expresses Godwin's belief that man is innately rational and benevolent, and that government and law only serve to warp and oppress human nature. *Caleb Williams* offers a darker vision of the impact of hierarchical, hereditary government upon human character and freedom. *Caleb Williams* seems to anticipate Godwin's subsequent disillusionment with radical politics, and his *Thoughts on Man*, published in 1831, repudiates some of the pro-revolutionary principles of the *Enquiry Concerning Political Justice*.

Godwin's personal life has been the subject of close scrutiny owing to his relationship with Mary Wollstonecraft. Following an intense period of friendship, the couple married when Mary discovered she was pregnant. Mary died, however, shortly after giving birth to the daughter who would go on to marry Percy Shelley and write the famous Gothic novel, *Frankenstein*. The relationship damaged the reputation of both parties and this was exacerbated following Godwin's publication of Mary's biography, *Memoirs of the Author of the Vindication of the Rights of Woman*, in 1798. Both of them were excoriated in the conservative press and Godwin became an increasingly isolated figure. He continued to write until his death, however, and his output remained diverse, including novels (*St. Leon*, 1799, *Fleetwood*, 1805, *Mandeville*, 1817) political and historical essays ('Of Population', 1820, 'History of the Commonwealth', 1828) and some works for children.

William Hazlitt (1778–1830)

Major Works: *Characters of Shakespeare* (1817); 'My First Acquaintance with the Poets' (1823); *The Spirit of the Age* (1825)

See also: *Literary Criticism*

Hazlitt was the son of a Unitarian minister and his father was part of a radical intellectual circle that included Joseph Priestley and Richard Price. Hazlitt was close to Wordsworth and Coleridge in their early career and wrote of his acquaintance with them in the important 1823 essay 'My First Acquaintance with the Poets'. Like the later Romantic poets, though, Hazlitt challenged the increasing conservatism of Wordsworth and Coleridge, regarding it as a betrayal of their earlier pro-revolutionary stance. He was influential as an essayist and journalist and wrote a number of social and political analyses that reveal his radical sympathies (see *Reply to Malthus's Essay on Population*, 1807, and *Political Essays*, 1819). As a journalist and parliamentary reporter, he contributed to a variety of the period's key magazines including the *Edinburgh Review* and Leigh hunt's *The Examiner*.

As a literary critic, Hazlitt helped shape the literary movements of his time. His lectures on the English poets (1818) influenced John Keats in the development of his idea of 'negative capability' and his 1817 *Characters of Shakespeare* was a key work of Shakespearean criticism. His most well-known work is *The Spirit of the Age* (1825), an analysis of the leading artists and thinkers of the period in which Hazlitt privileges the romantic emphasis on feeling and experience over the rationalist, utilitarian philosophy emerging in the work of Thomas Malthus and Jeremy Bentham.

Felicia Hemans (1793–1835)

Major Works: 'Casabianca' (1828); *The Records of Woman* (1820)

Hemans was a precocious child who published her first volume of poetry at the age of fourteen. The collection came to the attention of Percy Shelley who praised her talent in a letter to Thomas Hogg in 1811. Like many literary women of the period, though, Hemans had a difficult personal life; following her separation from her husband in 1818, she was left to bring up five children and needed to write for money. She therefore wrote prolifically, publishing nine volumes of poetry between 1819 and 1830 and contributing regularly to the leading periodicals of the time. Her work was widely praised in the 1820s and the *Literary Chronicle* acclaimed her 'the first poetess of the day' in 1826.

Hemans was a particular favourite of the Tory press, which appreciated her patriotic stance during and after the Napoleonic wars. Hemans was a complex figure, however, whose patriotism was tempered by empathy with the victims of war (see the famous poem 'Casabianca' of 1828) and especially with the suffering of women. The 1820 volume *The Records of Woman* is quite daring in its treatment of the condition of women and Hemans' concerns extend beyond the troubles of women of her own class and nation; 'Indian woman's Death Song', for instance, laments the suicide of an Indian woman deserted by her husband. Hemans' death in 1835 was commemorated by Wordsworth who re-published his 'Extempore Effusion on the Death of James Hogg' in 1837 with an extra stanza dedicated to Hemans.

Leigh Hunt (1784–1859)

Major Works: 'The Story of Rimini' (1816); Editorship of *The Examiner* (1808–1825)

See also: *Journals, Periodicals and Magazines*

Although not one of the six canonical Romantic poets, Hunt was central to the second generation Romantic movement. He was close to Keats, Shelley and Byron, and through his editorship of various periodicals (notably *The Examiner*) he helped to publish and promote the poetry of the late Romantics.

Hunt was a political radical and a vocal critic of the Regency establishment. His attack on the Prince Regent in 1812 resulted in his imprisonment for sedition. He was also a poet (his most famous work was the long narrative poem 'The Story of Rimini', 1816), though his work was not always well received outside his immediate circle and was often lambasted by the Tory press. Indeed, Hunt was frequently the subject of vitriolic attacks in journals such as the *Quarterly Review* on account of his politics and background, as well as his literary work: along with Keats and Hazlitt, Hunt was classed as part of the 'Cockney School' of poetry, a disparaging term designed to draw attention to the lower social class of these radical writers.

John Keats (1795–1821)

Major Works: 'On First Looking into Chapman's Homer' (1817); 'Endymion' (1818); 'To Autumn' (1819); 'To Psyche' (1819); 'To a Nightingale' (1819); 'Ode on a Grecian Urn' (1819); 'Lamia' (1819); 'The Eve of St Agnes' (1819)

See also: *Poetry and the Poet*

Keats revealed ambitions to be a writer very early in life, but his family was not wealthy, and following the death of his father he became an apprentice apothecary with a view to training as a surgeon. When he began to write poetry seriously, he was helped to publish his work and establish his name by his friends and mentors, Percy Shelley and Leigh Hunt. Keats' work did not enjoy a great deal of initial success, however, and his long 1818 poem

'Endymion' received very harsh reviews in the conservative press (though the radicalism of Leigh Hunt, with whom Keats was associated, had something to do with this). His work from 1819 showed greater maturity and versatility and Keats is perhaps best known today for the odes published in the summer of that year (for example, To 'Autumn', 'To Psyche', 'To a Nightingale'). Keats also developed the notion of 'negative capability' which he defined as the state of 'being in uncertainties, mysteries, doubts, without any irritable reaching after reason'. Keats privileged the imagination as the faculty consistent with negative capability, and thus his aesthetic has points in common with the aesthetic thinking of Wordsworth and Coleridge. Keats felt, though, that the earlier poets were rather too given to the rationalization of the poetic impulse, towards 'consecutive reasoning' as he put it.

Much of Keats' work has a rather dark, almost Gothic aspect and is infused with a sense of transience, suffering and decay, often mediated through an ambivalent female figure: see for instance the longer poems written in 1819 – 'The Eve of St Agnes', 'Lamia' and 'La Belle Dame Sans Merci'. These poems had a good deal of influence upon nineteenth-century art and literature: 'La Belle Dame Sans Merci' became a favourite subject for the pre-Raphaelite painters whilst 'Lamia' influenced the Gothic writer Edgar Allan Poe. It is possible that the sense of mortality and melancholy present in Keats' work of this period reflected the poet's sense of his own mortality: he nursed his brother to his death from consumption in 1818, having done the same for his mother seven years earlier, and he had a strong intuition that he, too, would meet an early death. This intimation of mortality might also have accounted for Keats' extraordinary productivity after his brother 's death. Keats did indeed succumb to consumption in February 1821.

Hannah More (1745–1833)

Major Works: *Poems on Several Occasions* (1785); 'Slavery: a Poem' (1788) 'Sensibility: A Poem' (1782)

See also: *Abolition of Slavery*

More was an extremely successful writer in her time and made a considerable fortune through her diverse writings, which included works of poetry, drama and influential religious, political and educational essays. Her tragedy *The Inflexible Captive* (1773) was admired by the actor Garrick who became a close friend and mentor of More, introducing her to some of the leading artists and thinkers of the day. It was through Garrick that More met Elizabeth Montagu of the 'Blue Stocking' movement and More herself became a prominent Blue Stocking; her most famous poem, 'Sensibility', was inspired by the group. The 'Blue Stocking Ladies' was a diverse collection of well-educated women who organised cultural and literary gatherings, supported each other's work and campaigned around some of the key issues of the moment, including slavery and improved education for women. More was an ardent anti-slavery campaigner and worked alongside William Wilberforce in the abolitionist movement. Unlike certain other Blue Stocking women (Anna Barbauld, for example), More was conservative and anti-revolutionary in her politics and did not support the radical position of some of her female contemporaries in respect of the rights of women. More emphasized the traditional role of woman as homemaker and mother, though she did advocate education for women on the grounds that it would enhance women's capacities to contribute effectively to the stability of home and nation. More was also staunchly Christian and her faith informed her writing and her social activism. The poem 'The Sorrows of Yamba' combines abolitionism with the Christian evangelism that characterizes much of her work. In her later career, More produced mainly religious and didactic texts and she played a key role in the formation of the Sunday School movement.

Thomas Paine (1737–1809)

Major Works: *Common Sense* (1776); *Rights of Man: Being an Answer to Mr. Burke's Attack on the French Revolution* (1791); *The Age of Reason* (1794)

See also: *Revolution*

Paine was one of the foremost advocates in England of the American and French revolutions. His reputation as an outspoken propagandist was established while he was working as a journalist in Philadelphia; here, in 1776, he published the pamphlet *Common Sense* in which he defended American independence, and between 1776 and 1783 he produced a series of pamphlets entitled 'Crisis' in support of the revolution. His most famous work, published in 1791 in response to Edmund Burke's *Reflections on the Revolution in France*, was *Rights of Man: Being an Answer to Mr. Burke's Attack on the French Revolution*. Paine argued in favour of a democratic republic, asserted the natural equality of all men and condemned hereditary monarchy for reducing the people to the status of chattels beholden to the monarch. To avoid a charge of treason consequent upon the publication of this work, Paine fled to France where he was elected to the National Convention before falling victim to the 'Terror' in 1793. Paine was imprisoned in France from 1793–4 and during his incarceration he wrote *The Age of Reason* in which he vociferously attacked the Christian church. As a result, Paine became an even more controversial figure in England and he spent the final years of his life back in America. His influence declined considerably during these final years when he was plagued by ill health and financial problems. He died in relative obscurity and was buried in New York in unconsecrated ground. Paine was nevertheless central to the radicalism of the early Romantic period and he has been regarded (along with contemporary figures such as Godwin and Wollstonecraft) as an inspiration to emancipationist movements since.

Thomas De Quincey (1785–1859)

Major Works: *Confessions of an English Opium Eater* (1822); 'On Knocking on the Gate in Macbeth' (1823); 'On Murder Considered as one of the Fine Arts' (1827); 'Suspiria de Profundis' (1845)

See also: *Autobiographical Writing*

De Quincey was throughout his life plagued by financial problems and ill health (often the result of his opium addiction). He ran away from his Manchester home in 1802 and ended up destitute in London. His situation improved following his reconciliation with his family a year later. He attended Worcester College, Oxford, and befriended Samuel Taylor Coleridge who introduced him to Wordsworth in 1807. Wordsworth had long been a hero of the young De Quincey who had read the *Lyrical Ballads* aged 15 and even contemplated seeking Wordsworth out at Dove Cottage after running away from home. Their friendship cooled after some years, however, as De Quincey became increasingly addicted to opium. The estrangement was complete following the publication of a series of De Quincey's reminiscences in *Tait's Edinburgh Magazine* in the 1830s which greatly offended Wordsworth in their treatment of the 'lake poets' (De Quincey famously accused Coleridge of plagiarism, for instance, in 1834).

Journalism was a key source of income for De Quincey and he contributed extensively to diverse leading periodicals of the day, including *Blackwood's*, *Tait's* and the *London Magazine*. These journals published some of De Quincey's finest essays: 'On Knocking on the gate in Macbeth', 'On Murder Considered as one of the Fine Arts', 'The Glory of Motion' and 'The Vision of Sudden Death'. De Quincey is best known for his 1821 *Confessions of an English Opium Eater*, one of the most frank and vivid examples of Romantic-era autobiography. It was a sensation at the time and has been influential since as a literary work (its style is darkly Romantic, and influenced Edgar Allan Poe and Charles Baudelaire) and a as a psychological study of addiction.

Ann Radcliffe (1764–1823)

Major Works: *The Mysteries of Udolpho* (1794); *The Italian* (1797) 'On the Supernatural in Poetry' (1826)

See also: *Gothic Fiction*

Ann Radcliffe was the most successful Gothic novelist of the 1790s and although her work attracted some negative critical and satirical treatment (Austen famously satirised aspects of Radcliffean gothic in *Northanger Abbey*), her fictions were best sellers in their time and earned Radcliffe a good deal of money. Her first novel, *The Castles of Athlin and Dunbayne* (1789), indulged the contemporary interest in medievalism and Celtic tales; set in the highlands of Scotland, the romance introduces the themes of vengeance, disrupted bloodlines and persecution (often of vulnerable young women) that recurred throughout Radcliffe's work and that were staples of Gothic fiction in the period. Her next four novels (*A Sicilian Romance*, 1790; *The Romance of the Forest*, 1791; *The Mysteries of Udolpho*, 1794; *The Italian*, 1796) are set in southern Europe and frequently turn upon a mystery surrounding the origin of the female protagonist whose search for identity drives the narrative. Radcliffe's concern with questions of female identity and its vulnerability to distortion and misappropriation has led critics to associate her work with a particular variety of Gothic writing: 'Female Gothic'. The Female Gothic novel tends to foreground the fragile, often threatened subjectivities of women and to problematize the patriarchal systems of authority that construct such subjectivities.

Radcliffe's last novel, *Gaston de Blondeville*, was published in 1826 along with an essay entitled 'On the Supernatural in Poetry'. This essay theorizes the aesthetic of 'terror' which had become associated with Radcliffe's Gothic style and which Radcliffe sets in opposition to the aesthetic of 'horror' popularized by Matthew Lewis's controversial Gothic novel, *The Monk*, in 1796. Radcliffe celebrates the capacity of 'terror' writing to expand the imagination of the reader through the evocation of suspense and obscurity. The essay also reveals the considerable influence of Shakespeare and Milton upon the development of the literature of terror in the late eighteenth century.

Walter Scott (1771–1832)

Major Works: *Waverley* (1814); *The Heart of Midlothian* (1818); *Ivanhoe* (1819)

See also: *Prose Fiction*

Scott, like Burns, has become a writer associated with the Scottish landscape and with the formation of a certain Scottish national identity during and after the Romantic period. Scott, unlike Burns, was born into a prosperous old Scottish family; his father was a solicitor and Scott followed his father into the legal profession, becoming clerk to the Court of Session in Edinburgh in 1806. Scott's family history (he was related to old families on both sides of the border) sparked his interest in the folk tales and legends of the border country, and his first works were collections of poems based upon tales of the border region.

Scott's later career was beset by financial difficulties following his establishment of a publishing house with James Ballantyne. The business faltered and Scott took on an immense amount of debt. This took its toll on Scott's health; he suffered polio as a child and though he was nevertheless a physically robust man, long hours writing (in his diaries he refers to himself as 'a sort of writing automaton') left him in considerable pain. In spite of these difficulties, Scott was a prolific writer of fiction and is best known for his Scottish historical novels set from the medieval period to the seventeenth and eighteenth centuries (*Waverley*, 1814; *Guy Mannering*, 1815; *The Antiquary*, 1816; *Old Mortality*, 1816; *The Heart of Midlothian*, 1818; *Ivanhoe*, 1819).

In the early-to-mid twentieth century, Scott's popularity waned; he was disparaged as a novelist by the influential critic F. R. Leavis, for example. Scott's legacy has since been critically acknowledged, however, and it is now accepted that Scott's fiction had a considerable formative influence upon the development of the historical novel throughout Europe.

Mary Wollstonecraft Shelley (1797–1851)

Major Works: *Frankenstein* (1818); *The Last Man* (1826)

See also: *Gothic fiction*

Mary Shelley was the daughter of Mary Wollstonecraft and William Godwin. She met Percy Shelley in 1816 and the two become close over the next few years, eventually marrying in 1816 following the suicide of Percy's first wife, Harriet. Mary Shelley's first novel, *Frankenstein*, was also her most famous, and the circumstances surrounding its composition have become almost as well known as the novel itself. Shelley was staying at Lake Geneva in 1816 with Percy Shelley, Byron and their friend John Polidori. Byron initiated a ghost story competition and the following night Mary had a dream which she claimed inspired her to write *Frankenstein*. The novel also reveals Shelley's interest in the scientific debates of the period and her close artistic alignment with the Romantic movement.

Percy and Mary remained in Italy during their marriage, with Mary returning to London following Percy's death in 1822. She continued to write, though none of her novels achieved the fame or the critical acclaim of her first. *The Last Man* (1826) presents an apocalyptic vision of humanity in the twenty-first century and to some extent it reflects its author's increasing political disillusionment in later life. Of her other fictions, the best known is *Mathilde* (commenced in 1819, but unfinished), which contains many details pertaining to Mary's relationship with her husband and father. *Valperga* (1823) is set in fourteenth-century Italy, whilst her final two novels – *Lodore* (1835) and *Faulkner* (1837) – were works of romance and intrigue that were somewhat at odds with the changing literary tastes of the period. Shelley also published short stories, a well-received travel narrative (*Rambles in Germany and Italy*, 1844) and the first authoritative collection of Percy Shelley's poems in 1839.

Percy Bysshe Shelley (1792–1822)

Major Works: 'Queen Mab' (1813); 'Alastor; or, the Spirit of Solitude' (1815); Mont Blanc (1816); 'Hymn to Intellectual Beauty' (1817); 'Ode to the West Wind' (1819); Prometheus Unbound' (1819); 'Adonais ' (1821); 'A Defence of Poetry' (1821)

See also: *Poetry and the Poet; Literary Criticism*

Shelley was a 'second generation' Romantic poet, close to Keats, Leigh Hunt and Lord Byron. He was born into an aristocratic family and educated at Eton and, briefly, Oxford. He was expelled from university, however, following the publication in 1811 of his essay 'The Necessity of Atheism'. Shelley had a strong personality and lived an unconventional and controversial life in some respects. William Hazlitt described him as having 'a fire in his eye, a fever in his blood, a maggot in his brain, a hectic flutter in his speech which mark out the philosophical fanatic'. Shelley eloped with and married Harriet Westbrook in 1811, but left her three years later to elope with Mary Wollstonecraft Godwin whom he married following Harriet's suicide in 1816.

Shelley's first major poem was 'Queen Mab' (1813), a work that reflects the radical influence on the young poet of William Godwin and that anticipates the revolutionary impulses of later poems. Like Byron and Hunt, Shelley was politically radical, castigating Wordsworth for his betrayal of revolutionary politics and writing some of the most politically powerful poetry of the late-Romantic period. In response to the Peterloo massacre of 1819, Shelley wrote 'The Mask of Anarchy' which was perceived by his friend and publisher Leigh Hunt to be so potentially inflammatory (and therefore dangerous in the politically repressive climate of Regency England) that Hunt refrained from publishing it until after Shelley's death.

Like Wordsworth (whom Shelley greatly admired, before Wordsworth's turn away from radical politics), Shelley explored in his work the personality and role of the poet and attributed to the poet a prophetic, political function capable of rousing and giving direction to the revolutionary impulses of the people (see 'Ode to the West Wind' and the essay *A Defence of Poetry*). Shelley's poetry is also complex and ambivalent in its treatment of the imagination, nature and the divine. Shelley's longer poems ('Mont Blanc', 'Alastor', 'Hymn to Intellectual Beauty', 'Prometheus Unbound') are often philosophically bleaker than Wordsworth's; they offer no certainty as to the existence of a divine power, nor as to any transcendental spiritual or aesthetic meaning to the 'sense sublime' of Wordsworth's 'Tintern Abbey'.

Charlotte Smith (1749–1806)

Major works: *Elegiac Sonnets* (1784); *Emmeline* (1788); *The Old Manor House* (1793); 'Beachy Head' (1807)

See also: *Prose fiction*

Charlotte's Smith's importance as an early Romantic and, indeed, the extent of her influence at the very origin of the Romantic movement in the 1780s and 90s has come to be acknowledged increasingly since the 1980s. In 1784, Smith published the *Elegiac Sonnets* in the *European Magazine*. The collection was very well received and Smith expanded it considerably over the next decade until in 1797 it was published in two volumes. This work influenced Wordsworth and Coleridge who sent drafts of their early work to Smith for her consideration. One of her major poems, 'Beachy Head' (1807), is a key Romantic work in which Smith might be said to have appropriated for herself (through her conceptualization of the sublime, nature and the imagination) the artistic authority associated culturally with the male Romantic poet.

Although Smith's main literary focus was initially poetry, her family's financial difficulties (her husband was imprisoned for debt in 1783) required her urgently to earn a living through her writing, and in the five years between 1788 and 1793 she published five novels: *Emmeline* (1788); *Ethelinde* (1789); *Celestina* (1791); *Desmond* (1792); *The Old Manor House* (1793). These novels, like Smith's poetry, were critically well received and the Gothic sensibility of novels such as *Emmeline* and *The Old Manor House* influenced the development of gothic romance in the 1790s, especially through the work of Ann Radcliffe.

Robert Southey (1774–1843)

Major Works: 'Madoc' (1805); *A Vision of Judgement* (1820)

See also: *Journals, Periodicals and Magazines; The Abolition of Slavery*

Southey was a poet and essayist with a particular interest in history: see *Life of Nelson* (1813) and *History of the Peninsula War* (1822–32). He was close to Wordsworth and Coleridge (whose sister-in-law he married) and he shared their pro-revolutionary politics in the 1790s. Southey was a strong opponent of the slave trade. He also planned, with Coleridge, to found a commune in North America according to the principle of egalitarian self-government which they termed 'Pantisocracy'. Like Coleridge and Wordsworth, though, Southey became more conservative in the early years of the nineteenth century and was a significant contributor to the Tory *Quarterly Review* following its establishment in 1809.

The later Romantics were critical of Southey's increasing conservatism and Byron in particular regarded Southey as a weak man and a poor writer. Byron wrote a scathing attack on Southey, *The Vision of Judgement*, which satirizes Southey's own *A Vision of Judgement* published in 1820. Southey was also satirized in Thomas Love Peacock's 1817 novel *Melincourt*. In spite of this disapprobation, however, Southey was well regarded as a poet in his time; he was appointed Poet Laureate in 1813 and his longer epic poems were especially popular: see 'Thelaba' (1801); 'Madoc' (1805); 'Roderick' (1814).

John Thelwall (1764–1834)

Major Works: *Poems written in close confinement in the Tower and Newgate* (1795); *The Natural and Constitutional Right of Britons to Annual Parliaments, Universal Suffrage and the Freedom of Popular Association* (1795); *Poems chiefly written in retirement* (1801); Editor of *The Tribune* (1795–6)

Thelwall was a poet, journalist, essayist and one of the most committed radical activists of the 1790s. He was a member of the pro-revolutionary London Corresponding Society which attracted the attention of the increasingly oppressive government of William Pitt after the outbreak of war with France in 1793. Following a mass meeting of the society in April 1794, Thelwall was arrested along with leading members of the group and charged with treason. The suspension of the law of Habeas Corpus that same year allowed for the detention of prisoners without trial and Thelwall was in prison for five months before his acquittal in October. Following his release, Thelwall continued his activism at great personal risk. He edited the radical journal *The Tribune* between 1795–6. He was under constant surveillance and the meetings he organised were regularly broken up. The 'Gagging Acts' of 1795 (forbidding meetings of fifty or more without a licence) was in the main a government response to the activism of Thelwall and his group.

In the late 1790s Thelwall struck up a friendship with Coleridge and Wordsworth. He was attracted by Wordsworth's principle that the language of poetry should be the language of the common man. His best known poetry was written during this period and reflects the influence of Wordsworth and Coleridge: see 'Lines Written at Bridgewater' and 'To the Infant Hampden', both written in 1797.

Helen Maria Williams (1762–1827)

Major Works: *Poems* (1786); 'The Bastille: a Vision' (1790); *Julie* (1790) *Letters containing a Sketch of the Politics of France* (1795)

See also: *Women*

Williams was a politically radical writer who was a part of the intellectual circle that included Paine, Godwin and Wollstonecraft in the 1790s. She was also known to Wordsworth, whose first published poem in 1787 was entitled, 'On seeing Miss Helen Maria Williams weep at a Tale of Distress'. Her first collection of sonnets in 1786 was a considerable success, attracting 1500 subscribers. Her most famous literary work was the 1790 novel, *Julia*, which re-worked Rousseau's influential fiction, *La Nouvelle Heloise*.

Williams remained a supporter of the French revolution even following her arrest in Paris in 1793 along with all British subjects who were confined to houses of security. During this period, she wrote *Letters containing a Sketch of the Politics of France* (1795) which contains one of the few contemporary accounts of the role of women in the revolution. Williams' political affiliation with revolutionary France was controversial and regarded by many as traitorous. Her reputation suffered further when, following her release from prison in 1794, she moved to Switzerland with a married man, fellow radical John Hurford Stone. Her commitment to France continued, making it difficult for her to return to England during the war; she finally became a citizen of France in 1817 and remained unapologetically radical in her politics until her death in 1827.

Mary Wollstonecraft (1759–1797)

Major Works: *A Vindication of the Rights of Men* (1790); *A Vindication of the Rights of Woman* (1792)

See also: *Women*

Mary Wollstonecraft was one of the most outspoken radical writers of her generation, particularly with regard to the position of women. Her first published work was the pamphlet *Thoughts on the Education of Daughters* in 1787 and she briefly established and ran a school for girls with her sisters and her friend, Fanny Blood. Wollstonecraft was required to earn her own living from her late teens and following an unsuccessful period as a governess and the closure of the girls' school, she turned to writing professionally and worked initially for the liberal journal the *Analytic Review*. It was in this capacity that Wollstonecraft met Thomas Paine and William Godwin, and in 1790 she published her first major work, *Vindication of the Rights of Men*. The work was a response to Edmund Burke's *Reflections on the Revolution in France* and it was in fact the first of several radical refutations of Burke to be published in the aftermath of the revolution. Indeed, Wollstonecraft's reply to Burke was published in the *Analytic Review* a matter of weeks after Burke's *Reflections*. It presents a detailed critique of Burke's defence of the *ancient régime*, and Wollstonecraft's commitment to the cause of female emancipation is already evident here: she deplores Burke's celebration of the conservative and, in Wollstonecraft's estimation, oppressive ideal of femininity embodied for Burke by Queen Marie Antoinette. Two years later, Wollstonecraft published *Vindication of the Rights of Woman* in which she identifies the role that education and culture play in the construction of gender identities that society regards as natural and fixed. Wollstonecraft argues for the transformation of female education so as to produce rational, independent women capable of contributing to society on an equal footing with men. She took up this theme later in her unfinished novel *Maria: or, The Wrongs of Woman*, published posthumously in 1798.

Wollstonecraft's life was highly unconventional for a woman in this period and as a consequence she became something of a hate figure in the conservative press. She travelled alone to revolutionary France in 1792 and in Paris met and fell in love with Gilbert Imlay with whom she had a daughter, Fanny, in 1794. In 1796, she travelled alone to Scandinavia as Imlay's business representative and her travel narrative *Letters written during a short residence in Sweden, Norway and Denmark* was very well received and influential even after her death. Following the breakdown of her relationship with Imlay (she twice tried to take her own life after learning of his numerous infidelities), Wollstonecraft became increasingly close to her friend, William Godwin, eventually marrying him and giving birth to their daughter, Mary, in 1797. Wollstonecraft died that same year, eleven days after the birth of Mary.

Dorothy Wordsworth (1771–1855)

Major Works: *The Alfoxden Journal* (1798); *The Grasmere Journals* (1800–1802)

See also: *Autobiographical Writing*

Following the death of her mother, Dorothy was brought up apart from her brother, William, and the two were only reunited in early adulthood. They then remained together throughout the rest of their lives, settling in Dove Cottage in 1799 where they were eventually joined by William's wife, Mary. It was in the Lake District that Dorothy wrote the work for which she is now famous: *The Grasmere Journals*. The journals are of significant literary and historical interest in terms of their account of the Wordsworths' daily life, their friendship with Coleridge and the excursions that inspired some of her brother's most famous work. Yet the journals are also of literary interest in their own right; they demonstrate Dorothy's keen eye for detail and her range of literary expression. They share and undoubtedly helped to shape the artistic vision of her brother, revealing an empathic identification with the people and landscape of the region, and the difficult, mundane routines of rural life at the turn of the century. This same perspective is evident in Dorothy's poetry, some of which (unlike the journals, which were private diaries never intended for publication) was published during her lifetime. Dorothy suffered from dementia later in life, though she survived her brother for five years and was nursed through her final illness by Mary Wordsworth.

William Wordsworth (1770–1850)

Major Works: *Lyrical Ballads* (1798); 'Preface' to the second edition of *Lyrical Ballads* (1800); 'Tintern Abbey' (1798); 'Composed upon Westminster Bridge' (1802); 'Surprised by Joy' (1815); 'Mutability' (1821); 'The Excursion' (1814); *The Prelude* (1850)

See also: *Poetry and the Poet; Literary Criticism; Autobiographical Writing.*

William Wordsworth is the poet most closely associated with the Romantic movement, certainly in the popular imagination, and his *Lyrical Ballads*, published jointly with Coleridge in 1798, articulates some of the key precepts of Romanticism: the definition of poetry as 'the spontaneous overflow of powerful feelings'; the understanding of a poet as a 'man speaking to men' in the language of the common man; the notion that the circumstances of ordinary life were an appropriate subject for poetry. Wordsworth had a lengthy writing career stretching from the 1780s (he published his first poem, 'Sonnet on Seeing Miss Helen Maria Williams Weep at a Tale of Distress', in 1787) to the 1840s (he was appointed Poet Laureate in 1843). Wordsworth was born in Cockermouth to a relatively prosperous family, but the death of his mother in 1778 and his father in 1783 came close to ruining the family financially. Wordsworth suffered financial hardship for some time afterwards and this shaped his early political radicalism. At Cambridge in the late 1780s, he developed an interest in revolutionary France, and in 1790 took a walking tour of France, Germany and Switzerland which consolidated his support for the revolution. Wordsworth returned to France in 1791 and began a friendship with the pro-revolutionary aristocrat, Michel de Beaupuy; as this friendship deepened, so too did Wordsworth's revolutionary commitment, and he briefly considered joining the radical Girondist faction in Paris. During this period, Wordsworth also began an affair with Annette Vaillon who gave birth to their daughter, Caroline, at the end of 1792. Wordsworth's intention seems to have been to remain in France and marry Annette, but financial constraints required him to return to London before the birth of his daughter. The outbreak of war between England and France in 1793 separated Wordsworth from Annette and Caroline and they did not meet again until the brief respite in Anglo-French hostilities in 1802. The mid-1790s were years of hardship for Wordsworth, but this was nevertheless a productive creative period which saw the publication of important early poems such as 'The Ruined Cottage' (1797) and 'Tintern Abbey' (1798), and which marked the beginning of his collaboration with Coleridge.

Wordsworth's life and career stabilized to some degree during the first decade of the nineteenth century. He married Mary Hutchinson in 1802 and the family's financial situation improved. The household (which included Wordsworth's sister Dorothy) settled at Dove Cottage in the Lake District and Wordsworth entered into a period of introspective conservatism that intensified as he grew older and that is reflected in the most influential of his poems of this period, 'The Excursion' (1814). By 1818, Wordsworth was campaigning for the Tories in the general election and this departure from his early radicalism was regarded as something of a betrayal by second gener-ation Romantics: see Shelley's sonnet 'To Wordsworth' (1816) and Byron's satirical treatment of Wordsworth in 'Don Juan' (1819).

Following Wordsworth's death in 1850, one of his most influential works, *The Prelude*, was finally published. Wordsworth had been working on this long autobiographical poem since the late 1790s, but shared it only with his closest family and friends and continued to revise it until his death. Because of Wordsworth's lifelong work on the *Prelude*, there are several versions of the poem, including the Thirteen Book Prelude of 1805 and the Fourteen Book Prelude of 1850 (there are two earlier manuscripts dating from 1799 and 1804). The poem's emphasis on the emotional development of the poet, the impor-tance of childhood, the transformative impact on the mind of psychological and spiritual crises and the role of memory in the formation of self-identity make this work a key text of British Romanticism and it has been especially influential upon later conceptualizations of selfhood, creativity and confes-sional writing.

Ann Yearsley (1753–1806)

Major Works: *Poems on Several Occasions* (1785); 'On the Inhumanity of the Slave Trade' (1788)

See also: *Abolitionism*

Described by the Critical Review in 1787 as 'the Bristol milkmaid', Yearsley was born into a poor family, had no formal education, married at the age of 18 and had six children in six years. Nevertheless, she wrote poetry of such quality that Hannah More agreed to become her patron on reading some of her early work. More ensured distribution of Yearsley's *Poems on Several Occasions* to a number of influential subscribers, including members of the Blue Stocking group, and the volume was very well received. Tensions arose between More and Yearsley, however, following the successful publication of the collection in 1785, whereupon More insisted upon holding the profits in trust for Yearsley and her children. Yearsley came to resent More's control over her finances and in 1786 she secured the patronage of Frederick Hervey, Bishop of Derry. She wrote a number of political poems, including the 1788 Poem 'On the Inhumanity of the Slave Trade', and her work is often characterized by a political urgency in relation to questions of poverty and social injustice that is perhaps lacking in the work of more privileged writers. In addition to poetry, Yearsley wrote a play (*Earl Goodwin*, 1791) and a Gothic novel (*The Royal Captives*, 1795). She finally achieved financial independence through the establishment of a successful circulating library in 1793.

Contexts, Genres and Movements

Abolitionism
Representative Figures: William Wilberforce; Thomas Clarkson; Hannah More; Josiah Wedgwood; Robert Southey; William Cowper; Anna Laetitia Barbauld; William Blake; J. G. Stedman; Olaudah Equiano; Toussant L'Ouverture.

Before the abolition of the slave trade in Britain in 1807, Britain was a key force in the institution and perpetuation of the transatlantic slave trade. The 1807 legislation was preceded by an acrimonious struggle beginning with the protests of the Quakers in the American colonies and spreading throughout Europe in the late-eighteenth century. By the 1790s, the abolitionist campaign had strengthened considerably and slavery had become one of the key political issues of the moment. The movement received added momentum from the success of the Haitian revolution in 1804. Since 1791, the Haitian slaves, under the leadership of Toussaint L'Ouverture, had been involved in violent struggle against the French colonial rulers; the rebellion eventually culminated in the establishment of a Republic governed by the black population – the first of its kind and a powerful inspiration to abolitionists elsewhere.

The Society for Effecting the Abolition of the Slave Trade was formed in 1787 in England by a group of Quakers, though its political influence was limited by the fact that members of dissenting faiths could not stand for parliament. The society thus sought and received support from several Anglican campaigners, including Thomas Clarkson and Granville Sharp, who helped found the Committee for the Abolition of the Slave Trade to promote the cause in parliament. Clarkson was especially active in establishing abolitionist groups across the country and in promoting lectures and pamphlet campaigns nationwide. The campaign was joined in 1791 by William Wilberforce who helped drive the Abolition Bill through parliament. The issue often crossed party political lines. Wilberforce himself was an independent MP who was deeply conservative in some matters (he was opposed to the French revolution, for instance, and supported some of the politically repressive measures introduced by the government in the 1790s). Hannah More was another conservative who campaigned against the slave trade alongside Wilberforce and she was also one of a number of writers who turned to poetry to advance the cause: she published 'Slavery: a Poem' in 1788. Other notable anti-slavery poems included Anna Letitia Barbauld's 'Epistle to William Wilberforce' (1791), Ann Yearsley's 'On the inhumanity of the slave Trade' (1787); William Cowper 'The Task' (1784) and 'The Negro's Complaint' (1788); Robert Southey's sonnets against the slave trade in *Poems* (1797). William Blake, as well as writing anti-slavery poems, produced a number of vivid illustrations depicting the ill-treatment of slaves to accompany J. G. Stedman's 1796 publication, *Narrative of a Five years' Expedition Against the Revolted negroes of Surinam*. Josiah Wedgwood, meanwhile, produced one of the most influential images associated with the abolitionist cause: a medallion featuring a slave kneeling in chains and bearing the slogan, 'Am I not a man and a Brother?' Wordsworth and Coleridge also combined their early radicalism with anti-slavery writings; Wordsworth wrote a sonnet in 1803 celebrating the leader of the Haitian revolution, Toussaint L'ouverture, and Coleridge delivered lectures against slavery in Bristol in the 1790s.

Many of these white British writers appealed in their writings to patriotic and religious sentiments, contending that England was too civilised and too Christian to tolerate the barbarity of slavery. Other voices came from the notable community of African writers and campaigners in the country at this time; these writers had personal experience of slavery and their work considerably influenced anti-slavery debate and activism. Phyllis Wheatley was an African poet celebrated in London literary circles in the late-eighteenth century and Olaudah Equiano's *The Interesting Life of Olaudah Equiano, or Gustav Vasso, the African*, is the best known of a number of first-person slave narratives of the period.

Changing Landscapes
Representative Figures: John Clare; William Wordsworth; William Gilpin; John Constable; J. M. W. Turner

The late eighteenth and early nineteenth centuries saw the rise of urbanization, industrialization and changes in agricultural production that had a significant impact upon the landscape of certain areas of the country. It became more difficult for rural workers in some areas to make a living from traditional agricultural practices and the Enclosure Laws passed during the period effectively saw the privatization of vast tracts of open land. Romantic writing responded in various ways to the changing rural and urban landscape and often set the 'populous city' negatively against 'nature's genuine beauty': see Charlotte Smith's 'The Emigrants'; see many of the poems in Wordsworth and Coleridge's *Lyrical Ballads*, and see Wordsworth's *Prelude* and 'Tintern Abbey'. The poetry of John Clare expresses an especially powerful personal reaction against the impact of enclosure on the landscape of Clare's native Northamptonshire and his critique often broadens out into an attack upon the political establishment responsible for cynical, brutal attacks against what Clare regards as the physical body of the nation (see poems such as 'The Mores', 'Lament of Swordy Well', 'To a Fallen Elm', 'The Flitting').

Those landscapes that remained relatively untouched by industrialization (the mountains of Wales, the Lake District and Scotland, for instance) became places of almost sacred refuge for the Romantic poets and a place of escape for people who could afford to enjoy these locations recreationally. In this period, we see the rise of what might be termed 'landscape tourism' and an aestheticization of the land that was related to concepts of national heritage and personal, spiritual development. This tendency was reflected not only in Romantic poetry, but in the Romantic-era novel, travel literature, landscape painting (see the work of Constable, Turner and Gainsborough) and in an emerging genre of guidebook writing: Wordsworth, for instance, wrote a *Guide to the Lakes* in 1810. The influence of contemporary aesthetic notions of the 'picturesque' (see William Gilpin's *Three Essays* of 1792 and Uvedale Price, *An Essay on the Picturesque*, 1796) and the 'sublime' contributed to the romantic conceptualization of certain landscapes as providing a particularly productive artistic, spiritual and even moral experience, and ultimately this tendency within Romanticism developed into a wider movement for the preservation of areas of outstanding natural beauty.

Childhood
Representative Figures: Anna Laetitia Barbauld; William Blake; William Wordsworth; Jean-Jacques Rousseau

The notion of childhood as a separate developmental stage in the life of an individual became more fully realized in the late eighteenth and early nineteenth centuries than it had been previously; the child was no longer necessarily understood as an adult in miniature, or as a chattel of the patriarchal family. Jean-Jacques Rousseau was influential in proposing new systems of education for children and in developing an idea of childhood in terms of a natural innocence that was contrasted sharply with the artifice and corruption of civilization (see *Emile*, 1762). A central feature of the Romantic conceptualization of childhood was precisely this sense of a purity, innocence and authenticity that associates the child, in some Romantic writings, with a prelapsarian state of grace. This idealization of the child is very evident in William Blake's *Songs of Innocence and Experience* and in Wordsworth's 'We are Seven', 'Lucy Gray' and 'Ode: Intimations of Immortality', for instance. This characterization of the child is often accompanied by a nostalgia specifically for the lost innocence of childhood, and more generally for a mythologized past for which the poet yearns. Representations of childhood thus mediate Romantic anxieties concerning a perceived cultural 'loss of innocence' in the context of growing industrialization and urbanization.

The Romantic era also saw the development of literature written in a variety of styles especially for children. Anna Laetitia Barbauld was a pioneer of early children's literature and much of her work had a highly didactic tone: see *Lessons for Children* and *Hymns in Prose for Children* (see also Maria Edgeworth's *The Parents' Assistant* and *Moral Tales*). Other writers sought not only to instruct but also to entertain the child reader, and the work of Charles and Mary Lamb, the American Washington Irving and the famous Grimm brothers helped to establish children's literature as a distinct genre of creative writing in the nineteenth century.

Drama
Representative Figures: David Garrick; Joanna Baillie; Edmund Kean; Sarah Siddons

Although drama has not been regarded as a major genre of Romanticism – largely owing to the dominance of the 'Big Six' poets over the period – the Romantic poets did at times appropriate and experiment with verse drama: see Wordsworth's *The Borderers* (1787); Coleridge's *Remorse* (1815); Shelley's *Prometheus Unbound* (1819); Byron's *Manfred* (18180; Leigh Hunt's *The Descent of Liberty* (1814). Moreover, recent re-evaluations of Romanticism have recognized the contribution of women writers to drama in the Romantic era; indeed, it is possible to argue that drama was largely a female form in this period and that it was through the work of women that 'Romanticism' found expression in this genre: see the work of Felicia Hemans, Charlotte Smith, Sophia Lee, Hannah More (a friend of David Garrick), Mary Robinson, Elizabeth Inchbald and Joanna Baillie. Baillie was the most famous dramatist of the period. She was extremely prolific, acclaimed by Walter Scott as the Shakespeare of her generation, and her work often gave dramatic expression to the introspective sensibility associated with Romanticism: see *De Montford* and *The Plays on the Passions*.

Theatre was also popular in spite of the restrictions on performance still in force under the Licensing Act of 1737. The influence of the great eighteenth-century actor David Garrick, who also managed the Theatre Royal at Drury Lane and did a great deal to bring Shakespeare to mass audiences in this period, was still apparent (he died in 1779), and actors such as Edmund Kean, John Kemble and Sarah Siddons became widely known and celebrated in the Romantic period. Comedy in particular thrived, as did Gothic drama, pantomime and melodrama. The plays of Shakespeare were regularly performed, the productions often featuring lavish sets and costumes. Shakespeare was seen to have considerable contemporary political relevance; *Julius Caesar* was banned under the censorship laws because of its depiction of regicide and William Hazlitt asserted that Edmund Kean's performance of Coriolanus would 'save[any man] the trouble of reading Burke's reflections or Paine's *The Rights of Man*' (*Characters of Shakespeare's Plays*, 1817). Indeed, theatre in general was often caught up in the political maelstrom of the 1790s and early 1800s with elaborate theatrical spectacles used to promote revolutionary and anti-revolutionary sentiments.

Gothic Fiction
Representative Figures: Horace Walpole; Ann Radcliffe; Matthew Lewis; Mary Shelley

See also: *Prose Fiction*

The Gothic originated as a literary form with the publication of Horace Walpole's *The Castle of Otranto* in 1764. This short novel established the key conventions of the eighteenth-century Gothic romance and triggered a number of imitators; one of the most successful, Clara Reeve's *The Old English Baron* (1778), acknowledged the influence of Walpole in its preface, although Reeve, like certain other Gothic writers of the period (notably Ann Radcliffe), eschewed what she regarded as an excessive and irrational supernaturalism in Walpole. Gothic fiction grew in popularity in the years following the French Revolution and the revolution certainly provides a significant context within which to situate the Gothic's concern with abuses of power, the problematics of patrilineal inheritance and the recurring themes of wrongful imprisonment, paranoia and retribution.

Two of the most famous Gothic novelists of the 1790s were Ann Radcliffe and Matthew Lewis. Out of their work emerged two distinct modes of Gothic writing: 'Terror' and 'Horror'. Radcliffe, the most successful Gothic novelist of the decade, promoted the aesthetic of 'terror', according to which the imagination of the reader should be left to respond freely to subtle and suspenseful evocations of dread. Radcliffe's *The Mysteries of Udolpho* influenced Lewis' publication of *The Monk* in 1796, but Lewis' novel went well beyond Radcliffe's in the explicit depiction of violence and the supernatural that has become characteristic of Gothic horror. In 1797, Radcliffe's *The Italian* re-affirmed the aesthetic of terror against Lewis and her posthumously published essay 'On the Supernatural In Poetry' (1826) presented a sustained analysis of both forms of Gothicism as well as a consideration of two crucial influences upon the late eighteenth-century Gothic novel: Edmund Burke's aesthetic of the Sublime and the plays of Shakespeare.

The relation between Gothic and Romanticism has received a good deal of critical scrutiny and the Gothic in this period can be understood as a distinctly Romantic phenomenon. Gothic fiction evokes the Sublime frequently as a means of heightening terror and suspense, and the Gothic also often reshapes and interrogates Romantic concerns regarding the self, body and mind, creativity and the relation of the individual to nature and society: see Mary Shelley's *Frankenstein*; James Hogg's *Confessions of a Justified Sinner*; Charles Maturin's *Melmoth the Wanderer*. There are also notable examples of the appropriation of Gothicism in the work of the romantic poets: see Coleridge's 'Christabel' and 'The Ancient Mariner'; Byron's 'Manfred' and 'The Giaour'. The Gothic also influenced the 'dark Romanticism' associated with the work of Coleridge, Byron, John Polidori, Mary Shelley and, later in the nineteenth century, the American writers Edgar Allan Poe and Nathaniel Hawthorne.

Journals, Periodicals and Magazines
Representative Figures: William Blackwood; Leigh Hunt; John Gibson Lockhart; John Scott; Lord Byron; Percy Shelley

A diverse range of journals and periodicals thrived during the Romantic era promoting various political and cultural agendas and becoming the forum for occasionally acrimonious debates over the significant issues of the day. The 1790s saw the launch of a number of publications concerned with the turbulent politics of the decade. John Thelwall's *Tribune* published many of Thelwall's radical political lectures, while at the other end of the political spectrum, the conservative *Anti-Jacobin Review* was noted for its scathing anti-revolutionary satire. The conservative *British Critic* and *Monthly Magazine* carried influential literary reviews, essays and poetry and many of these magazines (radical and conservative) had as their editors, founders or proprietors key figures of the Romantic movement (for example Coleridge's short-lived *The Watchman* and Leigh Hunt's *Examiner*). The *Quarterly Review* and the influential *Blackwood's* magazine (founded in 1817 by William Blackwood), both politically Tory, published the poetry of Coleridge, Southey and Shelley, among others, and also offered some scathing reviews of writers with whom the journals were out of sympathy: both journals bitterly disparaged the work of Leigh Hunt,

John Keats and William Hazlitt, for instance, dismissing their poetry as belonging to an uncultured 'Cockney School'. So scathing were some of these reviews that Shelley even blamed the *Quarterly Review's* lambasting of Keats' 'Endymion' for causing the poet's premature death.

The Whig-supporting *London Magazine* and the *Edinburgh Review*, meanwhile, existed in stark opposition to their Tory rivals, especially *Blackwood's*; indeed, the *London Magazine* editor John Scott was killed in a duel with an agent of *Blackwood's* in 1821 over allegedly libellous material published in the journal under the editorship of John Gibson Lockhart. Lockhart was an influential editor who contributed to the often rather combative tone of *Blackwood's* in its early years.

Another controversial journal of the time was the *Examiner*. Its founder and editor, Leigh Hunt, was imprisoned for seditious libel in 1812 after writing and publishing an article critical of the Prince Regent. Hunt went on to found another radical magazine, *The Liberal*, with his close associates Byron and Shelley; they published the journal in Italy to avoid prosecution and, although short-lived, it published some important work, including Byron's *Vision of Judgement*. The literary allegiances and powerfully partisan stances of these leading journals formed a vital component of the political landscape of the Romantic period

Literary Criticism
Representative Figures: William Wordsworth; Samuel Taylor Coleridge; William Hazlitt; Percy Shelley

See also: *Poetry and the Poet*

Many key figures of the Romantic period produced important works of literary criticism, published often as essays in the leading magazines. Like the poetry of the period, criticism reacted against the principles of early eighteenth-century 'Augustan' or 'Neo-Classical' aesthetic theory. Although the Romantics often acknowledged the importance and influence of Classical literature (see Thomas Love Peacock's *The Four Ages of Poetry*, 1820), writers turned away from what they regarded as the rule-bound, restrictive practices of Neo-Classicism. The emphasis in the Romantic era was upon a freer expression of feeling and imagination; Wordsworth's definition of good poetry as 'the spontaneous overflow of powerful feelings' carried over into a great deal of literary criticism which privileged imagination over reason and spontaneous expression over adherence to the literary precepts of Augustanism. William Hazlitt, a major literary critic of the period, contended against Alexander Pope's 1711 *Essay on Criticism* that the creation and appreciation of literature was not reducible to strict rules of composition.

The critical work of Coleridge (*Biographia Literaria*) and Shelley (*In Defence of Poetry*) went further, attributing an almost spiritual or mystical quality to poetry. For Shelley, the poet is akin to a prophet whose work has significant transformative power, not only artistically but socially: the poets, he says, are 'the unacknowledged legislators of the world'.

This period also witnessed a revival of critical interest in Shakespeare who came to be admired for precisely those qualities of sensibility and imaginative freedom for which he had been denigrated in the previous era. William Hazlitt and Coleridge saw in Shakespeare's work an anticipation and vindication of their own literary project and their criticism did much to guarantee the reputation of Shakespeare as a writer central to the nation's literary tradition over the next century (see Hazlitt's *Character of Shakespeare's Plays*, 1817, and Coleridge's lectures on Shakespeare delivered in 1818).

Nationhood
Representative Figures: Napoleon Bonaparte; William Pitt; Edmund Burke; Daniel O'Connell

Conceptualizations of national identity in the Romantic era were tied closely to pro- and anti-revolutionary ('Jacobin' and 'anti-Jacobin') positions in the aftermath of 1789, and yet more so after the outbreak of war between England and France in 1793. Anti-revolutionary figures such as Edmund Burke and William Gifford (founder of the journal the *Anti-Jacobin Review*) defined and defended national identity in terms of the political, social and cultural virtues of the ancient constitution, the Christian religion and the systems of lineage and hierarchy that in their view guaranteed stability and freedom under monarchical rule. Radicals such as William Godwin, Mary Wollstonecraft and Thomas Paine argued the opposite: that the constitution in its contemporary form was outdated and at the very least in need of reform, and that it imposed a burden on the people that it was the duty of the true patriot to overthrow. Their revolutionary sympathies allowed their opponents to portray these activists as traitorous anti-patriots, however, and ideas of nationhood and national identity were largely forged through vociferous anti-French and, often specifically, anti-Napoleonic sentiment throughout the period of the Napoleonic wars (1799–1815).

The expansion of the British state to include Ireland was also central to questions of Romantic national identity. Following a decade of agitation, political control of Ireland passed from Dublin to London following the Act of Union in 1800, but the new union was almost immediately beset by crisis, including the resignation of Prime Minister William Pitt in 1801 over the issue of catholic emancipation, and a failed Irish rebellion in 1803. The cause of Irish nationalism and Catholic emancipation gained momentum in the 1820s under the leadership of Daniel O'Connell, and the Catholic Relief Act of 1829, together with the Reform Acts of the 1830s, lifted many of the restrictions on Catholic participation in political and civic life.

Romantic literary responses to the Union, and its affirmation of the political power of the English Protestant ruling class, were varied and often deeply ambivalent. Maria Edgeworth's *Castle Rackrent* (1800) was deeply critical of the social and economic degradation wrought by English absentee landlords, though its overall perspective remained Anglo-centric in its treatment of that nation. Sydney Owenson's *The Wild Irish Girl* attempted a reconciliation of English and Irish interests through the marriage of an English aristocrat and an Irish heiress, though the novel could not successfully resolve the tensions inherent in a Union (and a marriage) premised upon an unequal co-existence of two distinct cultures in one newly constructed, Anglocentric 'British' nation.

Poetry and the Poet
Representative Figures: William Wordsworth; Samuel Taylor Coleridge; Percy Shelley; John Keats

See also: *Literary Criticism; Autobiographical Writing*

The publication of the *Lyrical Ballads* in 1798 marked a shift away from previous theories of poetry that had emphasized the importance of reason and regularity in poetic composition. John Dryden's *Essays of Dramatic Poetry* (1667–8) criticized Shakespeare's use of blank verse, for instance, arguing instead in favour of the more disciplined and, in Dryden's view, elegant poetry of the Classical civilizations. Wordsworth's preface to the second edition of the *Lyrical Ballads* (1800) re-defined poetry in terms of the free expression of the imagination, and this elevation of imagination over reason (see also Coleridge's *Biographia Literaria*) was coupled with an increased emphasis on interiority and individuality that was influenced by Jean-Jacques Rousseau's proto-Romantic autobiographical work, the *Confessions*. Here, Rousseau makes a typically Romantic claim for his own status as a unique human subject: 'I dare believe that I am not made like anyone in existence'. As a consequence of the Romantic poets' belief in the uniqueness of their experience, identity and creative impulse, poetry became more expressive than mimetic; that is to say, its chief concern was to capture the emotional state of the author rather than to represent external reality. This, in turn, had an effect upon Romantic poetic genre. The first-person lyric poem became a major form in this period on account of its capacity to reflect the emotion of the speaker; the 'I' that narrates the Romantic lyric poem became more closely associated with the poet's own life experiences than had previously been the case (see the lyric poetry of William Wordsworth, Percy Shelley and John Keats, for instance). The same is true to some extent of the Romantics' (and especially Wordsworth's) appropriation of the sonnet form, and of the dramatic poem as a means of intense personal revelation.

What is also evident in Romantic theorizations of poetry and the poet is an elevation of the cultural status of the poet as a uniquely gifted artist whose creativity owed more to intuitive individual genius than the observance of literary tradition or established aesthetic principles (see Shelley's *In Defence of Poetry*, for example). Critics have also contended (see chapter 6 below) that the elevation of the status of the poet was accompanied by a gendering of the identity of the poet: Romantic poetry was culturally coded 'masculine'. This came to be reflected in the later formation of the Romantic canon which excludes the work of the many successful female poets writing in the period; Charlotte Smith, whose work influenced Wordsworth and Coleridge in the 1790s, is a case in point. In tension with what might be regarded as a rather elitist under-standing of poetry, however, was a belief in the transformative, democratic power of poetry; Wordsworth in the preface to *Lyrical Ballads* (1800) contends that poetry ought to be concerned with the circumstances of ordinary people and that it should be written in the language of the 'common man' (Coleridge famously disagreed – see the *Biographia Literaria*). Moreover, a great deal of Romantic poetry was explicitly political, engaging in an accessible manner with the key social issues of the time and often displaying sympathy with revolutionary or reformist causes. It is not true, therefore, that Romantic poetry turned entirely inward and away from social and political concerns: from the abolitionist poetry of William Cowper to Shelley's impassioned condemnation of the Peterloo massacre in 1819, Romantic poetry retained a radical dimension that grew out of the revolutionary movements of the 1770s, 80s and 90s.

Prose Fiction

Representative Figures: Jane Austen; Walter Scott; Ann Radcliffe; Frances Burney

See also: *Gothic Fiction*

In spite of the later critical tendency to define Romanticism in terms of the poetry of the period, the novel was the most popular form of literature of the time and it was during the late eighteenth and early nineteenth-century, notably through the fiction of Jane Austen and Walter Scott, that the novel acquired its recognizable modern form in Britain. Romantic fiction can be broadly categorized in terms of the novel of sensibility, the novel of manners, Gothic romance and the historical novel, though many works incorporate elements of two or more of these sub-genres.

Novels of sensibility developed in the mid-eighteenth century in response to a wider cultural and philosophical validation of the role of 'feeling' in the moral, spiritual and social development of the individual: see David Hume's *Enquiry Concerning Human Understanding* (1748) in which it is argued that feeling, as opposed to reason, is the basis of morality; see Samuel Richardson's novels *Pamela* (1740), *Clarissa* (1748) and *Sir Charles Grandison* (1753); Henry Mackenzie's *The Man of Feeling* (1771); Frances Burney's *Evelina* (1778). Novels of sensibility had points in common with the Gothic romance which likewise privileged refined sensibility in its protagonists (especially its heroines) and which also relied upon the heightened emotional affect associated with senti-mental fiction in its production of terror. The novel of manners also placed emphasis upon the role of proper sentiment in the production of appro-priate forms of social behaviour, though there is a tension, evident in Jane Austen in particular, between wholesome sentiment and excessive, poten-tially destructive passion (see *Sense and Sensibility*, 1811).

The novel of sensibility and the novel of manners were both deeply class-based forms of fiction reflecting the values of an emerging middle class seeking advancement through the formulation of appropriate codes of conduct, or 'manners' (see the work of Austen, Frances Burney, Charlotte Smith, Maria Edgeworth and the 'Silver Fork' novelists of the late Regency period). Even as they endorse the social value of middle class 'manners', however, these fictions often have a richly satirical vein through which they express sometimes quite caustic criticism of the triviality and insincerity of contemporary social mores.

Sir Walter Scott is the writer most closely associated with the development of the historical novel in this period, though the influence of earlier Gothic romance writers, many of them women, should not be underestimated: Sophia Lee's *The Recess* and the highly popular Gothic fictions of Ann Radcliffe helped shape the conventions of the historical novel in the two decades before Scott. Scott's historical fiction defined the genre as one in which the conflicts of the past were seen to hold important lessons for the present, and in which complex and often contradictory aspects of national identity were woven into a seemingly more coherent whole. What was created thereby was a narration of national identity and history that had significant implications in terms of the conceptualization of nationhood in the Romantic period and beyond, and Scott's work had an immense influence upon historical fiction throughout Europe in the nineteenth century.

Religion
Representative Figures: John and Charles Wesley; Joseph Priestley; Hannah More; Samuel Taylor Coleridge; William Blake; Percy Shelley.

The Romantic period in Britain saw the emergence of increasingly diverse religious discourses that to various degrees challenged the established Anglican faith of the nation. Since the 1689 Act of Toleration, non-conformist faiths had been freer to organize and promulgate their beliefs, and certain Protestant sects that grew out of Anglicanism began to attract fairly numerous converts. Of these groups, Methodism (founded by John and Charles Wesley in the mid-eighteenth century) was amongst the most successful, attracting over half a million converts between the mid-eighteenth and mid-nineteenth centuries. Unitarianism (co-founded by Joseph Priestley) was also a growing movement in the late-Romantic period, and in political terms this was one of the most radical faiths; it appealed especially to women seeking opportunities to preach and practise a less patriarchal, less hierarchical religion. The Quaker movement was likewise a dissenting faith that coupled its religious evangelism with various political agendas, most notably the abolitionist cause. Members of these movements, along with influential Anglican evangelicals such as Hannah More, also played a key role in promoting the Sunday School movement.

Anglicanism remained dominant in religious and political terms during the Romantic era, however, and religious dissent was barely tolerated within the establishment. It was necessary to be of the Anglican faith in order to take degrees at Oxford and Cambridge, for example, and Percy Shelley was expelled from Oxford in 1811 for publishing the essay The Necessity of Atheism. In spite of the intellectual and political influence of Anglicanism, however, many Romantic writers were hardly orthodox in their religious beliefs. Many (such as Percy Shelley, Byron, Mary Wollstonecraft, Thomas Paine, William Godwin) were at the very least agnostic; Coleridge was a Unitarian minister in the late 1790s before returning to Anglicanism in 1814 and publishing several Anglican texts (*Lay Sermons*, 1817; *Aids to Reflection*, 1825; *The Constitution of Church and State*, 1830); William Blake despised institutional religion and developed a highly idiosyncratic mythology that reflects a deeply personal, mystical and at times Gnostic spirituality. Even Wordsworth, who throughout his life professed a staunch Anglicanism, manifests in some of his work a spirituality that approaches mysticism or even pantheism (see books one and two of the *Prelude* and 'Tintern Abbey', for instance). Certainly, what is evident in Romantic writings is a validation of – indeed often an insistence upon – the priority of subjective spiritual experience over the organized, dogmatic expression of religious belief. Religious discourses in the Romantic era thus express the movement's broad emphasis upon individualism and the creative freedom of the Imagination.

Women

Representative Figures: Mary Wollstonecraft; Helen Maria Williams; Hannah More; Anna Laetitia Barbauld; Charlotte Smith; Ann Radcliffe; Joanna Baillie; Maria Edgeworth; Jane Austen; Felicia Hemans

Women in this period suffered, as they had for centuries, from strict legal, social and cultural limitations upon their personhood and potential for self-determination. Legally, women had very few rights over property and were placed under the guardianship of fathers or husbands; only unmarried adult women (referred to in law as 'femmes sole' – 'women alone') had limited rights to own and dispose of property on their own terms. The property of married women passed to their husbands and in marriage women had little freedom to negotiate the terms of the relationship, either legally or culturally. Although the right to divorce did exist in English law, it was exceptionally difficult for either party to obtain, but especially so for women; a wife could not rely solely on the grounds of adultery, for instance, but had to prove some additional aggravating factor. The law in this respect reflected the cultural double standard, whereby the behaviour of women was subjected to a degree of control that did not apply to men, especially as regards sexual and marital relations. Women also had limited opportunities for education; they were barred from taking university degrees and entering the professions and such education as higher class women were afforded tended to be restricted to 'accomplishments': a smattering of French, music, needlework and so on. The position of women of lower social classes was much more precarious: denied the dubious protection of the sexual codes that applied to middle- and upper-class women (and that existed to protect the property interests of fathers and husbands through the enforced chastity of daughters and wives), poorer women often had no choice but to take what work they could, often in domestic service or the new industries that employed women and children, and they were vulnerable to gross sexual and economic exploitation.

The position of women came increasingly to be interrogated from a range of political and cultural perspectives in the eighteenth century and further into the Romantic period. The novel of sensibility, for example, often served as a means for even socially conservative writers to explore and condemn the injustices suffered by women (Samuel Richardson's *Pamela*, 1740; Frances Sheridan, *The Memoirs of Miss Sidney Bidulph*, 1761). In the years following the French Revolution, the question of women's rights came into sharper focus: Mary Wollstonecraft's *A Vindication of the Rights of Woman* was and remains a powerful, systematic attack not only upon the legal and political restraints imposed upon women, but upon a culture which constructed 'femininity' as passive, weak and artificially chaste in order to serve the interests of men. Other women, though not always as politically radical as Wollstonecraft (and some, such as Hannah More and Felicia Hemans, were conservative politically), explored, explicitly or implicitly, the restraints and injustices suffered by women: see the novels of Charlotte Smith and Ann Radcliffe (whose Gothic romances, although often socially conservative, depict the debilitating influence of patriarchal institutions upon vulnerable women); the poetry of Anna Laetitia Barbauld (see 'The Rights of Woman', 1795) ; Helen Mary Williams' writings on the revolution (which uniquely offer an account of the involvement of women in French revolutionary politics); the novels and essays of Maria Edgeworth (see *Letters for Literary Ladies*, 1795; *Belinda*, 1802); Felicia Hemans (*Records of Woman*, 1820)

It is also vital to appreciate that women were often very successful and influential as writers during this period. Jane Austen is a case in point. Ann Radcliffe and Hannah More were best-selling writers in the 1790s (and More was also an influential abolitionist campaigner). The best known dramatist of the era was Joanna Baillie. Although she was more successful as a novelist, Charlotte Smith's poetry influenced Wordsworth and Coleridge in their early career. Since the late twentieth century, critics have increasingly acknowledged the political, cultural and literary significance of women writers and the extent to which the post-Romantic process of canon formation has excluded women writers and the genres with which they were most associated.

3

Case Studies in Reading 1: Literary Texts

Rhian Williams

Chapter Overview

Introduction: Critical Perspectives

Close reading does not take place within a vacuum; it is always informed by critical and theoretical perspectives and thus my aim here is to introduce students to the practice of close reading by foregrounding a certain critical approach that focuses on what I term the 'ecology' of Romantic poetry. I begin with the following quotation that offers a point of access into this approach and the primary texts considered in this chapter:

> [T]he reading of great poetry might well be associated with the study of Nature, since there is no great poetry which can be dissevered from Nature (Thomas, 67).[1]

When Edward Thomas asserted – in 1909 – that there is an essential bind between reading poetry and 'Nature', this formed part of his broader conviction that 'Nature-study' should 'widen the culture of child and man' (68). This he saw exemplified by the author and churchman, Mark Pattison, who had cultivated his own appreciation of the natural world through a combination of outdoor pursuits and indoor reading. But it was in reading

William Wordsworth that Pattison found that his in- and outdoor lives converged:

> [W]hen I came in after years to read *The Prelude* I recognized, as if it were my own history which was being told, the steps by which the love of the country boy for his hills and moors grew into poetical susceptibility for all imaginative presentations of beauty in every direction. (68)

Thomas and Pattison's shared appreciation of Wordsworth's 'love of [...] hills and moors' focuses what many generations of readers have found not only in Wordsworth's poetry, but in Romantic writing more broadly. In recent decades this appreciative and celebratory recognition of Romantic engagement with British and Continental landscapes (found in writing by canonical poets such as Wordsworth, Samuel Taylor Coleridge and Lord Byron) has however been extended and complicated by critical reappraisal, not least in response to the growing attention now paid to other writers of the period such as John Clare and Charlotte Smith. The intense familiarity with the material conditions of a worked landscape found in the rural labourer Clare's writing, and the exploration of a landscape increasingly understood both emotionally and scientifically in Smith's poetry provide just two of many recently recovered counterviews to the canonically recognized Romantic engagement with the natural world.

One effect of introducing such counter-voices into the conversation about Romantic period engagements with 'Nature' has been to draw attention to the cultural and ideological imprints that literary representation both draws on and leaves behind in its aestheticizing of phenomena such as 'hills and moors': each of these writers brings a specific cultural position to their encounter with the natural world, and each of them leaves a specific cultural imagining of that encounter behind. In these crossing paths the notion of 'Nature', however, is apt to be treated as a 'cultural representation' (Soper, 124)[2] rather than a material reality. The effects of such characterization are grave, as has been asserted in recent decades: 'it is not language that has a hole in its ozone layer; and the "real" thing continues to be polluted and degraded even as we refine our deconstructive insights at the level of the signifier' (Soper, 124).

Since Thomas' assertion, the fragility of that concept 'Nature' (capitalized in order to register its status as both material reality and human-constructed aesthetic category) has become compellingly and urgently apparent through the increasing realization of man's involvement with ecological crisis. If the human culture that once grandly esteemed nature through literature is now also one whose infrastructures of capitalist globalization accelerate its destruction, then with such recognition comes the imperative to become more mindful in our study of writing that engages with landscape and the natural world. To look to the practice of literary criticism in the context of global ecological disaster may seem to indulge in tinkering as Rome burns, but to attend to linguistic representation is to address the very modes through which we come to know – and therefore might be prompted to feel for – nature's dynamics and our part in them. At a time when threats to the biosphere are momentous and on-going, when the idea of landscape is as likely to mean destruction and loss as it is beauty and familiarity, Thomas' assertion that reading poetry is intrinsically linked to 'Nature' indicates that a radical shake up will simultaneously be registered at the level of literary appreciation. As Cheryl Glotfelty asserted in her introduction to a vital 'green studies' publication, 'literature does not float above the material world in some aesthetic ether, but, rather, plays a part in an immensely complex global system, in which energy, matter, and ideas, interact' (p. xix)[3]. Vital for Western culture here is the legacy of Romantic writing about nature.

My intention is to explore the implication of this turn to ecological mindfulness in literary study for the process of close reading, by which I mean the act of spending sustained periods in intense engagement with the material aspects (sound, rhythm, rhyme, line length, arrangement and imagery) of a poem. I would like to attend to what Soper terms 'a problematic legacy' (123) by asking what might it mean to close read poetry of the Romantic period in an age of ecological crisis? How might the complexities of that period's engagement with landscape's material conditions be brought out in the context of our contemporary compulsion to reconnect with the material fate of our planet? By extension, we implicitly ask how might poetry (and the reading of poetry) be 'ecological'? How might we reconsider our practice of close reading such that it critiques, rather than re-inscribes, the 'problematic legacy' of 'romantic ideology', which Soper warns has 'as readily lent [it]self to the expression of reactionary sentiment' as 'radical critique of industriali-zation' (123)?

The series of close readings I undertake here concentrate closely on the text in hand, but their method implicitly acknowledges a body of scholarship that has radically reassessed writing of the Romantic period much more broadly. Recent decades have witnessed the emergence of a 'transformed intellectual agenda' that registers scepticism regarding the capacity for 'poetic-textualist issues' fully to account for how Romantic period writing emerged from and intervened in the complex materiality of its historical period, demanding instead 'an eclectic approach that borrows as much from developments in cultural studies, social history and critical theory as from literary criticism' (Benchimol, 2005: 51)[4]. Given the long-standing association between Romantic poetry and the natural world, this new agenda has significantly shaped the cognate discipline of eco-criticism, whose most compelling readings have often been focused on 'the way symbolic interpretations of landscape in the [Romantic] period were used to engage with urgent social and political issues' (Benchimol, 2007: 92)[5]. In the light of such scholarship, readers must now acknowledge that just as the 'hills and moors' we encounter through Romantic writing are coloured by our contemporary experience of them as threatened, so were they fundamentally politicized at the time of composition, registering as they did the pervasive effects not only of aesthetic categorization in terms of the sublime, the beautiful or the picturesque (and their attendant ideological implications), but also by the economic and material restructuring of, for example, the Highland clearances, acts of enclosure, and rapid industrialization of urban and rural modes of production. Our own ecological mindfulness, indeed, re-engages an ecological mindfulness of the past. What the introduction of an eclecticism of approach in the context of ecological change most compellingly demonstrates, however, is the necessity to replace notions of fixity more generally with those of flux. While this has been well established in terms of cultural materialist readings of the period, the interruption of the human imagination into the natural scene (as might describe the creation of a poem in response to nature) is still apt to prompt *close* readings that register at some level a sense of settling or fixing in their trace of a poem's translation of the material aspects of the natural world – 'River, fire, and mud', to use Michel Serres' arresting trio (p. 2) into the transcendent immortality of the printed page[6].

This tendency may be noticed in even the most deft and elegant eco-textual analyses, such as those by Jonathan Bate (see chapter four below), who prominently and importantly drew early attention to the ecological implications of Romantic writing[7]. In his ecological close readings, Bate echoes Pattison and Thomas in his enthusiasm for poets who draw on 'reverie, solitude, walking' since 'to turn these experiences into language is to be an eco-poet' (2000: 42)[7]. In executing such alchemy, Bate suggests, poets provide us with 'the myth of a better life that has gone' which is 'no less important for being myth rather than history. Myths are necessary imaginings, exemplary stories which help our species to make sense of its place in the world' (25). Accordingly, for Bate, the ecological potential of Romantic poetry is contained in its presentation to the sensitive reader of an integrated experience between man and nature, implicitly imaged in the integration of word and image across the poem's structure as a whole: 'the world of the poem thus comes to resemble a well-regulated ecosystem' (106)[7]. This is seen as distinct from (and apparently superior to) writing that is 'pragmatically green' since 'a manifesto for ecological correctness will not be poetic because its language is bound to be instrumental, to address questions of doing rather than to "present" the experience of dwelling' (42). Bate's Empsonian method thus shapes not only his literary-critical approach (emphasizing the integrity of the text), but also his canonical preferences and his characterization of poetry's contribution to ecological thought – identified not by its revelation of demanding uncertainty, but by its execution of moments of insight that become a capacity to establish an organic and integrated order. This is poetry – and Romanticism – as the repository of wise reminders.

Methods of close reading thus emphasizing myth over history, while they raised the profile of literary-ecological agendas, are clearly out of step with the 'transformed intellectual agenda' apparent in studies of the Romantic period outlined above. Practical criticism's legacy of isolationism of the text is too apt here to bury Romantic-period literature's interrogation of cultural mythology (prompted by material historical change) under a nostalgia that would write eco-criticism as the celebration of human-centred 'insights' into the natural world. Yet, rather than rejecting close reading altogether, it is apposite to take the opportunity offered by eco-criticism's recognized affinity with the 'a transformed intellectual agenda' to re-think this practice itself and to consider how it might become methodologically ecological. This might be explored through the notion of 'dwelling' – touched on by Bate – which speaks explicitly to an ecological perspective (the term 'ecology' derives from the ancient Greek *oikos*, meaning house or dwelling) but simultaneously holds out possibilities for the process of close reading and the practice of poetry. Ecology's etymological connection to dwelling ignites the potential in Martin Heidegger's assertion that 'poetry is what really lets us dwell', elaborated by David Borthwick's claim that 'ecopoetry describes a mode of metaphysical enquiry which recognizes our profound alienation from the natural world and suggests ways of enacting a reconnection' (64)[8]. However, there is a danger here that the fixing tendency of close-reading methods – the idea of scansion, for example, as an imposed ordering and dividing of a poem along rote lines – will promote a non-contingent essentialism that is blind or deaf to history. Here I want to draw on the potential of Burnside's view that 'the lyric poem ... raises the most interesting question concerning ... the identity of the individual, based upon a notion of continuity' (2007, par. 16)[9] while avoiding his half-wish that 'art is neither a political pursuit, nor a historical event' (2006: 93)[10]. This chapter emerges, then, from suggestions made in a paper with Emma Mason that sought to 'allegorize ... the process of scansion as forever evolving and spontaneous' (2009: 516)[11] by employing a method of 'reciprocal scansion' where '"reciprocal" names a backward-forward movement, and "scansion" brings with it a visual attention to the page' undertaken in the process of 'a conversation between two or more readers' (ibid.).

In this fluctuating, provisional method of close reading the valency of 'dwelling' might bring out not only its sense of inhabitation, but also the action of abiding for a time (in time, not out of time) and, more discomfortingly 'dwell' as 'to lead into error' (*Oxford English Dictionary*). This notion of inhabiting, spending time and being led into, but then perhaps out of, error (which might mean mistake, but also means roaming or wandering, suggesting a happy deviation from norms) offers a modification of Bate's method of plucking and fusing images from the text in an incantation of his own. His wish to 'measure the motions of "Frost at Midnight"' through his list of 'the pattern of the frost; the flickering of the flame and the flapping of the film on the grate; the flowings of breeze, wave, cloud, thaw-steam, eavesdrop and icicle' (2000: 111)[12] can disregard the metrical, structural and temporal ways in which the poem seeks to illuminate the architecture of their connection. Rather, I suggest the appropriateness of a close reading method that echoes the terms of Serres' 'natural contract' (an ecological manifesto) and its appeal for a new mindfulness in the relation between man and nature:

> Back to nature, then! That means we must add ... a natural contract of symbiosis and reciprocity in which our relationship to things would set aside mastery and possession in favour of admiring attention, reciprocity, contemplation, and respect. (38)[5]

This chapter takes a series of Romantic poems written in iambic pentameter (five-stress lines), starting with blank verse and ending in an ode. The restructuring implied by a loosened close-reading method is mirrored in the pairings I suggest, which ask implicitly for a loosening of canon formation too by putting poems by writers only recently receiving critical attention (William Cowper and Clare) into conversation with well-celebrated canonical texts by Coleridge and John Keats. The disruptions and renegotiations these might prompt are first seen reflected in the establishment of the blank verse poem as one that is walking, roaming, unending, uncontained by rhyme or stanza, and so in process; the effect of such conditioning of iambic pentameter is then traced when it wanders into the formal ode.

 ## William Cowper, 'The Task' (1785)

I begin with *The Task* (1785), a six-book poem in blank verse by the poet and hymn writer William Cowper (1731–1800). Although marginal to the critically acknowledged Romantic canon, Cowper's example is vital to our understanding of Romantic experiments in poetic register. Coleridge and Wordsworth's project in the *Lyrical Ballads* of 'fitting to metrical arrangement a selection of the real language of men' (Mason, 56–57)[11] emerges directly

from the two men's enthusiasm for Cowper's carefully constructed yet collo-
quial expression. In a resonant phrase, Coleridge celebrated Cowper's 'divine
chit chat' (Griggs 1: 279)[13] and described him to William Hazlitt as 'the best
modern poet' (Wu: 1998, 107)[14] while Wordsworth, strikingly echoing the
aspirations he had for his own poetry, conveyed his 'exquisite pleasure in
seeing such natural language so naturally connected with metre' (Mason,
p. 57)[11] in Cowper's poetry. Cowper's appeal is thus centred on an essential
process of negotiation – the handling of the idiosyncrasies of spoken communication layered together with the constant, regulating pulse of metre. In this
conjunction we have not only the spoken with the written, but the individual
in harmony with the collective and – by implication – the local (speech
implies the vagaries of local accent and expression) in relation with the global
(metrical regularity implies broad cultural practice and also shapes the 'global
effect' of a poem). As I shall explore, this essential dual vision has important
ecological implications. Indeed, in creating his 'map of busy life, | Its fluctua-
tions, and its vast concerns' (*Task* 1: 55–56)) Cowper's blank verse *arranges*
words as if 'from the lips of an extemporary speaker' (King & Ryskamp 2:
10)[15], arguably allegorizing the conditions of ecological change itself, in which
structures are buffeted by the sudden and unexpected events of the moment.

Perhaps the most significant aspect of Cowper's poetry – and why it should
be afforded serious consideration by Romantic period studies – is its searing
critique of the cultural and ideological effects of contemporary rapid industrialization and its attendant establishment of new economic authorities. For
the purposes of this chapter, this is focused in his depiction of the damage
done to rural life: sporting huntsmen, irresponsible landowners, landscape
'improvers' and particularly global marketeers are the repeated scourges of
Cowper's gently conversational and lilting lines. For Cowper, the stuff of
modern life has a pressingly political materiality that repeatedly reveals the
global within the local (so nuancing the metrical conversation dynamic). The
poem's eccentric opening passage (in praise of the sofa on which the poet
was sitting) sets the poem's dual focus in motion, tracing as it does the seat's
material history that includes 'cane from India' (*Task* 1: 39) and 'firm oak' used
when 'no want of timber . . . was felt or fear'd | In Albion's happy isle' (57–58).
Such domestic whimsy has a profound moral import. Likening the newly
emerging capitalist entrepreneur's activities to those of casual plunderers of
local property, Cowper rails at the hypocrisy that dictated, 'thieves at home
must hang; but he that puts | Into his overgorged and bloated purse | The
wealth of Indian provinces, escapes' (1:736–738). While such anger might
risk Cowper's exclusion from Bate's category of 'ecopoetry', this attention to
the overlapping spheres of local and global, and commitment to the material
experience of eighteenth-century life is vital, in fact, to Cowper's other more
obviously 'eco-poetic' presentations of the 'experience of dwelling'. By

focusing here on a short 'walking' passage of this long poem we can see that it is shaped not by the presentation of a 'better life that has gone' (Bate, 25)[7], but by the contradictory and confusing experience of border crossing, a process that comes to typify the defamiliarizing effect on landscape of new economic structures. The recognition of Cowper in the Romantic canon then allows us to see that the mode so celebrated in Wordsworth's *The Prelude* (this passage anticipates Wordsworth's mode of boyhood memory revived in rural/poetic settings) in fact clearly derives from a writer whose verse persists in implying the necessity of thinking that is 'pragmatically green':

> For I have loved the rural walk through lanes
> Of grassy swarth close cropt by nibbling sheep,
> And skirted thick with intertexture firm
> Of thorny boughs: have loved the rural walk
> O'er hills, through valleys, and by rivers' brink,
> E'er since a truant boy I pass'd my bounds
> T'enjoy a ramble on the banks of Thames.
> And still remember, nor without regret
> Of hours that sorrow since has much endear'd,
> How oft, my slice of pocket store consumed,
> Still hung'ring pennyless and far from home,
> I fed on scarlet hips and stoney haws,
> Or blushing crabs, or berries that imboss
> The bramble, black as jet, or sloes austere.
> Hard fare! but such as boyish appetite
> Disdains not, nor the palate undepraved
> By culinary arts, unsav'ry deems.
>
> 1:109–125

While decorously fitting his speech to the demands of the iambic pentameter (note the repeated elision and syncope of 'E'er', 'T'enjoy', 'hung'ring') this sensuous and detailed passage is nevertheless suffused with notions of excess, expansiveness and even exploitation, disconcertingly unsettling any complacent picture of Romantic integration between man and nature and revealing instead the fracturing undercurrents of environmental dwelling in the later eighteenth century. The passage relates how the poet's love of rural walking developed from his boyhood travels along the Thames, the remembrance of which infuses the repetition of 'have loved the rural walk' in lines 109 and 112 with a sense that repetition marks both similarity and difference in the conditions of each of his walks. As the poet exploits the conjunction between a walking pace and an iambic beat he begins by constructing through sound the 'intertexture firm' that latterly shapes his rural walking:

the modesty of an unrhymed blank verse arrangement is challenged by the richness of interior echo – the alliteration and assonance of 'close cropt', the accumulating stickiness of 'skirted thick with intertexture' at the back of the mouth, the swishing sibilance of 'grassy swarth'. This enclosed agricultural space is then contrasted by the second walk, 'o'er hills, through valleys, and by rivers' brink' where the replacement of the boundaries of 'thorny boughs' with the fluidity of 'rivers brink', coupled with the raised profile of vowel sounds ('through / truant', 'valleys', 'rivers' brink' and finally 'ramble / banks'), intimates a looser harmony in these conditions, a shift that retro-spectively perhaps characterizes the colon of line 112 as a 'but' rather than an 'and' (yes, I have loved walking in enclosed space, but I have loved walking in open ones ever since I 'pass'd my bounds'). Such subtle handling not only draws attention to the specifics of rural space, it also elicits a dynamic around the establishment of controlled and regulated agriculture and its subsequent breach.

Having 'pass'd [his] bounds' to reach the Thames, Cowper's broader awareness of increasingly globalized commercial networks leads us to recognize, however, that this signals not an escape into the liberty of a natural, nourishing environment (as might be encouraged by a post-Wordsworthian perspective on this passage) but rather as a profound moment that realizes the economic structuring of rural experience. The Thames' status as a trade route implies the infiltration of global markets into the very heart of England – and it is along its banks that the school-boy comes to speak of his 'pocket store' as a barren consumable. The passage's first interruption to the regular iambic beat soon follows in the pyrrhic (stressless) foot that ends 'pennyless' which then prompts the boy's mobilization of the natural world as a resource for human survival. So the fading of poetic stress is fused with economic and physical weakness and thence with ecological plunder: 'I fed on scarlet hips'. The boy's revived spirits provoke a burst of aesthetic exuberance as nature provides a harvest imaged in the beautifully rich colour repetition of 'scarlet' in 'blush', and expressed in soft 'b' sounds that intertwine with silky 's' sounds to engage the reader's lips and teeth in recitation. This bountiful rush of sensual memory looped together through the conjunctions 'and' and 'or' locates a scene of accumulation and excess in the poet's past that can then infuse the present with the added accumulation of time passed. Yet hidden in this richness are intimations of moral decline and suffering – hung'ring, austere, the jet black berries (suggesting mourning), hard fare, the implied depravity of cultivated tastes – ultimately infected by the oddity of 'berries that imboss | the bramble'. With 'imboss' Cowper revives an arcane word to liken the abundant and bursting excess of berries on the thorny branches to the foam at the mouth of an animal hunted to exhaustion (*Oxford English Dictionary*). With such characterization we might glimpse the associated exhaustion (and entrapment) of market-driven overproduction along the banks of a commercial waterway, providing the antithesis to the modestly 'nibbling sheep' who keep the 'grassy swarth close cropt'.

By spending time with this poem – following the path it iambically beats – we are encouraged to establish an intimacy with its tone that can become alert to these tiny 'off-key' moments, moments that prove to unlock a broader sense of unease in the poem's 'divine chit chat'. Rather than jumping to the conclusion that the love of rural walking must be the keynote to the passage, a close reading method of 'contemplation, and respect' (Serres, 38)[6] allows us to feel how such passages trace the complex reordering of both human experience and the status of the natural world in the new conditions of a newly emerging economic consciousness (the adolescent boy implies the adolescent economy). The ambivalent craving and moral discomfort this elicits in the boy and in the subsequently remembering poet is registered in the passage's movements between sensuous presentation and regretful intimation of loss and depravation. The natural world is something drawn on for aesthetic and emotional appreciation, but the impulse to express that through the lusty language of consumption reminds the poet and the reader of the material effects of aesthetics, effects that emphasize nature's vulnerability in the face of man's rapacious desires of all kinds. A passage that had seemed to imply an idealized conjunction between man and nature therefore in fact contains within it fissures of anxiety, intimated by the excessiveness that pervades the modest blank verse arrangement, the occasional disruptions to the iambic beat, the sinister turns contained in the vocabulary's heritage. Here we can see how Cowper's poetry speaks to our own ecological moment – not by providing a blueprint for change, or by inculcating nostalgia for better times gone by, but by using the sensual appeal of aesthetic presentation to alert in the reader an ear and an eye for wrong notes, stumbles in the walking pace, fractures in the relationship between nature and human and disruptions to healthy and proportionate life systems.

Samuel Taylor Coleridge, 'Frost at Midnight' (1798)

The ecological nature of Cowper's conversational poetics is further uncovered by bringing his poetry into direct dialogue with Coleridge's celebrated 'Frost at Midnight' (1798). Much of Cowper's long poem is, in fact, set in winter, propelling the contrasts between external frost and internal cosy warmth that draw attention to the poem's larger principle of contrast, but it is in a passage that finds him in meditation before the fire that we may see the clearest template for Coleridge's later expression of wintery thought:

> But me perhaps
> The glowing hearth may satisfy awhile
> With faint illumination that uplifts
> The shadow to the ceiling, there by fits
> Dancing uncouthly to the quiv'ring flame.
> Not undelightful is an hour to me
> So spent in parlour twilight; such a gloom
> Suits well the thoughtfull or unthinking mind,
> The mind contemplative, with some new theme
> Pregnant, or indisposed alike to all.
>
> 'Task' 4: 272–281

In Cowper's handling this contemplative passage is brought to an end by 'the freezing blast' that 'restores me to myself' (303, 307). Intriguingly, however, the return to self becomes a turn to the world outside – 'I saw the woods and fields at close of day' (311) – related in exquisite detail and specificity: 'I saw far off the weedy fallows ... grazed | By flocks fast-feeding and selecting each | His fav'rite herb' (316–319). Yet the poet's access to the scene is of fragile and temporary duration since 'To-morrow brings a change ... though silently perform'd' (322–323) with almost clichéd connection between the sheep's coats and the coming snow: 'Fast falls a fleecy show'r' (326). This moment then provides the cue for Coleridge, whose poem remains close to Cowper's antecedent:

> The frost performs its secret ministry
> Unhelped by any wind. The owlet's cry
> Came loud – and hard, again! loud as before.
> The inmates of my cottage, all at rest,
> Have left me to that solitude which suits
> Abstruser musings, save that at my side
> My cradled infant slumbers peacefully.
> 'Tis calm indeed! – so calm that it disturbs
> And vexes meditations with its strange
> And extreme silentness. Sea, hill, and wood.
> This populous village! Sea, and hill, and wood,
> With all the numberless goings-on of life,
> Inaudible as dreams!
>
> (Wu, 2006, 624)[14]

Coleridge's poem may be seen in ecological terms by virtue of the domestic setting that speaks intimately to the act of 'dwelling'. Yet, this process is problematically connected to the natural world outside. In contrast to Cowper's evocation of the woods and fields as 'A variegated show' (312) implying multiple colours in pattern, Coleridge's iambic pentameter registers an inability to bring diverse elements satisfactorily together. The conversational lilt of Cowper's lines are immediately rewritten in interruption as the assonance of the owlet's cry ('owl / loud') unsettles the stress pattern of Coleridge's lines, bringing the second 'loud' literally hard on the heels of the initial cry. Still this onslaught of sound recedes into the aurally disorientating 'abstruser musings' (6) (the assonance of 'suits' bleeds over the line ending, establishing a discomfortingly claustrophobic soundscape to express the tunnelling of sound into the poet's inner thought processes) and finally into 'extreme silentness' (10), the hyperbole of which – there cannot be silence by degrees – implies a vexed paranoia rather than a reconciliation between self and world. The disorientation of silentness is, indeed, written into the incantatory phrasing that follows in the pyrrhic substitution of foot three (ending 'silentness') and the subsequent spondee of 'Sea, hill'. The poem's formal arrangement thus anticipates the admission of an essential unreality in the relationship between poet and environment: 'Inaudible as dreams!' (13). Engagements with the lived experience of the natural world appear only as a series of disruptions, or uncanny prayer-like chants that replace detailed observation of the natural world with repetitions of 'sea and hill and wood' (11). Here conjunctions serve the metre while detracting from the specifics of landscape, replacing Cowper's flexible changeability with the stalled monosyllables of generalization. Bate's answer to this lack of engagement with outside space is to read the poem instead as an ecology of the mind, aligning it with his sense that poetry induces and produces insight and final settling: 'by the end of the night both the environment of the cottage and the ecology of the poet's mind will have subtly evolved. The poet has learnt to dwell more securely with himself, his home and his environment' (2000, p. 110)[12].

Yet what if we find something else here? We might hear within this poem's dominant mode of hopefulness and contemplation a faintly panicked inability to access the natural world outside aesthetic representation (imaged in the sea, hill and wood's service to metre rather than material engagement). This would suggest the poignancy of an environmental experience that *only* has aesthetic representation to fall back on, revealing the dislocating loss that lies beneath Bate's belief in myth as a substitute for history. Such a sense would seem to propel the poet's famous turn to his baby son, and his wish that the child might grow into a more engaged environmental consciousness than was possible for the urban-dwelling Coleridge: 'For I was reared | In the great city, pent mid cloisters dim, | And saw nought lovely but the sky and stars' (56–58). The father's need for the son to rectify this is made more moving by Duncan Wu's editorial notes suggesting that Coleridge's desire that Hartley will 'wander like a breeze | By lakes and sandy shores' (59–60) is grounded in a misrecognition of natural landscape, since the poem was written before the poet had visited the Lake District and the 'sandy shores' owe more to Wordsworth's 'The Pedlar' (then in composition) than to the reality of British lakesides. What the poem traces, therefore, is a yearning after an idea of nature and the radical dislocation from its material reality (echoing in the precarious emptiness of a failed incantation), even anticipating the occluded relationship with nature produced by ecological crisis. This rings out in the poem's final wish that 'all seasons shall be sweet to thee | Whether the summer clothe the general earth | With greenness, or the redbreasts sit and sing | Betwixt the tufts of snow' (70–73): this collapse of seasonality shatters the lived familiarity of Cowper's feel for the temporality of 'golden harvest' (314) into a series of metonymies that mark distance as much as association. Rather than dwelling securely himself, the poet invests in his son and on him casts a general and provisional spell that anticipates the handing down of damaged ecological relations to the next generation to solve.

John Clare, 'The Nightingale's Nest' (1835)

Picking up on the last note of 'redbreasts' here, I move in the last part of this chapter to Romantic engagements with non-human environmental dwellers, concentrating on two encounters with the nightingale. Such a move allows us to see the human/nature engagement in specific relational focus. Continuing the rural walking seen in several poets' work here, Clare's 'The Nightingale's Nest' (1835) opens by carefully exploring his local terrain, allowing the iambic pentameter to chart the undulating path he treads towards the hidden home of a bird that is to him a regular feature of daily life: 'Up this green woodland ride let's softly rove | And list the nightingale – she dwells just here.' (1–2). The 'just here' of this line arrests us with its immediacy, and its intimation that it is also 'just here' in the poem that we might find the singing bird, encouraged by repetitions across the poem of the specifics of place: 'This very spot' (7), 'her secret nest is here' (53), 'So here we'll leave them' (92). Yet the poem can only describe the poet's location – 'here I've heard her' (5), 'There have I hunted ... To find her nest' (13–15) – while the bird herself shifts on and on, eager to cover her tracks, to remain hidden: 'I watched in vain: | The timid bird had left the hazel bush | And at a distance hid to sing again' (19–21). The poem then becomes a song of reciprocity with the bird's movements leading the poet's active participation. Burnside's view of poetry and place is useful here – 'the poem of place always contains an implied observer, whose identity is inextricably linked to whatever is being observed' (2007, par. 2)[9] – because it installs in our understanding of the lyric the vital energy of encounter: 'where does the self end, and the other begin? ... the defining line exists at the borderline of their transactions, that we define one another, that without Thou, there is no I' (ibid. par. 3), so asserting lyric poetry not as the establishment of one voice, but rather the exchange of relationship, a vital ecological imperative. And this is what we see in Clare's poem of seeking: the establishment of a poet's movements in direct relation to the bird's enchanting authority (implying that the bird is as much the author of this poem as the poet). Iambic pentameter's Romantic association with walking and charting is here employed to hunker down, rather than roam across:

> There have I hunted like a very boy,
> Creeping on hands and knees through matted thorn
> To find her nest and see her feed young.
>
> (12–14)

> Part aside
> These hazel branches in a gentle way
> And stoop right cautious 'neath the rustling boughs,
> For we will have another search today
>
> (46–48)

The poem thus charts spatially, temporally, literally the re-ordering of nature and human with man placed low down, to the side, in hushed silence; in such arrangements that the poet's ornithological understanding can be realized as his movement specifically picks up the language of a bird's dwelling: 'among | The hazel's under-boughs, I've *nest*led down | And watched her while she sung' (my italics, 17–19). Even though the poem implies the bird's excessiveness as she often eludes the poet's capture in verse – 'vain' he says three times; 'there she is' is quickly qualified by 'if rightly guessed' (42–43), illustrating Theodor W. Adorno's sense that 'natural beauty ... veils itself at the moment of greatest proximity' (p. 83)[16] – the poet's patient willingness to be quiet, to move carefully – indeed to adopt a poetic stance – affords him privileged access to scientific knowledge via emotional pathways: 'her renown | Hath made me marvel that so famed a bird | Should have no better dress than russet brown' (19–21); 'Deep adown | The nest is made ... Snug lie her curious eggs in number five' (87–89).

As this patterning between bird and poet is established then we are primed to realize that when her song bursts forth – and the language becomes metaphysical – so the bird's trembling ecstasy is understood to intimate the poet's, and by extension the reader's:

> Her wings would tremble in her ecstasy
> And feathers stand on end as 'twere with joy
> And mouth wide open to release her heart
> Of its out-sobbing songs.
>
> (22–25)

This poem puts the bird's unique dwelling at its centre – 'no other bird … weaves | Its dwelling in such spots' (76–78) – so insisting that the poet and reader's ecstasy is always responsive rather than directive. Such ordering of poet and bird speaks to the deep ecological imperatives of today that look to acknowledge and protect nature's ontological status, conferring on the poet a duty of responsibility that is charted here from 'Hush! let the wood-gate softly clap for fear | The noise might drive her from her home of love' (2–3) to 'So here we'll leave them, still unknown to wrong, | As the old woodland's legacy of song' (92–93): it is the eggs that provide the germ for tomorrow's song. The human is hushed so that nature may speak.

John Keats, 'Ode to a Nightingale', (1819)

To finish with Keats' famous 'Ode to a Nightingale' (1819), then, we might expect this to be the reverse. Celebrated for its lyrical expression of a poetic sensibility and notable for its early shift from the bird's 'full-throated ease' (10) to 'Provençal song' (14), this would seem to be a poem in which nature gives way human culture. Indeed, the contrast between this and Clare's intimate knowledge of the bird is focused in the difference between the bird's dress of 'russet brown' (21) and Keats' apostrophizing of 'thou, light-winged dryad' (7) of the trees: material reality translates to mythic form. Yet, reading it in *conversation* with Clare, we might uncover a materialized relationship between human and nature that reveals surprising similarities between the urban and rural poet's understanding of the bird's behaviour, and its effect on the human. By reading this poem after the others discussed here we can find the exploratory, discursive open-endedness of blank verse infusing the traditionally understood hermeticism of the iambic pentameter ode, with its emphasis on formal arrangement, internal patterning and facilitation of human insight; such idealism might be disorientated by flux.

Focusing on stanza five (but implying ways in which the whole poem's energies might be retraced), I suggest that these lines acknowledge and ignite an ecological dynamic that indicates and elaborates Keats' habitual knowledge of nightingales' habits and location which directs his disorientated environmental consciousness. This poem knows, like Clare's, that the bird hides and is as often elusively covered over by vegetation as it is soaring through the skies. This is evident in the echoes between Keats' feel for habitat – 'the forest dim' (20), 'thou among the leaves' (22) 'the verdurous glooms and winding mossy ways' (40) – that provide the context for the bird's 'pouring forth thy soul abroad | In such an ecstasy!' (58–59), and Clare's witness that 'Lost in a wilderness of listening leaves, | Rich ecstasy would pour its luscious strain' (32–33). Such dialogue opens up the cultural in Clare's encounter with the bird and the material in Keats'. But where Clare's poem indicates care and respectful retreat, Keats' stares into the abyss of a loss of groundedness only intimated by Clare's nightingale's elusiveness. For in Keats' poem we find a radical loss of material encounter:

> I cannot see what flowers are at my feet,
>   Nor what soft incense hangs upon the boughs,
> But, in embalmed darkness, guess each sweet
>   Wherewith the seasonable month endows
> The grass, the thicket, and the fruit-tree wild,
>   White hawthorn, and the pastoral eglantine,
>   Fast-fading violets covered up in leaves,
>   And mid-May's eldest child,
> The coming musk-rose, full of dewy wine,
>   The murmurous haunt of flies on summer eves.
>
> (41–50)

Here the poem speaks directly to the disorientating, melancholic, mournful interpretation of our contemporary experience of the natural world: 'I cannot see what flowers are at my feet' (41) resonates with poverty of experience in an age of ecological crisis. Alleviation is glimpsed in the ensuing accumulation of sensual experience, however, if we see it forming a battery against destruction as the experience of nature becomes guesswork grounded in sensuality. The combined intimation of loss ('embalmed darkness' (43), 'fast-fading' (47), 'murmourous haunt of flies' (50)) with sensory stimulation ('each sweet | Wherewith the seasonable month endows' (43–44), 'the coming musk-rose, full of dewy wine' (49)) writes the natural world not as solidified and external to the human, but as fragile, apt to dissolve and yet yoked to traces and memories in human experience. Here the two work together – nature's perfume implied in poetry's figurative excess – to establish a dynamic by which both might persist in time, with the seasonal setting establishing a timeliness that is both transient and repetitive. Such intertwining – which follows up on the poet's earlier recognition that he is 'too happy in thine happiness' (6) – anticipates Tom Bristow's reading of Burnside, in which 'the progression toward the metaphysical and the ecological can be read as a single move by the poet showing what it might be like to reconcile mind and matter, and being and world' (p. 51)[17]. In this stanza, the poet is effectively in physical exile, but metaphysical community, and from here the poet eventually returns across the ode (in ways that bring to mind Cowper's return from meditation to material reality) to 'my sole self!' (72). Such solitariness might seem like a loss in the context of the earlier fusing of bird and poet, but the poem's final note of bewilderment, produced in aftermath and as the poet witnesses the bird's onward progression, suggests a profound restructuring of the self and a destabilization of certainty: an exile and return that seems to illustrate Bristow's identification of an 'element that allows for the self to be read as an effect of the world' (p. 57). In this final example of 'close-read ecology' then we have the radical shift of environmental thought: the recognition of selfhood as *effect* – contingent, provisional, and hence environmental:

> Thy plaintive anthem fades
> Past the near meadows, over the still stream,
> Up the hillside, and now 'tis buried deep
> In the next valley-glades:
> Was it a vision, or a waking dream?
> Fled is that music – do I wake or sleep?
>
> (75–80)

My readings here have attempted to avoid promoting a reading of poetry that reaches after certainty, settling, fixing or transcendent insight. But they have also sought to work around the distancing effect of history (a narrative that, at least by implication, demarcates the then and now). Rather, I want to suggest that poetry's charting and tracing is effected rhythmically, in echoes and spatial arrangements that draw on an emotional and sensual methodology traditionally understood to be ignited in the reader as well as the poet. I offer close reading of poetry of the Romantic period, therefore, as a methodological interface between then and now, a space in which we might be induced to respond to regularity, but from there become sensitized to disjunction, 'wrongness', disorientation, so implying the ecological wisdom that 'defamiliarization encourages reconnection' (Bristow, 59)[17]. While this might sound similar to – and indeed acknowledges the potential of – Burnside's characterization of the lyric poem as 'a kind of metaphysical space, which is essentially empty, a region of potential in which anything can happen' (2007, par. 2),[9] it is imperative that his notion of 'timelessness' (ibid. par. 1) is qualified by history; a discipline of which Burnside is deeply suspicious (2006, 92)[10]. The attentive accessing of Romantic period writing from our historical moment of ecological crisis necessitates the understanding that the Romantic scene we encounter was and is not fixed, but has a cultural materiality of its own, uncovered through Romantic studies' 'transformed intellectual agenda'. Our close readings of Romantic poetry should always be mindful of, and ideally in dialogue with, the circulation of cultural ideologies in its source. Romantic 'natural' scenes, therefore, do not stand as settled focuses for nostalgia, but as exposed spaces that were politicized, changing, threatened and negotiated, dynamic spaces that produced poetry that draws on, inscribes, challenges or disrupts the politics of expression. Recognition of this allows close reading to become an active engagement, not a passive totting up of effects, and the encounters with landscape and nature so revealed are articulated in dialogic, conversational terms that open up the collective fate of the land and its inhabitants. In such readings, the material conditions of now ignite with the material conditions of then, characterizing the Romantic poem not as a fixed and hermetic expression, but as a structure promoting on-going resonances and rethinking. Just as the dream with which Keats' poem ends suggests not an end but a beginning, so 'incompletion does not spell unfathomability; it offers the embodiment of potential ... alive to the world unfolding' (Bristow, 65)[17]. I finish then with process – a notion that speaks to the material reality of the natural world and fuses it with the energy of the Romantic poem:

> A great poem is a fountain forever overflowing with the waters of wisdom and delight; and after one person and one age has exhausted all of its divine effluence which their peculiar relations enable them to share; another and yet another succeeds, and new relations are ever developed, the source of an unforeseen and unconceived delight.
>
> (Shelley (1840), p. 269).

Further Reading

Adams, T. (2008), 'Representing Rural Leisure: John Clare and the Politics of Popular Culture', *Studies in Romanticism* 47, 371–392.

Baird, J. D. and Ryskamp, C. (eds.) (1980–1995), *The Poems of William Cowper*, three volumes (Oxford: Clarendon Press).

Bate, J. (ed.) (2006), *I Am: The Selected Poetry of John Clare* (New York: Farrar, Straus and Giroux).

Bate, J. (1997), *The Genius of Shakespeare* (London: Picador).

Coupe, L. (ed.) (2000), *The Green Studies Reader: From Romanticism to Ecocriticism* (London: Routledge).

Devall, B. and Sessions, G. (1985), *Deep Ecology: Living as if Nature Mattered* (Layton, Utah: Gibbs M. Smith).

Pite, R. (2002), '"Founded on the Affections": A Romantic Ecology', in *The Environmental Tradition in English Literature*, ed. J. Parnham (Aldershot: Ashgate), pp. 144–155.

Shelley, P. B. (1840 [c. 1821]), 'A Defence of Poetry', in *Poems and Prose*, ed. T. Webb (1995) (London: J. M. Dent), pp. 247–78.

Tayebi, K. (2004), 'Undermining the Eighteen-Century Pastoral: Rewriting the Poet's Relationship to Nature in Charlotte Smith's Poetry', *European Romantic Review* 15, 131–150.

Vardy, A. (2003), *John Clare, Politics and Poetry* (Houndmills: Palgrave).

Wallace, A. D. (2002), 'Picturesque Fossils, Sublime Geology? The Crisis of Authority in Charlotte Smith's 'Beachy Head', *European Romantic Review* 13, 77–93.

White, S. J. (2009), 'John Clare's Sonnets and the Northborough Fens', *John Clare Society Journal* 28, 55–70.

Wu, D. (ed.) (1998), *The Selected Writings of William Hazlitt*, nine volumes (London: Pickering & Chatto)

See also: Canonicity; Case Studies in Reading Critical Texts

Notes

1 Thomas, E. (2000), 'Studying Nature', in Coupe (ed.), pp. 66–69.

2 Soper, K. (2000), 'The Idea of Nature', in Coupe (ed.), pp. 123–126.

3 Glotfelty, C. (1996), 'Introduction: Literary Studies in an Age of Environmental Crisis', in *The EcoCriticism Reader*, eds C. Glotfelty and H. Fromm (Athens, Georgia: University of Georgia Press), pp. xv–xxxvii.

4 Benchimol, A. (2005), 'Remaking the Romantic period: cultural materialism, cultural studies and the radical public sphere', *Textual Practice* 19, 51–70.

5 Benchimol, A. (2007), 'Debatable Geographies of Romantic Nostalgia: The Redemptive Landscape in Wordsworth and Cobbett', in *Romanticism's Debatable Lands*, eds C. Lamont and M. Rossington (Basingstoke: Palgrave-Macmillan), pp. 92–104.

6 Serres, M. (1995), *The Natural Contract*, trans. E. MacArthur and W. Paulson (Ann Arbor: University of Michigan Press).

7 Bate, J. (1991), *Romantic Ecology: Wordsworth and the Environmental Tradition* (London: Routledge).

8 Borthwick, D. (2009), 'The Sustainable Male: Masculine Ecology in the Poetry of John Burnside', in *Masculinity and the Other: Historical Perspectives*, eds H. Ellis and J. Meyer (Cambridge: Cambridge Scholars Press), pp. 63–84.

9 Burnside, J., (2007), 'Poetry and a Sense of Place' *Nordlit* 1, http://www.hum.uit. no/nordlit/1/burnside.html>.

10 Burnside, J. (2006), 'A Science of Belonging: Poetry as Ecology', in *Contemporary Poetry and Contemporary Science*, ed. R. Crawford (Oxford: Oxford University Press), pp. 91–106.

11 Mason, E. and Williams, R. (2009), 'Reciprocal Scansion in Wordsworth's "There was a Boy"', *Literature Compass* 6, 515–523.

12 Bate, J. (2000), *The Song of the Earth* (London: Picador).

13 Griggs, E. L. (ed.) (1956–1971), *Collected Letters of Samuel Taylor Coleridge*, six volumes (Oxford: Clarendon Press).

14 Wu, D. (ed.) (2006), *Romanticism: An Anthology*, 3rd edn (Oxford: Blackwell Publishing).
15 King, J. and Ryskamp, C. (eds) (1970–1986), *The Letters and Prose Writings of William Cowper*, five volumes (Oxford: Clarendon Press).
16 Adorno, T. W. (1997), 'Nature as "Not Yet"', in Coupe (ed.), pp. 81–83.
17 Bristow, T. (2009), 'Negative Poetics and Immanence: Reading John Burnside's "Homage to Henri Bergson"', *Green Letters: Studies in EcoCriticism* 10, 50–69

4 Case Studies in Reading 2: Critical Texts

Sue Chaplin

Chapter Overview

Introduction

The late 1970s marked a watershed in the critical study of the Romantic period and the aim of this chapter is to assess some of the key critical works in Romantic scholarship over the last thirty years. Earlier critical work, it is fair to say, tended to focus on an extremely narrow selection of authors: the 'Big Six' of Romanticism as they are commonly known. Indeed, it is arguably the case that few literary periods or movements have been interpreted so tightly and to the exclusion of so many, often prolific, writers. The definition of Romanticism through the work of Wordsworth, Coleridge, Shelley, Byron, Keats and (later) Blake arose out of key critical texts of the mid-twentieth century (such as M. H. Abrams' *The Mirror and the Lamp*, 1953; Northrop Frye's *Fearful Symmetry*, 1947) that brought a certain aesthetic and cultural perspective to the study of the period. In the work considered in this chapter, the ground begins to shift considerably and it is important for students to recognise that the point of departure of these texts is often also a point of fracture as they define their approach *against* the dominant critical paradigm of the mid-twentieth century. An understanding of this critical history and the on-going debates and controversies within the discipline is essential to the study of Romantic scholarship and its varied and challenging historical and theoretical perspectives.

Paul de Man, *The Rhetoric of Romanticism*

Edition cited: *The Rhetoric of Romanticism*. New York: Columbia University Press, 1984.

This text brings together a number of essays written over two decades by the poststructuralist critic Paul de Man. His work poses a significant challenge to the foundational assumptions of earlier Romantic scholarship. Romanticism had been associated with the search for a harmonisation of mind and nature that would reconcile the division between the interior self and the exterior world, between 'subject' and 'object'. Central to this project aesthetically was a perceived transition at the end of the eighteenth century from allegorical to symbolic imagery. Writing in *The Statesman's Manual* in 1816 on the distinction between allegory and symbol, Coleridge argued that a poet's use of allegory could not close the divide between an image (what Coleridge calls 'picture language') and the idea that a poet is attempting to express through the deployment of that image. Symbolic figuration, on the other hand, achieves what allegory cannot: the unification of the image *with* the idea *in* the symbol. Critics of Abrams' generation tended to adopt Coleridge's perspective, seeing in Romanticism the displacement of allegorical in favour of symbolic modes of expression. It is this notion that de Man's writing contests through poststructuralist readings of canonical Romantic works. Far from the disappearance of allegory in Romantic writing (and the consequent reconciliation of opposites poetically and philosophically), de Man contends that allegory continues to function in the new figurative language of Romanticism, a language that does not close the gap between interior and exterior realities, but which insists on the precarious contingency of the relation between self and object. I say 'precarious' since the Romantic conceptualization of the self and its relation to the world is, in de Man's estimation, deeply problematic. What is sought through symbolization is the unity of the eternal with the finite self; what emerges in poetic practice through allegory is a troubled acknowledgement of the contingency of the self. De Man describes this as the 'negative self-knowledge' of the Romantics (120) and allegory becomes its primary means of expression, precisely because allegory works against an illusory union of image and idea. While Romantic works struggle to assert a transcendental subjectivity beyond finite language and materiality, their complex rhetorical strategies reveal the impossibility of their intellectual project, argues de Man, and the essays in this collection assess canonical Romantic works for evidence of the textual fractures and contradictions that expose Romantic 'negative self-knowledge'. Here, I give an account of two of these pieces which will introduce students to de Man's method: 'Wordsworth and Hölderlin' and 'Shelley Disfigured'.

'Wordsworth and Hölderlin' is a comparative analysis of language, imagination and temporality in selected works of these two writers. My focus here is on de Man's analysis of Wordsworth's 'The Boy of Winander'. The poem begins with the boy apparently in union with the landscape he inhabits and thus the emphasis is on precisely that unity of man with nature that the Romantics (and later critics such as Abrams) tended to privilege: in the opening lines, 'The analogical correspondence between man and nature is so perfect', says de Man, 'that one passes from one to the other without difficulty or conflict, in a dialogue full of echo and joyful exchange' (51). Nevertheless, de Man contends that this seeming harmony between subject and object is in fact undermined by Wordsworth's rhetorical strategies in spite of and often against the intellectual and aesthetic trajectory of the poem. As the poem continues, 'another dimension opens up and replaces this illusory analogy' (52), introducing an element of uncertainty that for de Man is signified by Wordsworth's increasingly unusual choice of adjectives and verbs: 'The reassuring stability of the beginning disappears and gives way to the precarious adjective "uncertain" that is added to the key word "heaven"' in line 412, for example (52). Moreover, Wordsworth intriguingly chooses the word 'hung' to describe the boy waiting for the owls to respond to his mimic calls:

> Then sometimes, in that silence, while he *hung*
> Listening, a gentle shock of mild surprise
> Has carried far into his heart the voice
> Of mountain torrents.... (52)

The interweaving of man and nature figured in the opening lines through the echoing by the owls of the boy's 'mimic hootings' is suspended and the sense of unity between the self and the world begins to slip away. The verb reappears in the second half of the poem and establishes a thematic connection between the poem's two parts at the point where the young boy's grave is described: 'the Churchyard *hangs* | Upon a slope above the village school'. De Man comments that here the origin of the uncertainty introduced earlier in the poem is disclosed through the reiteration of this ambivalent term 'hangs': the uncertainty resides in an 'indubitable connection between the loss of the sense of correspondence and the experience of death' (53). The poem fails to establish a correspondence between nature and the self that might overcome the awful contingency of subjectivity, materiality and poetic language, and de Man's analysis reveals here a Romantic 'negative self-knowledge', the acknowledgement of which cuts against the grain of previous Romantic scholarship.

In the essay 'Shelley Disfigured', de Man considers Shelley's last enigmatic poem, 'The Triumph of Life', and contends that this work is representative of Romanticism itself: its mysterious questions 'are characteristic of the interpretative labour associated with Romanticism' (94). The poem narrates a fictive history of the French philosopher Jean-Jacques Rousseau whose work considerably influenced Romanticism. De Man focuses on the elisions and displacements that mark the figurative structure of the poem and that function to pose and defer a series of questions relating to Rousseau's identity and origin: 'The structure of the text is not one of question and answer, but of a question whose meaning as a question is effaced from the moment it is asked' (98). If the poem begins apparently as a quest, it rapidly mutates into something else as its sequence of events and figurative strategies repeat themselves, receding to an obscure moment of origin (the origin of Rousseau, the origin of thought itself) that appears to be incapable of coherent representation. The text seems deliberately opaque, says de Man, resisting interpretation and frustrating the process of understanding. In the act of narrating Rousseau's history in terms of the 'how' and 'why' of his origin, the text in fact effaces the 'how' and the 'why', and this is figured through the symbolic disfigurement of Rousseau: when he first appears in the poem his face (*figure* in French) is grotesque: he has holes where his eyes should be. Shelley's last poem, that is so representative of Romanticism for de Man, expresses something beyond even the 'negative self-knowledge' of earlier Romantics: it suggests the absence of any representable subjectivity, an absence figured here through the loss of a face. This dis-figurement extends not only to Rousseau's identity, but to a poetic language that is ultimately incapable of successful, meaningful figuration. De Man considers in particular the constant ambivalent interplay between opposites such as light and darkness, waking and sleeping, and, especially, remembrance and forgetfulness. If language is meant to guarantee the efficiency of memory and thus the coherence of the self, then it fails here: the demarcation between these states is so unclear that it becomes impossible for Rousseau to maintain a distinction between what is known and what is unknown, or forgotten, or dreamed or imagined. Rousseau's forgetfulness – his vague sense of having known some truth now lost to him – is associated, de Man argues, with 'a metaphorical strain that is present throughout the entire poem: images of the rising and waning light of the sun' (104). This metaphorical strain constitutes a complex system of figuration that nevertheless unpicks itself during the course of the poem. The key figure here is a mysterious 'shape of light' that appears to Rousseau and that seems to offer the prospect of enlightenment only ultimately to withhold it. This 'light of heaven' has only a 'half extinguished beam'; it does not shine strongly, but 'glimmers' (106); its movement is so obscure that it appears as 'the ghost of a forgotten form of sleep' (106). The appearance of this enigmatic light, says de Man, 'creates conditions of optical confusion that resemble nothing as much as the experience of trying to read 'The Triumph of Life', as its meaning glimmers, hovers and wavers, but refuses to yield the clarity it keeps announcing' (1060).

Far from offering the unity of language and experience that critics such as Abrams associated with the Romantic project, 'The Triumph of Life' dissolves all apparent certainties and unities, and nowhere is this more evident for de Man than in the entropy and randomness generated by Shelley's poetic language, figured ultimately in the 'shape of light' that resists interpretation. Moreover, insofar as this poem is, for de Man, 'characteristic of the interpretative labour associated with Romanticism', his poststructuralist reading signals a significant paradigm shift in the study of Romanticism.

 Jerome J. McGann, *The Romantic Ideology: A Critical Investigation*

Edition cited: *The Romantic Ideology: A Critical Investigation.* Chicago: Chicago University Press, 1983.

In the introduction to this seminal work, McGann makes a bold statement of intent: his aim is to define and interrogate what he terms the 'Romantic ideology' and, moreover, to demonstrate that 'the scholarship and criticism of Romanticism and its works are dominated by [this] ideology, by an uncritical absorption of Romanticism's own self-representations' (1). From McGann's Marxist critical perspective, ideology is understood as 'false consciousness', as a 'body of illusions' that is historicized in literary works. McGann's project is to analyse the forms of consciousness that prevailed within the Romantic period and the extent to which critics of the twentieth century who have aimed to study Romanticism objectively have in fact absorbed and reiterated its 'body of illusions'.

Romanticism or Romanticisms?

McGann identifies the key dilemma that he feels has confronted Romantic scholarship throughout most of the twentieth century, a dilemma lucidly articulated by Arthur Lovejoy in the 1920s: Romanticism seems incapable of coherent definition, such that scholarship has tended to reveal not so much a unified field of study, as, in Lovejoy's words, 'a discrimination of *romanticisms*' (17). McGann cites Abrams' conceptualization of Romanticism in terms of 'the secularization of Judeo-Christian tradition' as one 'discrimination' of a particular 'Romanticism' (21). Another 'discrimination' emerges out of the more recent work of Anne Mellor (*English Romantic Irony*, 1980) which offers an alternative model based on her understanding of Romantic irony and its various expressions. Mellor's model has the advantage of developing a broader understanding of the subject that is capable of embracing those aspects of Romanticism neglected by Abrams, most notably the work of Byron whose 'sceptical' and 'ironic' productions could not easily be accommodated within Abrams' scheme (22). Nevertheless, McGann argues that Mellor's account has its own blind spot: when Romantic irony terminates and the 'perception of a chaotic universe arouses either guilt or fear' in Romantic-era works, what happens then? What are we dealing with? McGann concludes that Mellor's critical model, for all of its strengths, constitutes another 'discrimination' that excludes from its remit elements of Romanticism that it is unable to explain according to its particular conceptual or historical reference points.

Geoffrey Hartman is another critic whose groundbreaking work, associated (like de Man's) with the Yale school of deconstruction in the 1970s and 80s, is regarded as nevertheless beholden to the Romantic ideology that McGann seeks to question. Hartman's arguments in his key essay 'Romanticism and Anti-Selfconsciousness' (1970) seem to McGann to be 'exact translations of those issues in Romanticism which are fundamental precisely because they were declared to be fundamental by the earliest Romantics themselves' (40). McGann returns to Coleridge for an elucidation of those 'issues' that have passed in a line of ideological continuity from the literature of the Romantic period to the criticism of the late twentieth century. Coleridge's aim is to develop an investigative method capable of unifying the disparate aspects of human knowledge and understanding; he fails because he 'neglects to consider the social and historical transformations which cultural studies are subject to. His philosophic, totalizing grasp of cultural history is not a universal, transcendent truth, but a limited and time-specific idea. It is, in brief, an ideology of knowledge' (44).

How does this 'limited and time-specific idea' translate into the Romantic ideology absorbed by twentieth-century critics, including Geoffrey Hartman? The key figure here is the German philosopher Hegel who synthesized a variety of Romantic ideas into a universal system of thought far more unified than anything that emerged out of Romanticism itself: his theory 'represents the transformation of Romanticism into acculturated forms, into state ideology ... and most scholars since have adopted some form of this Hegelian synthesis' (48). There is an alternative to this ideological approach, however, which for McGann emerges out of the work of Heinrich Heine in Germany in the nineteenth century. Students will probably be unfamiliar with Heine's work, but it is his *methodology* that is important here. To recap: for McGann, critics and philosophers from Hegel to Hartman have accepted without proper interrogation the authority of Romanticism's key self-conceptualizations: 'spirituality', 'creativity', 'process', 'uniqueness' and 'diversity'. Heine opposes this intellectual practice with a method that insists on the primacy of historically specific political and cultural transformations that will have influenced not only the work under consideration, but the critic also. To give an example, Heine's work *The Romantic School* considers poems by Ludwig Uhland that influenced Heine considerably. Heine dwells on the fact that he first read this work in 1813 and then again in 1833. The reader might ask: so what? Yet it is precisely this historical difference that matters to Heine and to McGann; there is an 'epochal division' between 1813 and 1833 and the different experiences of reading the text, when acknowledged by the critic, 'are important because they bring into focus certain objective historical circumstances' that are vital to an understanding of the production and reception of literary works (51).

History, Ideology, Criticism
Having defined the form of the 'Romantic ideology' in the first part of the work, McGann goes on to consider what can be said to differentiate Romanticism from earlier movements and concludes that it is precisely an awareness of cultural and historical specificity that characterizes Romantic works. McGann compares the work of John Donne with that of John Keats and contends that in Donne 'the culturally inherited grounds of judgement [are not questioned] for the very reason that he does not see those grounds as culturally determined' (75). By contrast, 'Keats' poetic materials are self-consciously recognised to be socially and historically defined' and, more broadly, 'Romantic imagination emerges with the birth of an historical sense, which places the poet, and then the reader, at a critical distance from the poem's materials' (79). Yet it is precisely this sense of historical and cultural contingency that Romantic works often seek to *efface*. This is a crucial element of the Romantic ideology and it has been absorbed into twentieth century Romantic criticism which has dehistoricized and universalized culturally determined Romantic self-representations. McGann follows the process of effacement of historical specificity in Wordsworth's 'The Ruined Cottage'. This is a poem which displays a very particular historical awareness and a

specific set of social concerns: the weaver Robert loses his livelihood and attempts to save his family from poverty by going to war. He disappears and his family faces ruin. McGann's contention, though, is that the poem's strategy is ultimately to efface these historical details through the transformation of a scene of socially determined suffering into a meditation by the mature poet, writing years later, upon 'the secret spirit of Humanity' (83). The extent to which the Romantic imagination works to make present and then efface material historical details is essential to the formulation and transmission of the Romantic ideology, argues McGann, and complex effacements and displacements of historical specificity in Romantic works ought to be understood as a key component of Romanticism.

To clarify further the relation between history, ideology and criticism, part three of *The Romantic Ideology* identifies three historical phases of romanticism: one brief primary phase and two secondary, or revisionist, phases (109). The first phase corresponds to the period before the political calamities of the 1790s and its works (such as Blake's *The Marriage of Heaven and Hell*) are marked by an enthusiasm that eschews the more troubled, self-reflective approach of work in the second phase. The work of Wordsworth and Coleridge after the Reign of Terror, during this second phase, differs from that of Blake, for example, 'in that they are already laden with self-critical and revisionist elements' even if these elements are often displaced and occluded (109). The third phase corresponds broadly to the second generation of Romanticism (1808–1824) and here the displacements and occlusions of history persist and to some extent intensify as Byron and Shelley confront with despair the tensions and contradictions of their age. McGann's point is that the work of the Romantics in each phase is always historically and socially specific, even and perhaps especially when it appears furthest removed from historical realities. Romanticism emerged out of the complex and conflicted historical conditions of the period and was defined by its historical limitations; the Romantics were aware of this and responded with strategies of displacement and escape which produced the 'grand illusion' of the movement – the notion that conflict and contingency could be overcome through the unifying, harmonizing processes of the imagination (137). Critics have made this 'grand illusion' the basis of their critical study of Romanticism, the uninterrogated ground of their scholarship, and for McGann this has dangerous political implications. The ideological uncoupling of criticism from history threatens to place literary scholarship at the service of an establishment that has a good deal invested in the obliteration of historical awareness and specificity. Since its publication in 1983, *The Romantic Ideology* has been influential in encouraging the development of a Romantic criticism concerned with assessing self-critically the capacity of ideology to distort scholarly activity.

Anne K. Mellor, *Romanticism and Gender*

Edition cited: *Romanticism and Gender*. New York, London: Routledge, 1993.

Mellor begins her study with a provocative question: does Romanticism have a gender? Her thesis is that Romanticism is indeed a gendered discourse and that even the most groundbreaking studies in the later twentieth century (including de Man's and McGann's) have tended to 'base their constructions of British Romanticism almost exclusively on the writings and thought of six male poets' (1). Mellor's project is twofold: to re-evaluate the work of women writers of the Romantic period; and to consider whether the male poets of the canon reveal a gender bias that subsequent critics have reiterated in their studies. The structure of the work reflects these twin objectives. Under the heading 'Masculine Romanticism', Mellor examines 'the role played by gender in the construction of literary texts' through an analysis of key male Romantic works (15). She then aims to identify the common concerns and ideological positions of women writers whose work produces, she contends, an alternative 'Feminine Romanticism'.

Mellor acknowledges the difficulties of conforming to this masculine/feminine polarity since it runs the risk of reproducing the very binary opposition that has worked against a recognition of women writers in the past. Nevertheless, this approach, says Mellor, has the necessary advantage of 'allowing us to see what has hitherto been hidden, the difference that gender makes in the construction of British Romantic literature' (3). It is also important to be aware that Mellor does not consider the terms of this opposition to be in any way naturally or biologically determined; in no sense is 'the feminine' an essential, universal component of female identity. Mellor agrees with Foucault that sexuality is a social construction and her deployment of the polarity 'masculine/feminine' refers 'to the products of the social definition and organization of gender' (4).

Masculine Romanticism

Mellor's aim is to interrogate the ways in which gender functions in the canonical texts of masculine Romanticism, and central to her argument is the relation between nature, imagination and the feminine. Beginning with Wordsworth's *Prelude*, Mellor considers the extent to which the poem initially genders nature as 'feminine' and associates the poet's imaginative power with nature, only then to efface the feminine through the transformation of nature from 'she' into a male 'brother' (18). It is not therefore that Wordsworth genders nature 'feminine' and sets 'her' power alongside his own imagination, but that he and other male Romantics absorb and masculinize this force, adopting it as a 'brother' to their 'glorious faculty' of imagination. In Keats' 'To Autumn', for example, the poet 'subtly empowers the male poet to utter the music of a female 'Other', to become the voice of autumn and translate her "mellow fruitfulness" into his own consciousness of mutability' (21). This effacement of the feminine (through its appropriation and masculinization) is crucial, argues Mellor, to the creative self-expression of masculine Romanticism and it carries over into the very definition of poetry articulated by the Romantics, a definition centred upon 'feeling'.

Evoking the influence of the discourse of sensibility in the mid-to-late eighteenth century, Wordsworth defines poetry as 'the spontaneous overflow of powerful feelings'. Shelley spoke of 'the instinct and intuition of the poetical faculty' (23, 24). This discourse of feeling and sensibility was traditionally associated with the feminine and although this association rested on a stereotypical cultural understanding of femininity, it did grant cultural authority to a certain socially sanctioned female subject, the 'woman of sensibility' who features so prominently in the fiction of the period. When Romantic poetry is defined in terms of 'feeling', we witness, argues Mellor, the appropriation by the male poet of another cultural domain traditionally designated feminine. Thus the feminine is not accommodated within masculine Romanticism in culturally conventional forms (such as 'Nature' or 'Sensibility'), but effaced; 'feminine' attributes and modes of expression are re-ordered as 'masculine' and absorbed into the identity and mode of expression of the male Romantic poet. This effacement of the feminine conceals the gendered identity of Romanticism itself: 'masculine' Romanticism is neutralized as 'Romanticism'.

Feminine Romanticism

The thesis of the second part of *Romanticism and Gender* is that the prolific work of women writers in the Romantic era should be understood as comprising a distinct 'feminine' Romanticism. Here, Mellor examines women's writings across a broad cultural spectrum that can be seen to have initiated diverse challenges to and renegotiations of normative ideals of femininity. Beginning with Mary Wollstonecraft's wide-ranging critique of late eighteenth-century patriarchal society, Mellor identifies the emergence of a revolutionary feminine Romanticism which permeated the work of women novelists whose fiction has only recently been critically acknowledged: these include Maria Edgeworth's *Belinda*, Helen Maria Williams' *Julia*, Susan Ferrier's *Marriage* and Elizabeth Inchbald's *A Simple Story*. Central to this body of work is a challenge to the subordination of all family members – not only women – to the rule of the father and what is proposed is a revised family politics based upon egalitarian domestic affections and a democratic, empathic ethics of care. Mellor moves on to consider the implications of this new domestic politics with regard to two of the key concepts of Romanticism: the Sublime and the Self.

The Romantic Sublime

In Romantic aesthetic theory and much twentieth-century criticism, argues Mellor, the sublime has been conceptualized in terms of an experience of power or transcendence that is implicitly gendered masculine. In the Romantic poets, a 'masculine' sublime is associated with the poet's own creative power, a power that asserts a unity between the self and its 'other' that symbolically effaces the feminine. Certain women writers, on the other hand, questioned this conceptualization of the sublime in their work and sought to construct a feminine alternative grounded not in sameness, individualism and transcendence, but in relatedness and otherness. Mellor identifies two traditions of female writing in which this alternative sublime appears. The Gothic fiction of Ann Radcliffe tends to associate the masculine Romantic sublime with a tyrannical patriarchal authority that terrorizes women and vulnerable men. The feminine sublime, on the other hand, prioritizes 'a sympathy and love that connects the self with other people' and that enables women to escape mentally from 'the oppressions of a tyrannical social order' aligned with the masculine sublime (95). The other tradition emerges out of the work of Susan Ferrier, Helen Maria Williams and, in particular, Sydney Owenson. Owenson's *The Wild Irish Girl* (1806) represents a sublime landscape explicitly gendered feminine and in so doing, argues Mellor, it asserts the aesthetic and ethical value of shared experience *in* nature as opposed to solitary transcendence *through* nature.

The Self

Turning again to Wordsworth's *Prelude*, Mellor discusses its representation of Romantic selfhood and contends that what emerges out of the poem is not the 'universal self' of Wordsworth's imagination, but a 'specifically masculine self' that aims, through the power if its creative imagination, to transcend the body and, by implication, the feminine (147). The poet's self-assurance is nevertheless precarious; it rests upon 'the arduous repression of the Other in all its forms' (149). Again, though, Mellor is able to identify an alternative to this uneasy denial of materiality and femininity; in the work of Dorothy Wordsworth, she finds 'a very different concept of self from the egotistical sublime proposed in her brother's poetry'. Like the feminine sublime in the work of Romantic women novelists, the feminine self represented in Dorothy's journals is a relational and, crucially, an embodied self. This alternative Romantic conceptualization of identity has significant, far-reaching implications for a more politically and cultural inclusive form of criticism:

Dorothy's *Journals* linguistically represent a self that is not only relational, formed in connection with the needs, moods and actions of other human beings, but also physically embodied – not a 'mighty mind', but an organic body that feels heat and cold and hunger, that sees and hears and smells, that defecates and 'washes her head', that suffers both psychosomatic and physical disease. Such bodies have been for the most part absent from the canonical male autobiographies which have attempted to construct a permanent, even transcendental, ego that endures beyond the limits of matter, time and space ... the canonical male-authored autobiographies have been for the most part the production of a leisured, bourgeois, racially dominant class of men who are at least temporally free from the physical depravations of hunger, cold and poverty and thus have the luxury of constructing a mind detached from a body. In contrast, Dorothy's *Journals* join much African-American, working class and female autobiographical writing in the inscription of the body as a determining condition of subjectivity (157).

Mellor adds an important qualification to this analysis, though; she is not contending that the feminine/masculine subject position can only emerge out of the work of female/male writers. Rather, she emphasizes the construction in Romantic discourse of varying modes of subjectivity that are capable of expression through the work of female or male writers. The final part of her argument develops this point through a comparative analysis of John Keats and Emily Brontë as 'ideological cross-dressers' (171). Mellor compares Keats' concept of self to that of Dorothy Wordsworth: it is 'unbounded, fluid, decentred, inconsistent ... a self that continually overflows itself, that melts into the Other' (175). Not only does Keats privilege this identity as properly belonging to the 'true poet', he also 'locates poetic expression in the realm of the feminine' and develops an understanding of knowledge and creative power, argues Mellor, that might even be said to gesture towards late twentieth-century feminist appraisals of 'women's ways of knowing' (175, 178). This counter-cultural privileging of the feminine, however, together with the contemporary view of Keats as 'effeminate', led to tension in the poet's work as he sought to affirm for himself some form of consistent, convincing masculine subjectivity, and feminist critics such as Margaret Homans ('Keats Reading Women, Women Reading Keats', 1990) have seen in this a reassertion of masculine bias. Mellor insists, though, that Keats' positive emphasis on feminine and especially maternal creative power is much more in keeping with feminine Romanticism.

Brontë, on the other hand, is 'a female writer whose personal history and ideological investments more closely approximate masculine Romanticism than feminine'. *Wuthering Heights* is seen here as an expression of the masculine Romanticism that Brontë took from her avid reading of Shelley, Byron and Wordsworth. Instead of articulating the feminine sublime of earlier women's Romantic fiction, for example, this novel engages a masculine mode of the sublime that privileges transcendence and autonomy. Similarly, its treatment of love seeks the obliteration, not the affirmation of difference; Catherine and Heathcliff are posited as one being and their love aligned with a primeval life-force that is set against a corrupt, insipid culture represented by the Linton family. As a woman, however, Brontë does critique the social constructions of femininity that inhibit herself and her protagonist, Catherine Earnshaw, from achieving Romantic self-affirmation. Masculine Romanticism in *Wuthering Heights* is therefore undercut by an implicit acknowledgement that the possibility of female transcendence and autonomy is dependent upon women's social position in relation to men.

In conclusion, *Romanticism and Gender* has been influential in at least two respects: it has encouraged critical engagement with previously neglected texts by women of the period, and presented a cogent argument for the re-reading of the canon in terms of its hidden ideological positions. Mellor's work demonstrates that to question the gender of Romanticism is to question the very *meaning* of Romanticism as it has been studied and taught over the last century.

 Tim Fulford and Peter J. Kitson (eds), *Romanticism and Colonialism: Writing and Empire, 1780–1830*

Edition cited: *Romanticism and Colonialism: Writing and Empire 1780–1830.* Cambridge: Cambridge University Press, 1998.

In the introduction to this work, the editors acknowledge the importance of Jerome McGann's *The Romantic Ideology* in encouraging a criticism that engages with 'the significance of ideologies of class and gender in the construction of Romanticism'. They observe, though, that 'Romanticism's relation with colonialism has been relatively little studied' and this collection therefore aims to interrogate from a variety of theoretical and historical perspectives the implication of Romanticism in the imperial projects of the period (1). Here, we consider two very differently focused essays from the volume to gain a sense of the critical diversity of approaches to the topic and the possibilities opened up by postcolonial readings of Romanticism.

Lauren Henry, 'Sunshine and shady Groves': What Blake's 'Little Black Boy' learned from African Writers.

In this essay, Henry considers primarily the influence of the African writer Phillis Wheatley on Blake's poem 'The Little Black Boy', though this analysis also serves as a case study in the wider influence of African literature in the Romantic period. Wheatley was the slave of a Boston family who, although she never lost her slave status, was more or less adopted into their household and became a successful poet in the 1770s and 80s. Along with Ottabah Cuguano and Olaudah Equiano, Wheatley was part of a highly visible community of African writers and anti-slavery campaigners whose work influenced not only abolitionists, but the wider literature and culture of Romanticism. Henry aims to recover the significance of African writing to the period through a consideration of Wheatley's 'An Hymn to the Morning' alongside Blake's 'The Little Black Boy'. Wheatley's influence on Blake has not thus far been acknowledged by critics who have tended to overlook, and in so doing to efface the visibility of the African literary community in late eighteenth-century England.

Wheatley's work has been read as affirming colonial ideology in certain respects; she seems to posit African culture as inferior to European and herself as the grateful recipient of a 'grace' that is spiritual and cultural: the European has saved her from sin and from Africa. Henry joins other postcolonial critics, though, in highlighting the extent to which Wheatley manipulates poetic form and language to challenge the conditions of her enslavement. The poem 'An Hymn to the Morning' takes a conventional European form: it is written in heroic verse as a 'Hymn'. Henry asserts that, on one level, the poem, 'was certainly meant to be read by its original English and American audiences as a melding of Classicism and Christianity' (75). However, the poem subtly affirms African religious and cultural influences and reveals a tension between these influences and the Christian religion to which Wheatley converts as a slave. The poem's initial welcoming of 'bright Aurora', evocative of the rituals of sun worship Wheatley remembered her mother performing before her capture, gives way to a more ambivalent treatment of the 'fervid beams too strong' of 'th' illustrious King of Day'. The poet seeks the protection of a 'shady grove' against the 'burning day' and, indeed, the 'burning' beams of this masculine deity are ultimately so fierce that they force the poet into silence: 'I feel his fervid beams too strong | And scarce begun, concludes th' abortive song'. Henry contends that the tension that emerges here between a lost African worship and a seemingly oppressive 'King of Day' is a consequence of Wheatley's ironic stance towards the Christian God she has been required to serve, but who makes it impossible for her, as an African slave, to worship and write freely.

Henry notes Harold Bloom's description of Blake's 'The Little Black Boy' as 'one of the most deliberately misleading and ironic of all Blake's lyrics' (67). It is extremely difficult to discern the attitude of the boy to Christianity, a religion that seems to guarantee his salvation while sealing his fate as an inferior subject. The only indication that the boy might contest his spiritual slavery, says Henry, is 'the irony with which the story is told' (85), and the poem's irony becomes more visible and comprehensible when the text is read alongside Wheatley's 'An Hymn to the Morning'. Like Wheatley's, Blake's poem 'makes the reader aware of irony and bitterness through the tensions and contradictions in its depiction of the sun and a 'shady grove' ... In both poems, the 'shady grove' is associated with an African speaker's struggle to construct an identity (either poetic or personal)' (80).

Henry also considers other historical and literary materials that might have influenced Blake's depiction of the boy and his fraught relation to African and European religion. She observes that Blake was a good friend of the painter Richard Cosway whose house servant was Ottobah Cugoano, one of the leaders of the country's black abolitionists and a close friend of the most famous black campaigner, Olaudah Equiano. Equiano's autobiography (and other slave narratives that Blake might well have come across through his social and literary connections) describes a spiritual struggle very similar indeed to that depicted in Blake's poem. Thus, by carefully situating Blake's poem within the context of African literary and political communities of the late eighteenth century, it is possible to read The Little Black boy as a subtle, ironic questioning of Christianity's role in enslavement that is indebted to the work of black writers campaigning for their own physical and spiritual emancipation.

John Whale, 'Indian Jugglers: Hazlitt, Romantic Orientalism and the difference of view'.

Many of the essays in this volume are influenced by Edward Said's work on Orientalism, although some contributors, including Whale, are seeking to expand Said's paradigm. For Said, the hegemony that supports Orientalism is complex, embracing multiple cultural and political discourses in the formation of its imperial projects in the East. Whale's aim is to retain this sense of complexity and multiplicity while deploying fresh conceptualizations of the orient that broaden Said's rather 'monolithic' construction of the East and the oriental Other (206). Psychoanalytic perspectives, for example, have exposed collective cultural anxieties that contributed, along with material historical forces, to the formation of Romantic Orientalism as a complex, unstable, often contradictory discourse. Whale seeks to interrogate the function of 'sympathy' and 'imagination' in the development of a Romantic aesthetics of the orient that uneasily affirms and contests the hegemony of imperialism. Romantic orientalist aesthetics produced categories of difference that provoked pleasure, anxiety and guilt in the British consumers of an orientalized Eastern culture. Whale takes as an example the entertainment provided by Indian jugglers, magicians and acrobats to London audiences in the late eighteenth century. He considers the pleasures and anxieties that accompanied the viewing of these spectacles and that are recounted in critical responses to them, particularly William Hazlitt's essay 'The Indian Jugglers'. Whale acknowledges that this is a specific and local illustration of the aestheticization of the east, but an analysis of the essay in its colonial context reveal it to be an interesting example 'of the assimilative and appropriative power of British popular culture in the regency period' (207).

Troops of Indian jugglers performed in London in this period in a variety of theatrical contexts, often staging their acts as interludes in pantomimes, melodramas or masks. They were hugely popular. The dexterity, elegance and exoticism of the performances produced a construction of the juggler as a fascinating and largely (though not entirely) unthreatening oriental Other, and Hazlitt's essay is typical of contemporary critical responses in this regard. The juggling is a mesmerizing magic act that becomes a signifier of the differences between East and West: what the jugglers do, Hazlitt writes, is, 'what none of us could do to save our lives, nor if we were to take our whole lives to do it in' (212). Hazlitt responds with a Romantic imaginative sympathy (the jugglers come to exemplify the ingenuity and tenacity of mankind) that is nevertheless called into question by Hazlitt's sense of an otherness that is not completely without its dangers. Shortly after his celebration of the jugglers in terms that simultaneously universalize and exoticize the performance, an anxious scepticism emerges as Hazlitt alludes to the 'dogmas and superstitions' of the Hindu Brahmins; the abstract, supernatural formulations of the Brahmin's faith conflict with the more mechanical, empirical skills of the jugglers. However, Hazlitt's very valorization of the skill of the jugglers in opposition to the superstition of the Brahmins conforms to an Orientalist hegemony that in fact effaces the individuality of the jugglers:

> Insofar as they are endorsed by Hazlitt's sense of the mechanical, which is rooted in the material world, they forfeit their cultural particularity. Defined as mechanical, the jugglers also lose the imprint of identity and the possibility of historical self-consciousness (215).

This moment is symptomatic for Whale of a more general problem with Hazlitt's Romantic understanding of imagination and sympathy. Imagination promotes sympathetic understanding between individuals and helps prevent the particular identity and circumstances of a person from being absorbed in dehumanizing generalities. Ironically, though, the example that Hazlitt gives of his sympathetic imagination at work is of an Indian man, taken completely out of his cultural context, observed by a white man on the streets of London. This 'wandering Lascar' becomes for Hazlitt a 'specimen' of his nation (217) and there is an affinity here between the 'wandering lascar' and the Indian jugglers: in each instance the specific cultural identity of the subject is effaced at the very moment when Hazlitt insists upon that very specificity as the key to a proper empirical and ethical understanding of the east. Hazlitt's response to the colonized 'other' tensely affirms even as it seeks to challenge imperialist appropriations, manipulations and elisions of cultural identity. Whale's essay and the others in this volume reveal the uneasy, complicit, conflicted relations of Romanticism to diverse colonial contexts.

 Jonathon Bate, *The Song of the Earth*

Edition cited: *The Song of the Earth,* London: Picador, 2001.

Bate's *The Song of the Earth* has been influential in developing and bringing into Romantic studies the movement known as 'eco-criticism'. Opposing what it perceives as humanity's violent, self-aggrandizing exploitation of the environment since the onset of modernity, eco-criticism asks, 'What is the place of creative imagining and writing in the complex set of relationships between humankind and environment, between mind and world, between thinking, being and dwelling?' (73). In answering this question, the emergence of the Romantic movement in the late eighteenth century is a key point of departure for Bate. Certain Romantic writers developed what he terms an 'eco-poetics' which initiated a movement of opposition within literature to the environmentally degrading processes associated with modernity. 'Eco-poetics' comes from the Greek 'oikos', meaning 'home', and 'poesis', meaning 'making'. Eco-poetics is a form of 'home-making', an attempt to find an intimate, sustainable place for humanity in the world and to generate a sense of living with, rather than against, the earth.

An anxious awareness of humankind's increasing alienation from the earth is evident in early Romantic poets such as William Cowper and in the novels of Austen, a writer not traditionally associated closely with the Romantic sensibility. An eco-poetic consciousness is thus not limited to Romanticism's 'big six'. Cowper's poetry and Austen's heroines (Fanny in *Mansfield Park* and Marianne in *Sense and Sensibility*, for example) lament contemporary 'improvements' to the land that frequently serve only to impoverish the earth and the communities that depend on it. In this, Austen and Cowper can be aligned with a broader Romantic celebration of and nostalgia for an original, natural state of being, the formulation of which owes much to the work of the French philosopher, Jean-Jacques Rousseau. Rousseau's *Discourse on the Origin of Inequality* represents, for Bate, 'modernity's founding myth of the "state of nature" and our severance from that state' (42); it is modernity's version of the Fall of Man. For Rousseau, civilization is the condition into which men fall as the state of nature gives way to social practices and prohibitions, which in turn give rise to ever more complex social organizations, hierarchies, wants and needs. A decisive and particularly alienating development in the transition from nature to civilization is the invention of private property; the appropriation of land, natural resources and the products of human labour initiates inequality, unrest and the final alienation of humankind from nature. It is important to bear in mind, though, that Rousseau's influential model of the state of nature is itself a product of civilization; it is a mythic construct that arises out of the tensions of modernity and that comes to function as an imaginative point of departure for Romantic explorations of nature, culture and the self.

Nature, Culture, Myth and Monstrosity – Mary Shelley's *Frankenstein*

Frankenstein has come to be acknowledged as a key text of British Romanticism and here Bate cites it as 'literature's primary myth of how the spirit of the Enlightenment creates an image of the natural man as a sign of its own alienation' (49). The ambitions of two characters – Walton and, of course, Victor Frankenstein himself – exemplify the Enlightenment project of colonial and environmental conquest. Walton at the beginning of the novel is en route to the North Pole in the hope of finding the north eastern passage and opening up new trade routes for the empire. Commercial and colonial ambition is aligned here with a destructive, predatory attitude to the earth; Walton travels on a whaling ship and in his letter to his sister half-jokingly compares himself to Coleridge's ancient mariner who shoots the albatross in a random act of violence and is divinely punished for it. Similarly, Victor is a 'cultivated' man who nevertheless pursues a brutal project of domination over the earth and, by implication, over the symbolic maternal function of nature. His act of creation is a 'transgression of nature' and a symbolic form of matricide (51). The monster, meanwhile, represents Rousseau's 'natural man', doomed to degeneration at the hands of an Enlightenment scientist who refuses even the monster's most basic desire for community – his longing for a mate. Eloquently (and, indeed, the creature's is by far the most eloquent voice in the novel), he pleads to be allowed to live peacefully with his partner in harmony with the living earth; his plea is a poetic evocation of the Romantic,

Rousseauan state of nature and almost stands as an early environmentalist manifesto:

> If you consent, neither you nor any other human being shall ever see us again. I will go to the wilds of South America. My food is not that of man; I do not destroy the lamb and the kid to glut my appetite; acorn and berries afford me sufficient nourishment. My companion will be of the same nature as myself, and will be content with the same fare. We shall make our bed of dried leaves; the sun will shine on us as on man, and will ripen our food. The picture I present to you is peaceful and human, and you must feel that you could deny it only in the wantoness of power and cruelty (53).

Ironically, it is the creature designated monstrous by Victor and his society that presents this picture of life as 'peaceful and *human*'. Victor nevertheless does refuse the request and thus denies the creature's vision; his creature's words stand in judgement on his 'wantoness of power and cruelty'. It is Victor, then, who becomes the monster here; he is posited as the agent of a cruel, inhuman power that denies not only the monster's yearning for a 'companion of the same nature as myself', but his vision of making a small part of the earth his 'peaceful and human' home.

Ecological Contexts of Romanticism

Byron's poem 'Darkness' was written in the summer of 1816 and presents a vivid apocalyptic vision of profound natural disorder and destruction: the sun is extinguished, the earth becomes 'A lump of death – a chaos of hard clay' (95). Bate's carefully contextualized reading of this poem relates it to actual climactic disturbances prevailing at this time as a probable result of the eruption of the Tambora volcano in Indonesia in 1815. The global effect of volcanic dust in the atmosphere lasted for several years and Byron's poem is read not only as an imaginative evocation of apocalypse, but as a real response to an ecological crisis that is 'powerfully prophetic' in terms of late twentieth century ecological anxieties.

Two other key canonical Romantic poems are also read by Bate as essentially ecological in their concerns: Keats' 'To Autumn' and Coleridge's 'Frost at Midnight'. Keats' poem is again placed within the context of the environmental circumstances of this period, as Bate puts it in the title to the fourth chapter, 'major weather'. As a consumptive, Bate points out that Keats would have been dependent for his health on good weather and in this context 'To Autumn' acquires a certain urgency in terms of its treatment of earth, weather and seasons. The poem stresses the interdependency of nature's complex and diverse ecosystems; the world of the poem 'resembles a well-regulated ecosystem' and man is not placed at the centre of this system, but in relation to it (109). It comprises a series of intricate links between humanity and nature established through metre, syntax, imagery and various aural connections, and ultimately it presents an 'image of ecological wholeness which may grant to the attentive and receptive reader a sense of being-at-home-in-the-world' (109). This is precisely what Bate understands by 'ecopoetry'.

Similarly, Coleridge's 'Frost at Midnight' takes a non-instrumentalist, relational approach to nature that challenges the Enlightenment separation of man from nature (Enlightenment 'Dualism', or 'Cartesian Dualism' after the seventeenth-century French philosopher René Descartes). The poet – significantly for Bate – finds fulfilment in gently nurturing his sleeping son and imagining his future not as one of conquest and ambition, but as a delicate dwelling in and with the earth. Bate contends that here the poet adopts a feminine subject position in relation to nature and his child, and that this is one of the most radical aspects of the poem:

> What is truly radical about 'Frost at Midnight' is Coleridge's self-representation as a father in the traditional maternal posture of watching over a sleeping baby. In ecofeminist terms, this realignment of gender roles clears the way for a caring as opposed to an exploitative relationship with the earth (112).

The notion of dualism is important to Bate, and to ecocriticism generally, since it defines theoretically and empirically the modern method of acting upon, rather than in harmony with the natural world. In chapter five, Bate relates Cartesian dualism to a significant Romantic aesthetic concept: the picturesque. This concept has had a profound (and, for Bate, a largely negative) influence upon later environmentalist movements, however much it might appear to have promoted increased ethical concerns over the impact of technology on nature. The notion of the 'picturesque' landscape was theorized and popularized by William Gilpin in the late eighteenth century. A landscape was to be admired in so far as it resembled the landscape painting of the period, hence the term 'picturesque'; nature was thus subordinated to art and in a sense conquered by the eye of the cultured, knowledgeable beholder who subjects the earth to aesthetic scrutiny. For Bate, this aestheticization of nature produced a certain form of environmentalism concerned to protect landscapes considered to be aesthetically valuable – rolling hills and woodlands, for example, rather than peat bogs. Citing the work of the Marxist philosopher Adorno, he argues that this response to nature is a necessary consequence of modernity's alienation of human beings from each other and from nature; in the face of the incessant commodification and exploitation of humanity and the earth, individuals seek refuge in an idealized 'nature' (the protected national park, for example) that belies the continuing debasement of the environment outside specially designated areas.

Bate sees in the work of Wordsworth an alternative to the artistic principles of the picturesque and he sets Wordsworth's 'ecopoetics' against the damaging environmentalism influenced by the picturesque aesthetic. Whereas the picturesque submits the landscape to the 'perceiving, dividing eye', Wordsworth's approach to nature in a poem such as 'Tintern Abbey' seeks the 'dissolution of the self from perceiving eye into ecologically connected organism' (145). Bate's approach here is therefore far removed from critics such as Anne Mellor who see in Wordsworth a masculinist, egocentric version of the sublime that ultimately constructs Nature and Woman as 'Other'. Instead of effacing the feminine, Bate contends that Wordsworth holds Woman to be 'the power that draws man back into integration with nature' (150). Following what he terms an 'ecofeminist' as opposed to an 'orthodox feminist' argument, he suggests that if anything is effaced in Wordsworth's poetry (he refers to book eleven of 'The Prelude' and 'Tintern Abbey' especially here), it is the judgemental Enlightenment rationality that oppresses woman, man and nature.

John Clare: *The Politics and Poetics of Place*

Clare has not traditionally been included in the Romantic canon and, during his life, his social position (he was known as 'the peasant poet') mitigated against a positive, scholarly reception of his work. Over the last two decades, however, critical interest in Clare has grown considerably and, for Bate, Clare is a significant Romantic figure whose ecopoetic sense of place contests the possessive, exploitative aesthetic that emerges out of Cartesian dualism and the Romantic aesthetic of the picturesque. In his reading of Clare's work, Bate draws from the work of the French philosopher Gaston Blanchard (*The Poetics of Space*, 1958). Blanchard develops a philosophy of space based not on notions of division and conquest, but on an intimate, nurturing habitation of the places we call home. This is not 'Nature' in the abstract, but a localized, protective dwelling place that grounds human identity in space and time. Similarly, the place that Clare inhabits is not a universalized Nature, but an intimate locality that is as much the home of birds, trees, insects and grass as it is of Clare himself. Another notable feature of Clare's poetry is its focus on the small things of the earth – birds, flowers and even weeds – as opposed to the expansive landscapes that are celebrated as sublime or picturesque. For Bate, Clare goes beyond other Romantic poets, including Wordsworth, in actually giving a *voice* to neglected places that were in Clare's time suffering the increasingly brutal divisions and transformations of the laws of enclosure. Clare emphasizes the destructive impact of these laws (which had a devastating effect upon his own Northamptonshire village of Helpstone) not on the landscape as Romantic *scenery*, but on trees, birds' nests, brooks, flowers, insects and so on. 'The Lament of Swordy Well', for example, is a poem 'written in the voice of a piece of land' (171); this is a land capable of being wronged and even of feeling pain. This notion of the land as sentient and as capable of having rights sets Clare, in Bate's view, ahead of even the most radical of his contemporaries; his ecopoetics anticipate some of the arguments of late twentieth-century 'deep ecology' movements to the effect that the land deserves consideration as an entity in its own right, and not only in so far as it facilitates or obstructs the technological projects of humankind.

What are Poets For?

This is the title of the final chapter of text. Here, Bate revisits his central contentions and moves beyond Romantic writing to consider more generally the relevance of poetry to the ecological concerns of the twenty-first century. Bate draws here on the work of the German philosopher Martin Heidegger for whom the question, 'What are poets for?' was inseparable from the question of what technology is for and how it has developed since the advent of modernity. For Heidegger, human beings are inherently technological beings, committed for their survival to the transformation of their world, and technology itself is not necessarily problematic. It is only in modern times that technology has acquired particularly destructive tendencies, since it is no longer a matter of technology effecting transformations that remain in connection with nature and with humanity's groundedness in nature (our 'being-in-the-world', or *Dasein*, as Heidegger terms it); rather, modern technology aims to systemize and instrumentalize nature, to turn it into a resource for human consumption. Thus a river becomes 'a water-power supplier', or, 'an object on call for inspection by a tour group ordered there by the vacation industry' (254). Heidegger terms this systemization of the world an 'enframing' of nature that alienates us from our authentic being – our 'being-in-the-world'. Now the question 'What are poets for?' acquires a particular urgency for Heidegger and for Bate when one is faced with the consequences of modern technological practices, for poetry is the one form of art capable of helping humanity to return to an appropriate place of dwelling in and with the earth. In his reading of Keats' 'To Autumn' in chapter four, Bate contended that the metre, syntax, imagery and rhythms of that work reflected the interconnectedness that the poem attributes to nature's complex ecosystems. This poem is a 'song of the earth' for Bate and he argues with Heidegger that poetry is the most able of all forms of literature to generate this sense of the interconnection between nature and a humanity increasingly alienated from its own earthly dwelling place. Crucially, poetry does not tell the reader anything in the sense of providing information about the objects of the world; rather, through its varied structures, spaces, pauses, sounds, rhythms and imaginative associations it evokes the rhythms, repetitions, contingencies and complex vitality of the earth. It is thus, for Bate, 'our way of stepping outside the frame of the technological' and possibly even of halting the technological practices that threaten to make a permanent reality of the apocalyptic scenario envisaged in Byron's poem 'Darkness'.

This is a bold claim and Bate admits that his argument cuts against the grain of much late twentieth-century literary theory. However, he stresses that his aim is not to insist on a definitive practice of ecocriticism that might promote a given ecopolitical agenda. This would be yet another act of systemization, of what Heidegger calls 'enframing', and this is precisely what poetry resists. Instead, he argues for an 'ecopoetics' that 'seeks not to enframe literary texts, but to meditate upon them, to thank them, to listen to them, albeit to ask questions of them' (268). This 'greening' of literary criticism, as it were, has opened up a new trajectory for twenty-first-century Romantic scholarship as witnessed by the growth since 2000 of critical works and academic conferences devoted to what has become known as 'Green Romanticism'.

 ## Eve Kosofsky Sedgwick, *Between Men: English Literature and Male Homosocial Desire*

Edition cited: *Between Men: English Literature and Male Homosocial Desire*, New York: Columbia University Press, 1985

Influenced by feminist and queer politics in the early 1980s, critics began to shift the focus of Romantic scholarship from canonical poets to non-canonical works that reveal in a variety of contexts new configurations of power, desire, sexuality and subjectivity in the Romantic period. One of the earliest works to express this new emphasis and orientation in Romantic criticism was Sedgwick's *Between Men: English Literature and Male Homosocial Desire*. This study is not focused exclusively on Romantic writing, but takes as its subject fiction from the mid-eighteenth to the late nineteenth centuries. Nevertheless, Sedgwick's consideration of homophobia and Romantic-era Gothic fiction make this an important work of scholarship for students of Romanticism.

Historical and Theoretical Perspectives

The term 'homosocial' is used in social science to designate social bonds between persons of the same sex. Sedgwick establishes a correlation between male homosocial behaviour (social interactions that, in a patriarchal society, work to consolidate male power, rituals of male bonding and so on) and male desire. 'Desire' here is not to be understood necessarily as sexual, or even as pertaining to a particular emotional state, but as 'the affective or social force, the glue, even when its manifestation is hostility, or hatred, or something less emotionally charged, that shapes an important relationship' (2). Sedgwick contends that in a patriarchal society, in which heterosexuality is normative and strictly (often violently) imposed, male homosocial behaviour is frequently accompanied by homophobia, 'a fear and hatred of homosexuality' (2). Male homosocial behaviour must be closely monitored in order to produce models of hetero-sexual subjectivity that exclude homosexual desire, and one result is that male homosocial desire (which for Sedgwick exists on a continuum with, and not in opposition to, homosexual desire) often expresses itself in the form of paranoid homophobia. As new relations of political, social and sexual power emerged in the early modern period, this paranoia took a variety of forms that Sedgwick sees as represented and interrogated through the complex tropes, devices and narrative strategies of Romantic-era Gothic fictions. These fictions portray in heightened psychological terms persecutory, hostile, eroticized relations between men and also, crucially, between women and men.

Sedgwick's analysis of sex, sexuality, gender and class is influenced by radical feminist thinking that has applied psychoanalytic and deconstructive theory to the cultural construction of gender difference. The French theorist Luce Irigaray, for example, has in Sedgwick's view considerably expanded theoretical understandings of the function of male homosexuality within patriarchal societies. Irigaray contends that social and symbolic relations between men provide the regulatory framework within which specific roles are allocated to individuals according to the patriarchal, heterosexual 'norm'. Irigaray therefore regards male homosexuality as a structuring principle, a 'law', according to which heterosexual behaviours acquire legitimate social and symbolic meaning. One difficulty with this approach for Sedgwick, however, is that it tends to efface or at least downplay the impact of histori-cally specific, material forces on the experiences of women and men in varied political and cultural contexts. Radical feminist conceptualizations of sexuality and gender often seem impervious to processes of historical change and to historically specific activities of embodied subjects, to the extent that Irigaray's account of male homosexuality 'turns out to represent anything but actual sex between men' (26). Sedgwick's solution is to combine a radical feminist approach with a more materialist, Marxist analysis of the production and perpetuation of structures of power. Thus she cites the work of Heidi Hartman and Gayle Rubin in support of her contention that 'in any male dominated society, there is a special relationship between male homosocial (*including* homosexual) desire and the structures for maintaining and transmitting power' (25). Male homosocial desire is a more flexible and historically nuanced concept than Irigaray's understanding of homosexuality (in the sense of symbolic and social relations between men) as a 'law' that universally structures heterosexual exchanges.

Another concept that is key to Sedgwick's analysis is drawn from the work of René Girard, though again Sedgwick modifies Girard's work in accordance with her own feminist method. Girard identifies in the male-centred novelistic tradition the emergence of triangular structures of desire within which two males compete over one woman. Sedgwick aligns Girard's 'erotic triangle' with Sigmund Freud's theorisation of Oedipal conflict, according to which the male child competes with the father for possession of the mother. The problem with these models, though, is that neither acknowledges the significance of historically specific, culturally constructed gender differences or the crucial point that the role of the woman within this structure is to mediate desire *between men*. Sedgwick refers to Gayle Rubin's influential theorization of patriarchal heterosexuality to argue that the erotic triangle permits 'the use of women as exchangeable, perhaps symbolic property for the primary purpose of cementing the bonds between men' (26). The Oedipal conflict discussed by Freud and the 'erotic triangle' posited by Girard provide social and psychological support for volatile systems of patriarchal power, but by themselves these models are insufficient to account for complex interrelations between gender, sexuality and class at any given historical moment.

Turning specifically to relations of class and gender in the eighteenth century, Sedgwick suggests that one significant outcome of the ideological struggle between the bourgeoisie and the aristocracy in this period was 'the feminization of the aristocracy', to the extent that the first modern stereotype of the homosexual male was very similar to the stereotype of the male aristocrat as seen by the middle classes. At the same time, an ideology of the bourgeois family developed which privileged middle-class women as chaste wives, mothers and daughters within a private family unit; fathers, husbands and sons, meanwhile, were expected to forge new political, economic and cultural relations of power through male homosocial interactions outside the home. In this volatile context, homosocial, homosexual and heterosexual relations became ideologically highly charged in terms of both class and gender. Gothic fiction emerged at this historical moment and articulated through vivid, psychologically intense and often violent dramas of persecution and Oedipal conflict its culture's homophobic paranoia.

Gothic Paranoia

Literary Gothicism and Romanticism arose contemporaneously and Gothic novelists are often seen to have expressed more overtly than the Romantics the social and sexual anxieties that mark this period of emerging modernity. In particular, Sedgwick identifies a variety of Gothic fiction that was especially concerned with changing forms of masculine self-identification, male bonding and male desire: she terms it the 'Gothic Paranoid'. In the work of William Godwin, James Hogg and Charles Maturin, she identifies and interrogates a severe cultural paranoia regarding sexuality, the dynamics of the bourgeois family and, especially, male homosocial desire and its effects:

> The Gothic seems to offer a privileged view of individual and family psychology. Certain features of the Oedipal family are insistently foregrounded there: absolutes of licence and prohibition, for instance; a preoccupation with possibilities of incest; a fascinated proscription of sexual activity; an atmosphere dominated by the threat of violence between generations. Even the reader who does not accept the Oedipal family as a transhistorical given can learn a lot from the Gothic about the terms and conditions under which it came to be enforced as a norm for bourgeois society (91).

In chapter six, Sedgwick offers a detailed reading of James Hogg's 1824 novel *Confessions of a Justified Sinner* in terms of her theory of male homosocial desire and homophobic paranoia. This choice of text is problematic since, Sedgwick admits, it is not conclusively a Gothic text. Like William Godwin's *Caleb Williams*, it lacks the conventions associated with the early Gothic: the sense of foreignness and antiquity; the persecution of the chaste female; the Gothic location of castle, convent or monastery; and, especially in this instance, the anti-Catholicism. Hogg's novel is set in Edinburgh in the early 1800s and its religious anxieties centre not on Catholicism, but on the Protestant doctrine of predestination. Nevertheless, this text has entered the Gothic canon and thus, in spite of its distance from the Gothic in its earlier forms, it merits consideration in these generic terms. Like Godwin's novel, this is a text that moves the Gothic towards its modern engagement with psychological conflict, repressed desire and paranoia. In particular, the novel employs the gothic trope of 'doubling' or 'pairing' in order to negotiate anxieties concerning family relations, sexuality and class identity. Indeed, the novel could be said to 'double' itself, since it offers two versions of the same events: one provided by an 'editor' and the other narrated by the protagonist, Robert Wringhim. Wringhim is apparently the son of a strict Protestant mother and a rather decadent Scottish laird; the novel encourages the reader to assume, however, that Robert is in fact the illegitimate son of a severe predestinarian preacher, also named Robert Wringhim, who takes responsibility for the boy and gives him his name. The elder Wringhim exerts an extraordinary degree of psychological control over the boy, negating the influence of his mother and, as Sedgwick argues, reformulating the family 'in homosocial terms as a transactive bond among God, old Wringhim and Robert' (110). Underlying and undermining this homosocial family unit, however, is a profound insecurity as to gender and class identity. The young Robert is an effeminate man who cannot claim legitimate aristocratic heritage; thus he clings to the notion of his predestined salvation through grace as evidence of his superiority over the rest of his family. Robert's marginalized position is expressed in the first half of the novel through his 'pairing' with his brother, George. George, like the laird, is a man entirely comfortable with and in firm possession of the privileges of masculinity and aristocracy. Unlike Robert, George is able to establish the homosocial ties that bind men together, often through heterosexual exchanges of women. Robert's response to his lack of aristocratic and masculine power in comparison to George is to persecute and ultimately murder his brother in a manner that appears almost supernatural and that exposes the dysfunctional violence of Robert's thwarted homosocial desire:

> In his abjection, Robert cannot desire women enough to desire men
> through them; instead, identifying himself hatingly [with women] he
> hatingly throws himself at the man who seems to be at the fountainhead
> of male prestige. The uncanny "pursuit" of George by Robert that is the
> subject of the Editor's Narrative offers a portrait of male homosocial
> desire as murderous resentment (102).

If homosocial desire emerges as a murderous pairing in the first half of the text, it takes the form of a more erotic and paranoid doubling in the second. Robert narrates his relationship with a mysterious stranger known only as Gilmartin to whom he feels an immediate attraction, an 'enchantment' as he puts it. Gilmartin is able to assume Robert's identity and perform acts of violent masculine self-affirmation that Robert, in his feminized abjection, cannot; thus, it becomes apparent in the second half of the novel that Gilmartin is responsible for many of the transgressions attributed to Robert. Gilmartin becomes Robert's double *and* the empowered male 'other' that Robert simultaneously fears, hates and desires. In a typical Gothic gesture – and one that is highly significant in terms of the homophobic paranoia articulated through the character of the effeminate Robert – Gilmartin turns out to be none other than Satan himself, who is able to drive his victim to damnation precisely because Robert is so certain of his predestined salvation. The spiritual compensation for his social and sexual ineptitude – the small space of empowerment that Robert carves out for himself – is his downfall. The space of his empowerment, an empowerment that he inherits as the illegitimate son of his lower-class father, becomes the site of a homosexual, demonic seduction. Robert ultimately embodies the paranoia and systems of prohibition that operate within the patriarchal, homophobic society that this and other Gothic fictions of the time depict.

See also: Changes in Critical Responses and Approaches

Key Critical Concepts and Topics

Adeline Johns-Putra

The Canon

The literature of the British Romantic age, perhaps more than any other, has been shaped by canonizing forces. Conventionally, the Romantic movement is discussed in terms of a small number of poets – the famous (or infamous) 'Big Six'. These major figures – William Blake, William Wordsworth, Samuel Taylor Coleridge, Lord Byron, Percy Bysshe Shelley and John Keats – are often further divided into first- and second-generation Romantics, the first three designated as the former and the second three as the latter.

Such a canonical formation – convenient but reductionist – does possess a certain coherent intellectual rationale. These six poets share common traits, as they could not have failed to be inspired and informed by the events during and immediately after the French Revolution. Sympathizing with the motives of the Revolution, what we now think of as the 'first generation' of Romantics, along with Robert Southey (Poet Laureate from 1813 to 1843), identified themselves as revolutionary and radical in some sense, in both their politics and poetry. Indeed, in the first decades of the nineteenth century, there was an increasing awareness that the Revolution and the poets who had responded to it were part of a coherent movement. Writing in the *Edinburgh Review* in 1802, the reviewer Francis Jeffrey (1802: 63–83) assigned Wordsworth, Coleridge and Southey to a school of poetry that he subsequently named 'The Lake School'; consequently, in his article on 'Young Poets' in his *Examiner* in 1816, Leigh Hunt confirmed Byron's place in such a school, and anticipated that the up-and-coming Shelley and Keats would make 'a considerable addition of strength' (1816: 761) to it. Thus, when William Hazlitt counted Wordsworth, Coleridge, Byron and Sir Walter Scott amongst the poets who had contributed to what he called *The Spirit of the Age* (1824), the ground for a Romantic canon of poets had been well prepared. It was not till 1863, however, that critic Hippolyte Taine applied to this grouping the word 'Romantic' (1965: III, 422), meaning fanciful or wonderful, and closely related to the kind of privileging of the imagination and the supernatural associated with the form of romance.

Nonetheless, the similarities that bind this canon go only so far. Tellingly, the grouping was resisted in its own time by the poets themselves. Wordsworth, for example, protested violently against the appellation of the 'Lake School', on the grounds of differences between himself and the others, excepting Coleridge (letter to John Thelwall, January 1804). Certainly, beyond the close collaboration and friendship shared by Wordsworth and Coleridge, resulting most significantly in the *Lyrical Ballads* (1798), and a comparable sense of camaraderie between Shelley and Byron, the Romantic canon bears little evidence of co-operation or coterie. Blake knew of, but certainly was not associated with, his early Romantic counterparts; Shelley corresponded with Keats and elegized him after his death, but Byron was dismissive and even disdainful of the younger poet. Meanwhile, the 'second-generation' Romantics first admired and then rebelled against Wordsworth as he emerged as a figure of the conservative establishment in old age.

Furthermore, as this account of Romantic canon-formation demonstrates, such an alignment conceals the breadth of literary activity that took place in Britain in the fifty years or so after the Revolution. For one thing, the established canon of the 'Big Six' tends to ignore poetry that is not so easily read under the rubric of revolutionary or radical fervour, consigning to the past a range of poets who were widely read in their own time, ignoring not just Southey, Scott, Robert Burns and Thomas Moore, but utterly marginalizing once-popular women poets, among them Anna Letitia Barbauld, Felicia Hemans, Letitia Elizabeth Landon, Anna Seward and Charlotte Smith. Effaced also are the writings of labouring-class poets, from John Clare to Ann Yearsley to Elizabeth Hands. By focusing on a group of poets whose output tended towards the lyrical, the canon elides, too, the diversity of poetic genres witnessed in the age, particularly the vogue for narrative forms such as epic and romance.

Indeed, the Romantic canon encourages a narrowing of the critical lens to poetry in general, so much so that it is easy to forget that this was also the age in which a major novelist such as Jane Austen emerged, and thus a significant moment in the development of the novel towards the high realism of Victorian fiction. This moment also includes the emergence of important genres, from the gothic made wildly popular by Ann Radcliffe, to the historical novel inaugurated by Scott.

Thus although the concept of a Romantic canon has provided a basis for a critical understanding in terms of broad brushstrokes, the past several decades have seen Romanticist scholarship move toward a more nuanced and less restrictive view – what one might figure as a shift toward recanonization. In short, while aware of the significance of the 'Big Six' as a kind of shorthand for Romanticism, recent revisionist criticism has yielded a more accurate and complex story of the age we call Romantic.

Class

The age of Romanticism, inaugurated as it was by a revolutionary fervour of egalitarianism and emancipation, was an age in which class barriers were subject to much interrogation. A consideration of class is therefore crucial to any understanding of Romanticism. Yet in such a consideration, it is important to distinguish between the radical politics of its major thinkers and writers on the one hand and the material experience of labouring-class writers – many still considered minor Romantic figures – on the other.

Most of the major Romantics certainly stated at some point in each of their lives a radical position in respect of class. For example, William Wordsworth wrote enthusiastically of the sweeping away of the aristocratic excesses of the French *ancien régime* with the Revolution, for example in *The Prelude* (1805), while the young Percy Shelley augmented the political statements of his pamphlets with what could be read as a deeply personal gesture in protest against class oppression, when he married the socially inferior Harriet Westbrook. Nonetheless, these political positionings are easily undermined, when one considers, for example, that Wordsworth shifted towards a conservative stance later in life, and Shelley's gesture seems to have been precisely that – a gesture – for the marriage broke down within three years and Harriet committed suicide shortly after Shelley eloped to France with Mary Wollstonecraft Godwin. Indeed, most of the poets we now think of as major Romantics belonged distinctly to the privileged educated classes, with the exception of William Blake and John Keats. Both Blake and Keats were obliged to work to support themselves, Blake's poetic activity supplemented by his professional engraving and Keats' choice to abandon a career as a surgeon resulting in financial difficulties. Nonetheless, it is worth considering that both poets were born into reasonably prosperous middle-class families, a fact which Keats' designation as part of the 'Cockney School of Poets' (Lockhart 1817: 70–76) tends to efface.

It pays to read, then, alongside the radical class politics of Romantic figures, the work of genuinely labouring-class writers of the time. This was the age in which poor working conditions and restricted suffrage, combined with economic depression at the end of the Napoleonic Wars, culminated in the Peterloo uprising and massacre, when a protest by about 80,000 working-class men and women agitating for political and economic reform was fatally and brutally put down by cavalry. But this was also a time in which the rise in literacy and the expansion of printing, signified by the sharp increase in periodical circulation, broadened opportunities for literary activity beyond the upper and middle classes. In addition, the innovation of publication by subscription that had become popular in the eighteenth century (St Clair 2004: 166) meant that the costs of publishing could be met by patrons whose responsibility lay not in meeting those costs but in the much less onerous task of introducing the writer to polite society and thus to potential subscribers. Such was the role of Hannah More in relation to Ann Yearsley, the so-called 'Bristol Milkwoman'.

In the writings of these labouring-class poets, the common Romantic theme of nature is framed by the experience of exploitation, want and marginalisation that were the lot of the rural working class. Wordsworth and Coleridge's *Lyrical Ballads* (1798) had sought to reflect, in Wordsworth's words, 'incidents and situations from common life ... in a selection of language really used by men'. However, it is in the poems of just such men – for example, John Clare and Robert Bloomfield – that we share the perspective of the labourer who works the land rather than the poet who appreciates the landscape. Thus Bloomfield's *The Farmer's Boy: A Rural Poem* (1800) claims not to know 'Nature's sublimer scenes' (I, 11) but to write of 'meaner objects' (I, 13), proclaiming: 'Live trifling incidents and grace my song / That to the humblest menial being belong' (I, 19–20). In a similar vein is Clare's poetic almanac, *The Shepherd's Calendar* (1827), which sets out, like Bloomfield's poem, an honest view of rural nature through the seasons. A sense of protest against the appropriation of nature by the leisured class is implicit in such poems, and is, indeed, an explicit theme of a poem such as Clare's 'The Flitting' (1832), which includes a disdainful mention of the poetic muse for whom 'splendour passes for sublime' (156) and who would 'sing and never see / A field flower grown in all her days' (182–183).

Oppression and objectification inform, too, the perspective of the labouring-class woman poet. A common theme in Yearsley's poetry is the horror of the slave trade that centred on her hometown of Bristol, given a poignant edge by her personal experience of disenfranchisement. And, just as Clare and Bloomfield interrogate and reveal the modes of production behind the Romantic masculine sublime, Elizabeth Hands critiques the exploitation at the heart of the ideology of domesticity, so dominant in middle-class women's writing of the time (see, for example, Landry 1990: 182–273). Hands' satirically autobiographical poems, 'On the Supposition of an Advertisement in the Morning Paper of the Publication of a Volume of Poems by a Servant-Maid' (1789) and 'On the Supposition of the Book having been Published and Read' (1789) cleverly map the ways in which middle-class domesticity is enabled by the labour and servitude of the working classes.

Thus questions of class inform much of the literature of the Romantic age, but in considering the class politics and dynamics of the day, the radical ideology to which the major Romantic poets subscribed must be read against the lived experience of oppression and deprivation to which less canonical, labouring-class poets testify. Most importantly, that the two sat uneasily alongside each other must also be borne in mind.

Gender

Considerations of gender have shaped Romanticist scholarship since the 1980s and 1990s, when a revisionist attitude to Romanticism was inaugurated by critics such as Margaret Homans, Stuart Curran and Anne K. Mellor. This reveals how what we conventionally understand as Romanticism is premised on masculinist assumptions, and seeks to recover other attitudes and ideologies. Such a project of gendered recanonization has clarified women's relationship with Romanticism and attempted to determine whether they were united by an alternative ideology.

The typical Romantic poet is easily read as male: he possesses a highly developed subjectivity, and his poetry represents the solitary achievement of an individual who understands both himself and his place in the world. The canonical Romantic poets are all men, and all compared, at one time or another, their poetic function to other traditionally masculine roles – the creator, the prophet, the legislator. Marlon Ross, for example, has suggested that such a masculinist sense of subjectivity is most clearly manifest in the Romantic poet's desire to control and conquer, specifically in the encounter with nature (1989: 15–55). In this, the Romantic poet not only projects his own perceptions on to nature but appropriates its procreative powers for himself. Thus, for example, gendered readings of William Wordsworth's poetics (for example, Mellor 1996: 144–169 and Wolfson 1994: 29–57), have pointed out that although the poet presents nature as a potent maternal and presumably procreative energy, he ultimately envisions himself as subduing and appropriating this energy in order to carry out his own creative acts. Thus it is possible to read, in canonical Romantic constructions of gender, a profound disempowerment of females and femininity. In much Romantic poetry, women are simply silent or unseen, from Wordsworth's dead Lucy to John Keats' Madeline, who fulfils her role in the love story of 'The Eve of St Agnes' (1820) almost entirely asleep. Alternatively they are placed in the realm of the fantastic and exotic, as are Keats' *Lamia* (1820) and 'La Belle Dame sans Merci' (1820) and Lord Byron's many Orientalist heroines.

To read women writers alongside the canonical male Romantics, then, is instructive. For one thing, a quite different set of ideals and interests emerges. Women writers of the Romantic age were preoccupied with the home and their position in it, and the increasingly influential notion of separate spheres became a dominant ideology. Emerging out of this concern with the domestic is an emphasis on the need for women to be educated as rational beings and therefore as useful wives and mothers. A range of women's writing addresses the gender norms of the day in this way, and even as wide a political spectrum as represented by Hannah More on the one hand and Mary Wollstonecraft on the other is united by a call for what Wollstonecraft labelled a 'female revolution in manners' to counter the revolutionary ideals of masculine Romanticism.

An awareness of gender requires a shift of attention to literary forms, such as letters, diaries and conduct books, once neglected because of their status as conventionally feminine genres. A critical reading of such texts enables a broader understanding of the prevailing gender norms of the day. Conduct literature by both men and women – for instance, Hester Chapone's *Letters on the Improvement of the Mind* (1773), Erasmus Darwin's *Plan for the Conduct of Female Education in Boarding Schools* (1797) and Hannah More's *Strictures on the Modern System of Female Education* (1799) – is particularly useful in this way. Further, traditionally personal modes of writing can reveal gender norms in the process of being affirmed or subverted: Wollstonecraft and Helen Maria Williams extended the private to the public as they used the letter form as a basis for political commentary, while Dorothy Wordsworth's journal entries demonstrate the extent to which we might consider Wordsworthian poetics as a silencing of the female.

At the same time, an account of gender allows an inflection of our understanding of more conventional genres, such as the novel. It is worth considering not just the increase in the number of women who were writing and reading novels at this time but how the novel, with its emphasis on psychological development and domestic ties, played no small part in the establishment of gender norms and domestic ideology (see, for example, Armstrong 1989: 28–58). Such novels were produced by and often for women – most obviously, the *oeuvre* of Jane Austen, but instanced also by Charlotte

Smith and Maria Edgeworth. Also relevant is the phenomenon of the Gothic, which reached the height of its popularity in the Romantic age thanks to writers such as Ann Radcliffe. In many ways, the standard Gothic plot, juxtaposing female confinement and escape, represents a subversion of established gender norms and reveals both their prevalence and the opportunities that existed to revise them.

Such a consideration of gender in approaching Romanticism is not, however, without its risks. It is important to bear in mind that a reductionist binary of male versus female Romanticism could be potentially retrograde to the aims of recanonization, for it facilitates the installation of an alternative female canon, rather than a questioning of the male Romantic canon, which would render women writers susceptible to a kind of canonical tokenism. Thus a gender-sensitive criticism of Romanticism would entail, ideally, an exploration of not one but several Romanticisms, always attentive to the gender politics of both male and female writers.

Nature

It is a critical commonplace that one of the central preoccupations of Romantic poetry is nature. Indeed, the conceptualization of nature as a distinct and unified entity seems to dominate in the Romantic age, so much so that modern environmentalism can be said to owe much to Romantic attitudes to and constructions of the natural world. Today's widespread environmentally informed attitude to nature as a source of imaginative inspiration and moral value, and therefore something to be admired, appreciated and preserved, has its seeds in Romantic conceptualizations of the external world.

In particular, such constructions of nature have their origins in the wonder and awe of nature (Bate 2000: 13) expressed in William Wordsworth's Preface to the *Lyrical Ballads*. The *Lyrical Ballads*, first published in 1798 as a collaboration between Wordsworth and Samuel Taylor Coleridge, appeared in a second edition in 1800, this time containing only Wordsworth's contributions and a preface, also written by Wordsworth. Although not meant explicitly to be a formal manifesto of any sort – Wordsworth would later state that he did not care 'a straw about the theory' (quoted in Simpson 1987: 57) – the preface sets out the rationale agreed by Wordsworth and Coleridge for a new set of poetics, and has come to be a convenient document by which to read the intellectual shifts at the heart of Romanticism.

This poetics consists of a reimagined relationship of the poet, his natural surroundings and the poetry he produces. In his preface to *Lyrical Ballads*, Wordsworth famously states that he has chosen to write of 'low and rustic life', because 'in that condition the essential passions of the heart find a better soil in which they can attain their maturity'. Crucially, for Wordsworth, the emotions of rural men and women are more representative of genuine human emotion not simply because they are relatively uncontaminated by social convention but because 'in that condition the passions of men are incorporated with the beautiful and permanent forms of nature' – because, indeed, they are closer to nature in a pure state. The poet, according to Wordsworth, is responsible for producing a poetry that deals with nature and men and women who live as close as possible to a state of nature, and for reproducing in his readers a genuine and elemental emotional state that replicates the emotions that occur in men and women who are in touch with nature. Throughout Wordsworth's poetry, and not just in the *Lyrical Ballads*, the poet is shown to be inspired by the forms of nature, which allow him to intuit a deeper understanding of the workings of both humanity and the universe that surrounds it. Such a belief reaches its apogee in *The Prelude*, in which nature is figured as a great teacher and enabler of poetic ability, the many forms and objects of the natural world functioning to reveal to the poet 'The types and symbols of eternity / Of first, and last, and midst, and without end' (VII. 639–40).

In construing nature in this way, as a symbol or even substitute for God, and as revelatory of universal truth, Wordsworth was building upon several aesthetic theories of nature that dominated in the eighteenth century and were influential in the Romantic age. The first of these is the theory of the sublime, a concept codified by Edmund Burke in his *Philosophical Enquiry into the Sublime and Beautiful* (1757), but conventionally traced to a treatise attributed to Longinus in the first century. The sublime in nature may be defined as that which induces awe and wonder, but that experience of awe and wonder encapsulates a complicated response to sublime objects, scenes and experiences, such as mountainous or stormy landscapes. This response involves not simply an intense rapture at feeling physically dwarfed or threatened, but includes a concomitant or consequent sense of transcendence from the physical, a sensation of being lifted out of the scene and into a mediation on the vastness of the natural world and thus of the universe.

Yet Wordsworthian and, indeed, Romantic nature also owes much to a very different theory, that of the picturesque. The school of the picturesque – as expressed in the writings of William Gilpin, Richard Payne Knight and Uvedale Price – placed much emphasis on the pleasurable capacities of certain types of landscape, specifically those marked by 'rugged' or 'interesting' qualities, not so smooth as to be dull, but not so rough as to induce sublime terror. It encouraged travel expressly with the aim of appreciating landscape, and highlighted the significance of painting and poetry as a way of capturing the beauty of landscape. Thus, its emphasis on the educational and civilizing potential of landscape informed and influenced Romantic attitudes to nature. Nonetheless it should be noted that Wordsworth came to denounce the sensibilities of the picturesque and to differentiate these from his own particular brand of poetics. It is worth ending, then, on Wordsworth's own juxtaposition of these, for this crystallizes the Romantic response to nature. In *The Prelude*, he defines the picturesque as a state in which 'the eye [is] master of the heart' (XI, 175), as distinct from his own practice, in which the poet is 'now all eye / And now all ear, but ever with the heart / Employed, and the majestic intellect!' (XI, 140–42).

Imagination

William Blake declared, 'Man is all Imagination, God is Man and exists in us and we in him' ('Annotations to Berkeley's *Siris*'). In much of Blake's poetry, the positive energy of the imagination, represented by the mythical figure Los, is juxtaposed with the reductive power of reason, embodied by the jealous god Urizen. Thus for Blake, reason restrains the ultimately sensual force of the imagination: 'Energy is the only life and is from the Body and Reason is the bound or outward circumference of Energy' (*Marriage of Heaven and Hell*). Towards the end of the Romantic age, John Keats similarly privileges the sensual over the rational when he declares, 'O for a life of sensations rather than of thoughts!' (letter to Benjamin Bailey, 22 November 1817).

Such outbursts remind us that the Romantics tended to celebrate the imagination as a victory of the instinctive over the ratiocinative, and that this was very much a reaction against neo-classical or Enlightenment emphases on knowing the world through logical induction and deduction, or empiricism. Leading Enlightenment thinkers from John Locke to David Hume through to Immanuel Kant may be said to have insisted on man's natural ability for reason – best expressed in Kant's injunction to 'Dare to be wise!' (*Sapere Aude*). Meanwhile the Romantics, spurred on by the revolutionary events of the late eighteenth century, reacted against this by celebrating the human gift for imagination, an attribute more easily recognizable as egalitarian. After all, imagination, when aligned with sense and instinct, could even be found in the 'low and rustic life' that Wordsworth so insistently foregrounds in his 1801 preface to the *Lyrical Ballads*.

Yet the imagination in Romantic terms is not always so far removed from Enlightenment thought. Locke's *Essay Concerning Human Understanding* (1698) distinguished between sensation and reflection, the one leading to simple ideas and the other building on and synthesizing those simple ideas to create complex ideas. But Hume's *Enquiry Concerning Human Understanding* (1748) had questioned whether reason was merely sequential in this way. Building on Hume's scepticism, Kant suggests in his *Critique of Pure Reason* (1781) a distinction between reproductive and productive forms of imagination, the former resembling the empirical method of reasoning described by Locke, but the latter referring to a much more spontaneous capacity for synthesizing ideas that actually precedes sensation. For Kant, the productive imagination allows us to take in all at once the many sensations we experience almost at the moment of – or indeed *a priori* to – actually experiencing them.

Kant's productive imagination is thus a necessary but little understood human faculty – 'a blind but indispensable function of the soul' – and informs one of the most important Romantic conceptions of the imagination. Samuel Taylor Coleridge's distinction in the thirteenth chapter of his *Biographia Literaria* (1817) between fancy and the imagination echoes the Kantian split between the reproductive and productive imaginations. For Coleridge, fancy 'has no counters to play with, only fixities and definite' while the imagination may be divided into primary and secondary modes. Recalling Kant's discussion of the imagination as pre-existing and indeed shaping experience, Coleridge defines the primary imagination as 'the living Power and prime Agent of all human perception' and the secondary imagination as 'an echo of the former, co-existing with the conscious will, yet still as identical with the primary in the kind of its agency, and differing only in degree, and in the mode of operation. It dissolves, diffuses, dissipates, in order to recreate'. He therefore distinguishes between the operations of the imagination before or at the moment of perception (primary) and after that moment (secondary), when the mind attempts to understand the manifold sensations of experience.

Coleridge greatly influenced Percy Shelley in his contradistinction between reason and the imagination, as we see in Shelley's *Defence of Poetry* (1821). For Shelley, 'Reason is the enumeration of quantities already known; Imagination is the perception of the value of those quantities, both separately and as a whole'. Shelley further goes on to discuss poetry as the 'expression of the imagination', in line with Coleridge's definition of the secondary imagination.

A final chapter in the Romantic conceptualization of the imagination is provided by Keats. Keats' notoriously difficult notion of 'negative capability' builds further on Coleridge's theories. In a letter to his brothers George and Tom on 21 December 1817, in which he discusses 'what quality went to form a Man of Achievement especially in Literature', Keats posits the concept of '*Negative Capability*, that is when man is capable of being; in uncertainties, Mysteries, doubts, without any irritable reaching after fact and reason'. For Keats, one is able to produce true poetry only when one renounces logical thought, when one rejects, indeed, fancy or the reproductive imagination – such a poet is in this way negatively capable. Strikingly, Keats singles out Coleridge in particular, for allowing reason to cloud the imagination:

Coleridge, for instance, would let go by a fine isolated verisimilitude caught from the Penetralium of mystery, from being incapable of remaining Content with half knowledge. This pursued through Volumes would perhaps take us no further than this, that with a great poet the sense of Beauty overcomes every other consideration, or rather obliterates all consideration.

Such constructions of the imagination as a creative force constitute a lynchpin of Romantic poetics. They posit that the poet or artist is able to create the world anew through his imagination, and accord him a status and a power over that of nature and even God.

Orientalism

The Orient – construed as the nations and peoples east of Europe – exerted a considerable allure over Romantic literature. From novels to poetic romances and lyrics, and from travellers' tales to scholarly studies of language and culture, a range of writings in the age of Romanticism betrays a deep-seated fascination with the East.

In the brief pre-history of Western representations of the Orient leading up to the Romantic age, we see the development of the sometimes contrary preoccupations that Edward Said (1979) identified with nineteenth-century Orientalism – the construction of the East as Other develops in tension with the desire to understand, and perhaps to bring under some kind of control, the apparent utter strangeness of this Other. What is remarkable about all these writings is not just their interest in the spaces of the East but an ethnographic intensity, the intention (not always realized) to outdo any previous writings in accuracy and detail.

From the early modern age, Persia and the Ottoman Empire exert a presence in Western consciousness, for they constitute the locus of Islam, which is increasingly understood in the eighteenth century as the polar opposite of Christianity. These Islamic lands thus help to define the bounds of Europe to the East in what is now Turkey. At the same time, the defeat of the Ottomans at Vienna in 1683 allowed a regulation of and increase in diplomatic and trade contacts with the Empire and beyond. Such travels resulted in a profusion of translations and fictions of the East, most notably in the case of Antoine Galland, who served as secretary to the French ambassador in Constantinople. Galland produced the *Mille et une Nuits* (1704–17), which appeared in English as the *Arabian Nights Entertainments* soon after, and which exerted a tremendous influence on the eighteenth-century and Romantic imagination. There is no shortage, either, of British writers and travellers in the eighteenth century, for example, Lady Mary Wortley Montagu with her *Turkish Embassy Letters* (1721). By the end of the century, the linguist Sir William Jones had produced a breathtaking body of Orientalist scholarship

– translations, grammars, academic analyses – dealing with a range of Eastern languages and literatures.

The example of Jones reminds us that the rise of Orientalism goes hand in hand with imperialism, and puts into focus those tensions between the desire for a sympathetic understanding and an impulse towards control. Although Jones' work (for example, his addresses to the Asiatick Society, which he founded in 1784) is remarkably sensitive and even-handed in its depiction and understanding of the East, it was enabled by the British Government's presence in India – it was Jones' knowledge of Arabic and Persian that earned him a post in the Supreme Court of Bengal and in turn led to his scholarly interest in Sanskrit. For the Romantic age was also a time of aggressive imperialist expansion, a period in which British rule in India was consolidated, and colonialist projects begun in Southeast Asia and Australia.

Such tensions reveal themselves in Orientalist poetry and fiction. The seductive imaginative appeal of the East is constantly underwritten by the impulse towards academic accuracy and control, signified by the copious notes that would become a defining characteristic of the genre. Certainly, scholarly paraphernalia had been made *de rigeur* by William Beckford's novel *Vathek* (1786). Moreover, in Orientalist romances such as Walter Savage Landor's *Gebir* (1798), Robert Southey's *Thalaba, the Destroyer* (1801) and *The Curse of Kehama* (1810), and Thomas Moore's *Lalla Rookh* (1817), the East is a space both of glorious spectacle and decadent luxury, both lavish and corrupt, and therefore held at arm's length even while it is the object of a desiring gaze.

Inevitably, Romantic depictions of the East circle around the harem. This over-mythicized space captures all the tensions implicit in Romantic Orientalism. While it is understood as utterly antithetical to the norms of heterosexual monogamy that lie at the heart of British constructions of identity, and therefore an aberration to be resisted and even destroyed by the heroes of Orientialism, it is also a site of sensual appeal, off limits to these heroes and therefore tantalizing in its sexual promise. Nowhere is this more obvious than in Byron's 'Turkish Tales', which include *The Giaour* (1813), *The Bride of Abydos* (1813), *The Corsair* (1814) and *Lara* (1814).

Terror, guilt, fascination, repulsion, will to power – the psychic contradictions within Romantic Orientalism fuelled a very public phenomenon of the consumption of Orientalist poetry. It would seem that not merely the Orient but the anxieties that surrounded it were ultimately reflected back towards the British Romantic reader.

Revolution

The age of Romanticism was an age of Revolution. The American Revolutionary War (or the War of American Independence) in 1783 had resulted, from the

British perspective, in a substantial circumscription of imperial power and had been a national disaster. Yet, it had also fired the imaginations of those in Britain who wished to see their government's power challenged and reformed. The decade seemed to promise progress and reform.

The French Revolution therefore constituted a real watershed for those who watched events as they unfolded across the Channel. Not only was this a Revolution in old Europe, and in powerfully close proximity, but it quickly became clear that this revolution was unlike any other in recent history in terms of its complexity and impact. Although 1789 is often designated as the year in which the Revolution occurred, the extraordinary events of its aftermath are equally significant in terms of assessing its influence on the literature and thought of British Romanticism.

The Revolution is conventionally dated to the fall of the Bastille in July 1789. In the months immediately preceding this, the French Estates General had declared itself the national assembly and decision-making body, in place of the King. The Parisians' storming of the Bastille, a hated symbol of tyranny by virtue of its established use as a political prison, was both the culmination of this political crisis and the beginning of a painful process of constitutional confusion. Initially, a 'national convention' was tasked to set up the constitution, and a constitutional monarchy successfully negotiated with the King and established in September 1791. However, this occurred amid political disagreement and serious – even deadly – unrest amongst clergy, republicans, and aristocracy. In 1792, the Palace of the Tuileries was stormed, led by prominent members of the Convention such as Maximilien Robespierre, and a Republic declared. The Republican government, riddled by factional infighting between the Jacobins and Girondins, ruled through 1793 and 1794 in a series of increasingly severe and paranoid measures, known as the Reign of Terror. The Terror came to an abrupt end when Robespierre was overthrown, to be replaced by the unpopular and unstable reign of the Directory, which was plagued by coups and finally overthrown by Napoleon in 1799.

The upheavals of the Revolution were met with corresponding confusions of loyalty in Britain. The Revolution was initially greeted with enthusiasm, both by those who were ready for reform in Britain and by those who felt that, at last, the benighted despotism of French Catholicism and aristocracy was giving way to the kind of enlightenment Britain enjoyed. The major Romantic poets, young and optimistic, celebrated it with a kind of heady optimism, Coleridge composing 'An Ode on the Destruction of the Bastille' in 1789 and Wordsworth remembering of this time of revolutionary fervour that 'Bliss was in that dawn to be alive, / But to be young was very heaven!' (*The Prelude*, 1805, x.693–4). More direct still was Thomas Paine, the veteran of the American Revolution, whose *Rights of Man* (1791–92) called for the French

Revolution's reforms to be introduced to Britain. Prosecuted for sedition, Paine fled to France, only to be imprisoned there during the Terror, prompting furious protests from his friend William Blake.

This is not to say, of course, that anti-Revolution feeling did not exist. An early conservative view was put by Edmund Burke, the prominent Whig MP and writer, in *Reflections on the French Revolution* (1790), which voiced a total opposition to the Revolution and included an emotive defence of the French Royal family, expressed, notoriously, as a somewhat over-gallant concern for the distress of Marie Antoinette. This prompted Mary Wollstonecraft's spirited response, *A Vindication of the Rights of Men* (1790), followed by *A Vindication of the Rights of Woman* (1792), which extended egalitarian principles to women.

Yet as the Revolution became bloodier and the Terror reared its head, optimism gave way to disillusionment – Wordsworth in the *Prelude* again provides a chronicle, recounting his despair at the Terror and relief at Robespierre's downfall. For the likes of Wollstonecraft and Helen Maria Williams, who had been prompted by the Revolution to move to Paris and build their lives there, the Terror was not just emotionally wrenching but life-threatening. Wollstonecraft held on to her revolutionary hopes for as long as she could, eventually abandoning both these and France in 1795; Williams retained a firm belief in the values of the Revolution and remained in France till the end of her life, leaving just once at the height of the Terror, when – imprisoned for a month and then released – she fled to Switzerland for six months in 1794.

Moreover, the Terror justified and heightened the anti-Revolution concerns of the kind expressed by Burke. These were intensified when Britain went to war with France in 1792, leading to a government crackdown on the Revolution's liberal sympathizers. The conservative backlash thus turned into easy accusations of spying and sedition: Wordsworth and Coleridge were followed by a Home Office agent in 1796, and Coleridge's good friend John Thelwall was arrested for treason. Such was the context in which conservative publications flourished; for example, the *Anti-Jacobin Review* and *Quarterly Review* launched attacks on Wordsworth, Coleridge and Southey, and deemed them enemy sympathizers.

As the worst of the Revolution's excesses – from the Terror to the spectre of Napoleon – subsided, its spirit of radical political reform remained a touchstone in the writings of later Romantics. It retains its urgency in a poem such as Percy Shelley's *Revolt of Islam* (1817), which depicts an idealized bloodless revolution. For Shelley, the French Revolution was 'the master theme of the epoch in which we live' (Letter to Byron, 8 September 1816), and, indeed, it defined British Romanticism.

Science

The Romantic age has sometimes been called 'the second scientific revolution' (see, for example, Heringman 2003: 2). The scientific revolution of the sixteenth and seventeenth centuries – culminating in Britain in the achievements of men such as Robert Hooke and Isaac Newton and in the founding of the Royal Society – ushered in the Enlightenment and enshrined the empiricist attitudes of modern science. It is possible to recognize, at the end of the eighteenth century, a second wave of new scientific ideas and discoveries, which created the discourse of science as we know it today. This second scientific revolution helped to shape – and was shaped by – the literature of the age.

While Enlightenment scientific ideals had been heralded by the foundation of the Royal Society, science in the Romantic age was framed by the aims and activities of the Royal Institution, established in 1799. The Royal Institution was set up expressly to put science to work in the service of public interest, whether in terms of improving general knowledge or increasing industrial productivity. Its public lectures put forward a very different model of scientific dissemination from the private correspondence and informal meetings between gentlemen that had previously been the primary mode of scientific exchange. Somewhat ironically, by locating science within the public domain in this way, the Royal Institution helped to turn science into the rarefied and specialized discourse that it is today; indeed, one could say that it was instrumental in the professionalization of science. It seems no coincidence that the word 'scientist' had been coined by the end of the Romantic age by William Whewell in the 1830s.

One of the most influential figures in Romantic science, and one of the most publically recognized scientists of the age, was Humphry Davy, who was appointed to a professorship at the Royal Institution in 1801. Davy's work in chemistry and physics – for example, his discoveries of various chemical elements using electrolysis and his experiments with nitrous oxide or 'laughing gas' – fired the public's imagination and brought him immediate celebrity, as did his idealistic views on science as a creative expression. Some of these ideas he had formed in conversation with Samuel Taylor Coleridge and in correspondence with William Wordsworth. For Coleridge, in particular, Davy represented the perfect type of the imagination at work, and he presented Davy as such in his journal *The Friend* in 1809.

Although Coleridge's views align the scientific and the literary in terms of their imaginative modes and methodologies, they also enable the recognition of a division between the two in terms of their application. The idea that science and poetry are twin forms of imaginative genius, propounded by Coleridge and embodied by Davy, inspired Percy Shelley. Shelley was of course impressively familiar with the latest scientific information, and his *Prometheus Unbound* (1819) borrows much from the astronomical advances enabled by Newton, the electrical experiments carried out by Davy and the botanical knowledge of Carl Linnaeus, as popularised by Erasmus Darwin. Yet in his *Defence of Poetry* (1821), Shelley makes a clear distinction between the uses of science and poetry:

> Ethical science arranges the elements which poetry has created, and propounds schemes and proposes examples of civil and domestic life ... But poetry acts in another and a diviner manner. It awakens and enlarges the mind itself by rendering it the receptacle of a thousand unapprehended combinations of thought. Poetry lifts the veil from the hidden beauty of the world; and makes familiar objects be as if they were not familiar...

Thus the scientific imagination works in a more or less mechanistic fashion, putting into play ideas and truths, the discovery of which is enabled by the poetic imagination.

Such a construction of scientific discovery as a mere arrangement of facts, alongside an idealization of the poetic imagination as revealing, in some more authentic fashion, the secrets of life, may be discerned in what is perhaps the most negative portrayal of science in the Romantic age – Mary Shelley's *Frankenstein* (1819). Like her husband Percy, Mary Shelley was influenced by Davy's example and Coleridge's construction of it. However, her vision of the scientist – Victor Frankenstein – is a damning portrayal of scientific experimentation as hubris, going beyond the deduction and description of nature to attempt the act of creation itself.

Thus the Romantic age bears witness to an extraordinary flourishing of scientific endeavour and a corresponding alignment of such endeavour with the type of poetic imagination that was also being valourized at the time. However, such an alignment also provides the basis for a split between the two domains, and the Romantic age is also responsible for the development of science and art, as C. P. Snow would memorably describe it, into 'two cultures' (1959; 1989).

Slavery

Debates around the question of slavery and the slave trade raged throughout the Romantic age. In the eighteenth century, the slave trade had been a highly successful industry, with major British ports owing much of their prosperity to the thriving business of transporting African slaves across the Atlantic via the so-called 'Middle Passage'; for example, some three-quarters of all

European slaving ships in the last two decades of the eighteenth century left from Liverpool. At the end of the eighteenth century, slavery was still legal in Britain's colonies and former colonies, and many British merchants with property and interests in these lands profited directly from the labour of slaves, often undertaken in the harshest conditions. It is easy to see why, in an age preoccupied with subjectivity and egalitarianism, slavery and the slave trade prompted searching moral and political questions.

The Romantic period is marked by significant milestones in the history of the abolition of slavery in Britain. In 1772 slavery was abolished in Britain itself; in 1778 the first legislative attempts to regulate the slave trade were made by the Prime Minister William Pitt; in 1787 the Society for the Effecting the Abolition of the Slave Trade was formed; in 1788 the Slave Trade Regulation Act was eventually passed; in 1807 the Slave Trade Act made the slave trade illegal; and in 1833 the Slavery Abolition Act finally put an end to slavery in Britain and most of the British Empire. The age is therefore framed on the one hand by the first attempts at abolition of slavery in Britain and on the other by their eventual success.

The Abolition movement, led for the most part by William Wilberforce, greatly influenced the literature of the last decades of the eighteenth century. One of the most powerful examples of this is the genre of the slave narrative, best represented by *The Interesting Narrative of Olaudah Equiano or Gustavus Vasa* (1789). Although this was preceded by examples such as *The Narrative of the Most Remarkable Particulars of Ukawsaw Gronniosaw* (1772) and the poetry of Phillis Wheatley, Equiano's extraordinary autobiography transformed him into something of a literary celebrity and one of the key figures in the British Abolition movement.

Perhaps just as significant is the profusion of anti-slavery poetry associated with the cult of sensibility, which advocated the cultivation of 'feeling' towards the slave condition, many of which were written in direct response to or association with the Abolitionist movement. Thus, William Roscoe's *The Wrongs of Africa*, William Cowper's 'The Negro's Complaint' and 'The Morning Dream', Hannah More's *Slavery*, and Ann Yearsley's *Poem on the Inhumanity of the Slave Trade* all appeared in 1788. Significantly, such poems, particularly those by women writers, discussed slavery not just in terms of an infringement of a basic human right, but as a violation of normal affective and familial bonds (Mellor 1996: 316–17).

The prevalence of sentimental anti-slavery writing by women brings into focus the potential for an intersection of race and gender in these texts. Yet, many British women writers tended to avoid highlighting the obvious parallels between the subjection of slaves and the oppression of women (Coleman 1994: 354). The most prominent exception, and a text that takes full advantage of such a comparison, is Mary Wollstonecraft's *A Vindication of the*

Rights of Woman (1792). In her treatise, Wollstonecraft has frequent recourse to the language of slavery and bondage to sharpen the edge of her polemic: 'Is one half of the human species, like the poor African slave, to be subject to prejudices that brutalize them...?'. Yet it must be acknowledged that such arguments function to elide the plight of the slave, reducing it to an alibi for the struggle for gender equality.

Slavery emerges into the nineteenth century as a theme in a range of novels, again mostly by women. It underpins, most famously, the plantation interests at the heart of the landed gentry of Jane Austen's *Mansfield Park* (1814), yet goes largely unremarked in that novel. More explicit in their concerns are Maria Edgeworth's *Belinda* (1801), in which the wealthy Creole Mr Vincent and his black servant, Juba, bring questions of slavery into the foreground, and Amelia Opie's *Adeline Mowbray* (1804), which includes in its narrative the trials and sufferings of the slave-woman Savanna. By the 1820s and 1830s, as the abolitionist movement achieved its most significant political successes, the theme of slavery was addressed in a variety of works associated with the political campaign, but no longer held such potent ideological force.

The Sublime

It is notoriously difficult to define the sublime exactly. For some Romantic-era writers, it is a power or sense that resides within the mind (the German philosopher Immanuel Kant termed it a 'sense super-sensible' in his *Critique of Judgement* in 1790). From the early-eighteenth century it came to be associated with a sense of grandeur and magnitude that had the power to inspire transcendence of mind, or terror. The sublime re-entered European aesthetic discourse at the end of the seventeenth century following a French translation of an essay by an ancient Greek philosopher, Longinus; this essay, entitled 'On the Sublime', associated the concept with that style of elevated rhetoric that had the capacity almost to transform the mind of the listener – to take the listener out of his or her ordinary reality. In 1704, the critic john Dennis published an important essay on poetry in which he also aligned the sublime with an elevating, almost transformational style of poetry able to reproduce rhetorically the awe-inspiring grandeur of certain natural landscapes. Later in the century, the sublime came to be increasingly associated with a power that was natural, or divine, and that enabled the human mind to reach its full, transcendental potential. John Baillie in his 'Essay on the Sublime' (1747) observed that: 'That object can only be called sublime which disposes the mind to this enlargement of itself, and gives her a lofty conception of her own powers'. In his 1757 *A Philosophical Enquiry into the Sublime and Beautiful* Edmund Burke asserted that the sublime 'is always some modification of power'; this is a power that originates in nature, or in

God, and it has the capacity to inspire 'Terror'. These conceptualisations of the sublime influenced Romantic poets for whom the sublime was central to the poet's experience of nature, and to the poet's understanding of the power of the imagination in response to nature: see Charlotte Smith's 'Beachy Head' (1807); Wordsworth's 'Tintern Abbey' (1798) and Percy Bysshe Shelley's 'Mont Blanc' (1817).

Some critics have identified different modes of the sublime operating in the work of male and female writers of the Romantic era. Anne Mellor argues that the sublime in what she terms 'Male Romanticism' works to facilitate a highly individualistic, self-affirming transcendence that disconnects the poet from a social sphere constructed as 'feminine' (and associated more with 'beauty' than with the sublime). She contends that certain women writers, on the other hand (Dorothy Wordsworth in her Journals, Ann Radcliffe in her Gothic fictions), produce a version of the sublime that emphasises relationality and empathy over transcendence and separation: see Mellor's *Romanticism and Gender* (1993).

See also: Historical Contexts; Literary and Cultural Contexts

6

Changes in Critical Responses and Approaches

Joel Faflak

Criticizing Romanticism

In chapter one we discussed how 1790s politics in Britain made the communication of information to the public a vexed issue. Discussions of literature were central to this issue because fictional writing made it easy to dissimulate historical events and thus communicate them differently, making it difficult to tell where the truth lay, or whose minds it might be changing. This shape-shifting was a potent political strategy when the charge of treason threatened anyone who dared to speak against the status quo. But it also made literature difficult to believe, begging the question of how or why it mattered, especially when contrasted with other emergent bodies of knowledge, like those of the sciences or political economy, which seemed to speak more immediately to the concerns of private and public life. The rise of the novel was one way that literature had been responding to these concerns for some time, and Romanticism's experimentation with all genres reflects this continuing adaptation. Of particular relevance in the Romantic period, then, is how literature gets consumed. This is where Romantic criticism comes in, for it marked not only the cultural importance of literature, but ensured its correct transmission to reading audiences.

The historical, social, and political conditions that determined the writing of Romantic criticism vary considerably. Who decides how and why Romantic literature and its study are important is tied to how and why they are compelled to make this claim. This process starts in the Romantic period itself, so this chapter's overview of changes in critical responses and approaches to Romanticism begins there and moves forward to give some sense of the current critical landscape. Because the chapters following this one discuss more current criticism at some length, this chapter will dwell equally on the history of Romantic criticism up to the later twentieth century in order to provide the back story to this later history. The 1950s onward were a time of particularly intense focus on Romanticism, during which time Romantic Studies proper can be said to emerge. But we sometimes forget how Romanticism gained its critical prominence as a distinct field of critical study. Gaining some sense of the critical fortunes of Romanticism and Romantic Studies before the later twentieth century tells us as much as recent criticisms about why it is that Romanticism continues to galvanize our attention, for better or worse.

Romantic Romanticism

All periods of literature go through ups and downs of critical acceptance. But perhaps no literary period has undergone such a fluctuation in critical responses and approaches as Romanticism. Part of the reason for this wavering goes back to the period itself, which often looks to us like a number of diverse characters in search of an author. The range of Romanticisms now apparent to us is the result of the period's shifting self-definitions. Yet perhaps it more crucially reflects the often turbulent critical marketplace of the past two centuries, when 'literature' emerged as a distinct body of knowledge. As we said above, at stake here is the issue of how literature gets consumed by its readers. The issue is by no means a new one: Plato worried that the divinely inspired poet, his rationality suspended in order to create, might similarly affect the judgement of his audience. Confronting the rise of the novel in the eighteenth century, Samuel Johnson worried that its attention too closely to everyday life, to the experience of a flawed human nature, and thus to the flawed nature of human experience itself, might leave the wrong impression on young or untrained minds. On the positive side, Johnson's concern reflects increased literacy rates among the middle and especially industrial classes, despite his infantilization of the latter. More people than ever before had access to printed material, an information economy that really starts to explode in the Romantic period. On the negative side, Johnson reflects anxieties about the expansion of a previously small class of learned readers to an increasingly diverse reading public whose consumption of literature cannot so easily be controlled. If more people than ever before were reading, who was going to say what they read – what they *should* read. The concern became especially urgent in the social and political upheavals of the Romantic period, when ideas about national, gender, sexual, racial, historical and class identity began to circulate in ways that threatened notions of what the status quo should be. Put another way, as selective as literary writers could be in what aspects of these identities they did or did not choose to include in their works, so criticism was equally selective when it chose to praise or condemn these works – and their writers – in turn.

Because literature became one of Romanticism's premier ways of making sense of the period's complex historical changes, to talk about the role of criticism in making sense of Romantic literature we have to ask why literature demanded criticism of and about it. We can think of the term in two senses: literature as 'literate' writing and Literature as a specific mode of this writing. The former is a rather capacious and hence problematic category, because it can expand to include any form of writing for any literate reader, from the most prosaic newspaper item to the loftiest poem or philosophical disquisition. Already we see in this implied division between 'high' and 'low' culture what is at stake in the work of the latter category, Literature, as a way of distinguishing forms of writing with a higher social and moral purpose from those that merely feed an audience's desire for information or entertainment. In his 1800 Preface to *Lyrical Ballads*, Wordsworth decried the public thirst for supposedly shallow or sensational literature[1]. Wordsworth has in mind specific forms of fictional writing, but his distaste implies a more general suspicion of literature that does not reflect the higher aspirations of the imagination, a key concern for the Romantics. In an essay on Alexander Pope, Thomas De Quincey, whose *Confessions of an English Opium-Eater* (1821)[2] might very well be considered as an example of the kind of sensational writing Wordsworth decried, distinguished between a literature of knowledge, which is the mere gathering of information, and a literature of power, which elevates the mind and soul to contemplate beyond the merely physical or material aspects of human experience. Percy Shelley takes a similar tack in his *Defence of Poetry* (1821)[3] when he speaks of poetry as a vital creative force necessary to animate the increasingly unwieldy body of knowledge produced for an increasingly diverse public hungry for information. That both pieces were written just after the final Regency Crisis we outlined in chapter one alerts us to the urgency of marking how literature should disseminate ideas to the public.

We can think of Wordsworth's, Shelley's, and De Quincey's essays as three of the earliest documents of a critical approach to Romanticism, documents that showed readers precisely how to read the very literature all three were writing themselves. Ironically, De Quincey's essay was for the *Encyclopaedia Britannica*, precisely the kind of knowledge compendium he, like Shelley in his *Defence*, was reacting against. Moreover, because De Quincey wrote almost exclusively for the periodicals that constituted what is commonly thought of as the 'golden age' of journalism in the first half of the nineteenth century, he was embroiled in the very matrix of a knowledge-based literature that he wanted the power of Literature to rise above. Such periodicals were the battleground for the time's culture wars about the moral and social purpose of literature in an increasingly modern age, a battle over who got to tell audiences what it was appropriate to read. Venues like the highly influential *Edinburgh Review* were in the business of shaping the identities of the audiences to which they were addressing themselves, a dynamic negotiation between knowledge and reader that helped to define the shape of print culture itself, both in periodical and book form, in the late eighteenth and early nineteenth centuries. As much as writers like Wordsworth, Shelley or De Quincey wanted to elevate Literature (which usually meant poetic writing) above the fray of the prosaic, then, they were increasingly aware of their dependence on a wider public readership to have their voices heard, a readership they were thus invested in training *how* to read their works.

Victorian Romanticism

In his *Defence of Poetry*, Shelley argues that the literature of England seemed to have been reborn in his own time. He also writes that poetry is like the shadows that futurity casts upon the present. Like prophets, poets anticipate a future that has not yet arrived, a potential yet to be realized. But as shadows, there is something latent and darkly apocalyptic about poetry, something doubly uncertain about its reflection of history: it expresses both a present uncertainty about the future and a future uncertainty about the present, as if to anticipate how the future will evaluate and judge the present, and thus to ensure the ambivalence of this time. This is perhaps why Shelley ends his essay by calling poets the *un*acknowledged legislators of the world. Writers like Shelley were also aware that other forms of writing, like the novel or drama, spoke more urgently, or at the very least more directly, to an audience increasingly distracted by the push and pull of modern life, a readership who had increasingly less time for sustained contemplation of the deeper issues of the time and of life. As poetry started to seem out of touch with his modernity, the task of redefining its function became crucial, which is why Shelley focuses on the genre of poetry, but also on poetry as a cultural and historical force animating all human endeavour.

Theorizing poetry in this way, however, was a mixed blessing, for in the decades following it became a way of attending less to the actual achievement of Romantic writers, the diversity of which only a much later criticism would recognize, than to the influence these works exerted. More often than not, then, Romanticism ended up being isolated either as an abstract imaginative power, a kind of intellectual or secular religion removed from the everyday, or as a spontaneous and thus dangerous overflow of feeling in need of containment. Romantic literature had emerged from and was strongly influenced by eighteenth-century ideas of sentiment, sensibility and sympathy, which valued the person whose highly-attuned and highly-cultivated individual feeling indicated a level of self-development that meant this person could properly interact with others. Such notions were the cornerstone of eighteenth-century notions of the enlightened, progressive and democratic evolution of a civil society. In the aftermath of Revolutionary and Napoleonic as well as domestic political and social upheaval, however, a Romantic sensibility was also viewed as an excessive or unruly threat to social order. Often this threat was figured as feminine and/or racially 'other', as a 'nervous', even hysterical force that needed containment. This became especially true as emergent Victorian notions of 'moral hygiene' came to re-emphasize the necessity of individuals controlling and thus properly deploying their feelings. Within this climate, again, Romanticism came to signify an inchoate, dangerous energy that exerted its influence beyond or below rational or conscious purview.

It is important to recall that while both De Quincey's and Shelley's ideas about literature's higher calling are considered part of the Romantic canon, they were published in the Victorian era, De Quincey's essay in 1842 and Shelley's *Defence* in 1840, though it was written in 1821. By the time the Romantic critic William Hazlitt memorialized the same 'spirit of the age' that Shelley claims had revitalized the literature of the opening nineteenth century, this literature's time had largely passed, along with several of its key figures: Byron, Keats, and Shelley himself. By the time De Quincey wrote his gossipy recollections in the 1830s of what were named the Lake School writers in the early nineteenth century (Wordsworth, Coleridge, Southey and others), a new generation of writers – Tennyson, the Brownings, Arnold, Carlyle – were emerging. Such figures were clearly indebted to the writers who came before them, but one senses some ambivalence about this relationship. For one thing, so many of the works of the previous decades, like William Godwin's or Mary Wollstonecraft's fiction and non-fiction, Byron's poetry or the excesses of Gothic writing, had been politically and morally suspect, or, like William Beddoes' *Death's Jest Book*, Keats' *Hyperion* or Shelley's *The Triumph of Life*, were aesthetically complex, indeterminate or simply unfinished or unpublished. Both the form and content of Romantic literature embodied the restlessness and upheavals of the period it reflected, making it difficult to make sense of its achievement after the fact. Those who did, like Mary Shelley in her prefaces to her husband's collected poems, published after his death, tended to underplay such problems by focusing on the morality implicit in the work's aesthetic qualities. The poet Robert Browning followed Mary Shelley's rehabilitating efforts: in an essay on Shelley he surmised that had Shelley lived he would have ended up a Christian, as if to suggest that the poet, otherwise known for his philosophical and political radicalism, would have found the right (i.e. conservative) path[4].

So when in *Sartor Resartus*[5] Carlyle urges his reader to 'Close thy *Byron*', whose writing was used in the Victorian era as a symbol of Romanticism's dubious morality, and 'open thy *Goethe*' (146), whom Carlyle champions for a more philosophical and transcendental sensibility, one senses that the times had shifted considerably. This is not to say that Carlyle's own text is an entirely unironic (or easy!) read, but when in his 1869 Preface to *Essays in Criticism*, entitled 'The Function of Criticism at the Present Time', the writer Matthew Arnold says that the literature of the first part of the nineteenth century had about it something 'premature' (240)[6], he expresses a certain dissatisfaction and discomfort with Romanticism's literary achievement, as if Romantic thought and writing were more on the side of recessive feeling than progressive action. Arthur Hallam and William Johnson Fox, reviewers of Tennyson's *Poems, Chiefly Lyrical* (1830)[7], both took pains to note that Tennyson's poetic voice, while full of Romantic feeling, also tempered this feeling with analysis. Arnold himself had given up writing poetry to focus on cultural criticism because his own poetry betrayed too much of Romanticism's ambivalence. Such sentiments were vast over-simplifications of the heterogeneous range of Romantic writing, but they came to signify a prevailing attitude toward Romanticism so long-lasting in its influence that it has only been thoroughly contested in recent decades.

In 1871 Walter Bagehot read Tennyson differently[8]. As if following Carlyle's notion in *The French Revolution*, published the same year as Victoria's ascension, of equating revolution, feeling and Romantic literature along with sensuality and falsehood, Bagehot disparaged the pre-Raphaelite writers as comprising 'the fleshly school of poetry'. For him the example of morbid and hysterical (read: too feminine) feeling had been set by Tennyson's *Maud* (1855), who had caught the 'disease' from the Romantics themselves. Or as Bagehot says of Robert Browning, his poetic corpus had degenerated from the more classical form of its earlier Wordsworth reflectiveness to a later, more grotesque Keatsian Romanticism that was all sense and no common sense, all body and no brain. By the end of the nineteenth century, then, Romanticism was figured in one of two ways: it was either the signal influence of a renewed aestheticism, an 'art for art's sake' that expressed the essential beauty disfigured by an overly industrialized, prosaic world; or it stood for the kind of degenerate, animalistic decline into pure sensation (or worse) that the late Victorians so intensely feared.

The Early Twentieth Century: Liberal Humanism and the New Criticism

Romanticism cast a long shadow on nineteenth-century literature and culture, but this influence had less to do with the survival of Romantic writers' bodies of work intact, or according to success in their own time (Shelley's verse hardly sold at all, and Blake was virtually unknown in his own time) than with the cultural use to which specific aspects of their writings could be put. Early twentieth-century critics understood Romanticism in relationship to the Victorian, and Victorianized, version outlined above, which followed Arnold's 'premature' view of Romantic writers, but also his notion of the moral virtues that accompanied the reading and teaching of literature. This notion was indebted to Coleridge's idea, promoted in his *On the Constitution of Church and State* (1829), of the philosopher-as-cleric, who embodies the highest intellectual values of the nation for whom he speaks. What Coleridge outlined in theory Arnold put into practice through his prose, which models the civilizing and spiritual force of criticism as a disinterested endeavour to ascertain the 'best that has been thought and said' in the world. Such a notion of the criticism's vital cultural function, coinciding with Britain's so-called 'civilizing mission' around the globe, finds its most cogent articulation in Arnold's *Culture and Anarchy* (1869)[9], which argues for culture as a necessary inoculation against the forces of anarchy that threaten Empire. Ironically, the political imperative – and antagonisms – of this civilizing function is elided by putting 'and' rather than 'versus' between the title's two themes. Arnold felt that criticism should be above politics, *about* but not *of* the everyday, and further establishes the idea of an ahistorical, universal category of 'literature' defined by the discrimination of those works that best exemplify a civiliza-tion's (i.e. English civilization's) highest cultural achievements. This cultural 'common sense' derived from the German philosopher Immanuel Kant's earlier notion of a *sensus communis* of aesthetic taste as the highest expression of a community's and nation's progressive state.

Of course, who or what defines this standard – more importantly, what writers or ideas it excludes from its register – becomes highly problematic, an expression of other forms of 'discrimination' left relatively uncontested until the later twentieth century, as we shall see. With few exceptions, criticism about the Romantics in the early twentieth century reflected a very narrow canon: Wordsworth, Coleridge, Keats, Shelley, sometimes Byron, rarely Blake, Mary Shelley, but only because of the success of *Frankenstein*. Arthur O. Lovejoy crystallized the problem in his 1924 essay 'On the Discrimination of Romanticisms'[10]. Lovejoy's plural spelling suggested Romanticism's resistance to categorization, unlike the supposedly singular and coherent identity of Victorian literature, which relied on the fixity of a monarch's reign. In his 1912 essay 'Romanticism and Classicism'[11] the poet and critic T. E. Hulme pits the carefully delimited finitude of Classicism (tradition, organization, etc.) against the formless infinity of Romanticism, which he calls 'spilt religion'. Hulme, who otherwise notes the enduring qualities of a Romantic spirit, reiterates the more dangerous excesses of Romantic vision as a symbol of a world order about to break apart in his own time (Hulme died on the Belgian front in WWI). Picking up on Hulme's notion of a classic tradition, the critic T. S. Eliot, an early student of Irving Babbitt before transplanting himself on to English soil and author of the time's defining poem *The Wasteland*, argues for a selfless critical practice that would have little in common with the (supposedly) self-centred poetry of the Romantics or their immediate Victorian heirs[11]. Such a sense of literature, focused less on the author's personality than on the formal aesthetic and cultural qualities of the work itself, was important to establish the objective status of a critical tradition to which the greatest writers made the most vital contribution (ironically, this idea of criticism is profoundly indebted to Shelley's idea of poetry as one great 'mind' to which poets contribute their thoughts).

It is not difficult to see how these critics might have been cathecting on to Romanticism, a time of turbulent historical change, as we saw in chapter one, a threat of anarchy felt in their own time. Their thought and writings came to symbolize a liberal humanism that defined criticism for at least the first half of the twentieth century on both sides of the Atlantic, especially at the universities of Harvard, Oxford and Cambridge, and continues to exert a strong influence. In Britain this humanism was exemplified by the Cambridge critic F. R. Leavis, whose *The Great Tradition* (1948)[12] extended well into the twentieth century Arnold's notion of the ability of the essentially moral vision of great literature to shape in turn the sensibility of its readers. For Leavis as for Arnold, this morality was self-evident, which made criticism (i.e. critique) of its assumptions rather difficult. By focusing almost exclusively on Victorian fiction, a genre he read as carefully engaged in expressing the cultural and social organization of the nation, Leavis' notion of criticism implicitly devalued Romantic literature, which to that point was read exclusively with a focus on a Romantic poetry that Arnold devalued as a writing largely out of touch with its time, except for Wordsworth (though ironically, such distance was, for Arnold, a necessary quality of criticism itself).

Criticism's quality of being involved in the times only insofar as it could step outside history to see its participation in and reflection of more universal standards of taste and morality typified the work of what became known as the New Criticism. New Criticism came to prominence in the 1920s and 30s, exerting its most powerful influence on the American academy in the 1940s and 1950s. The term is associated with a body of writers – I. A. Richards, John Crowe Ransom, William Wimsatt, Monroe Beardsley and William Empson, among others – for whose work the term New Criticism is a broad generalization. Nonetheless, the New Criticism can be said to emphasize the formalist study of literature detached from its historical, biographical and sociopolitical context. In this sense it is the logical extension of Arnold's idea of criticism's essential and necessarily disinterested approach to literature in order to distill the universal from the particular or local, the eternal from the historical and the everyday.

Perhaps most exemplary of this approach was Cleanth Brooks' *The Well-Wrought Urn* (1948)[13], which takes its title from a phrase in Keats' 'Ode on a Grecian Urn', and uses that text's internal struggle with ambiguity and ambivalence as a signal of literature's ability to work out and work through its own internal contradictions. Like his colleagues, Brooks argues that literary interpretation must be divorced from the socio-historical or political context of the poem's making, and from what Wimsatt and Beardsley called the intentional and affective fallacies of reading the text in terms of the author's cathexis with his own time. Earl Wasserman's *The Subtler Language* (1959)[14] and later *Shelley: A Critical Reading* (1971)[15] stand as monuments of the kind of nuanced close readings New Criticism could distill from Romantic poems. Such documents exemplified the power of what was known as the 'hermeneutic circle' of criticism: the fact that the text's recurrent and often contradictory perspectives on its own meaning staged in turn the critic's struggle to negotiate to the core of the text's labyrinth in order to bring back to the reader the golden thread of an ultimately coherent interpretation that in turn reflected the text's singular, coherent meaning. Yet history enters in other ways, for Brooks' own analyses, by demonstrating literature's – i.e. poetry's – ability to work through internal dilemmas separate from history, in turn offered literature as a powerful model for how socio-historical circumstance could be at once transformed and transcended, and thus implicitly exemplified literature itself as a profound historical force. If Leavis' liberal humanism symbolized the need for literature to express a stable cultural order, especially between the two World Wars, which witnessed the prolonged waning of the British global dominance post-Victoria, the New Criticism expressed the same stability on behalf of an ascendant American imperialism, though not without its turbulent experience of economic and social instability in the 1930s, virulent patriotism in the 1940s and simultaneous post-WWII optimism and paranoia in the 1950s.

Such transformations were in many ways a reaction against the somewhat earlier anthropological and psychological temperament of what was known as 'myth and symbol' or archetypal criticism. Taking its cue from James Frazer's

The Golden Bough (1890), a key influence on the Modernist concern with myth and allegory (Yeats, Eliot, Joyce), works such as *Mythology and the Romantic Tradition in English Poetry* (1937)[16] by the Harvard critic Douglas Bush, or the Oxford scholar Maud Bodkin's *Archetypal Patters in Poetry: Psychological Studies of the Imagination* (1934)[17], the latter indebted to the archetypal psychology of Carl Jung (1875–1961), reached its epitome in the archetypal criticism of Northrop Frye at the University of Toronto. In 1947 Frye published *Fearful Symmetry*, which single-handedly revived the study of William Blake, mostly forgotten during the nineteenth century. Via Frye's inductive critical method, Blake's vision reiterates the Biblical narrative of creation/fall/resurrection, which itself maps the larger mythic patterns, mapping at once human and cosmic experience, of which literature is the pre-eminent expression. Frye thus also recuperates the visionary power of Romantic mythopoiesis long undervalued in the critical study of Romanticism. For Frye, the movement in Blake's corpus from early or minor vision to major prophecy exemplified Romanticism's creative ability to overcome the particularities of sociohistorical circumstance which, left unredeemed – as mere history – symbolized for Frye humanity's unregenerate tendency. Whereas the New Critical agenda focused on shorter poetical works in order better to demonstrate literature's textual efficiency in overcoming ambivalence and overdetermination, Frye's formalist analyses addressed all poetry and much prose – at least those parts of it 'worthy' of reading in Arnold's or Leavis' sense. His post-Aristotelian masterwork, *The Anatomy of Criticism* (1956)[19], showed how the corpus of literature rewrote large the body politic of everyday life by expressing its archetypal, universal or mythic patterns of organization – a narrative (re)organization of human experience that expressed, for Frye, the essentially narrative nature *of* human experience itself.

Frye's critical vision constitutes at once the apotheosis of New Criticism's aesthetic universalism and a mid-century resurgence in interest in the Romantic imagination. In 1946 Walter Jackson Bate published *From Classic to Romantic* (1946)[20], which saw the shift from the Enlightenment to Romanticism less as a breach than a failed evolution in subjective empiricism. Bate may have been responding directly to the New Humanism of Harvard critic Irving Babbitt in his *Rousseau and Romanticism* (1919)[21], which typified the early twentieth-century reaction against what it saw as Romantic excess and feeling. In *The Romantic Imagination* (1949)[22] the Oxford critic C. M. Bowra isolated the distinctive imaginative achievement of the Big Five (Blake, Wordsworth, Coleridge, Shelley, Keats) and read its future influence on a variety of Victorian writers from Poe to Christina Rossetti, but again as a failed experiment in vision. By the time of Harold Bloom's *The Visionary Company* (1979)[23] and M. H. Abrams's *Natural Supernaturalism* (1971)[24], however, the focus was on Romantic imaginative transcendence rather than failure. Again addressing the Big Five (Byron being, as Abrams notes, too 'ironic' to fit any visionary scheme), both critics, like Frye, saw in the fearless and revolutionary energy of the Romanticism imagination an inherent human capacity to transform the political, if not always to set aside history. Such critical visions expressed the seemingly endless optimism of 1950s and 1960s North American culture and its elevation of what Frye called the 'educated imagination', the pre-eminent training of which took place in the literature departments of Canadian and American universities. This was perhaps the heyday of humanities education and criticism, in many ways the fulfilment of Arnold's or Leavis' vision of the civilizing function of literature's moral imagination, whether this criticism denounced Romanticism's excess or praised its creative potentiality, depending upon the times in which critics were writing. That such a vision remained uncontested for such a long time is a testament to its cultural power. All that was about to change.

After the New Criticism: Poststructuralism and Deconstruction

It is difficult to underestimate the changes in Romantic criticism in the 1960s and 1970s. In 1979 Bloom contributed to the seminal collection, *Deconstruction and Criticism*, which brought together a group of critics associated with Yale University – Bloom, Geoffrey Hartman, J. Hillis Miller, Paul de Man and Jacques Derrida. Arguably the most influential of these was de Man, who had met Derrida at a legendary conference on structuralism at Johns Hopkins University in 1966, where Derrida delivered his seminal paper 'Structure, Sign, and Play in the Discourse of the Human Sciences', perhaps the most important document of what became known as poststructuralism. Emerging in the wake of two World Wars, structuralism sought to map the universal grammar articulating all discursive models (Frye's anatomy is characterized by such an effort). Driven by the spectres of global destruction and genocide on one hand and 1960s' political and cultural radicalism on the other, poststructuralism went even further by contesting the very truth-bearing and truth-granting strategies of any structuralist project. It thus called into question the entire metaphysical tradition of Western thought and philosophy since Plato and Aristotle, particularly its presumptions and assumptions about its own truth value. In the specific realm of literary criticism, this struggle took aim at the immanent moral knowledge of Arnold's or Leavis' great tradition.

Under the influence of poststructuralism, de Man's analyses of English and German Romantic literary and philosophical writings practised what became known as deconstruction, a term specifically (and reductively) assigned to a Yale 'Mafia' because of its traumatic and hegemonic affect on the humanities. For deconstructors, the same textual ambivalences and overdeterminations that were for New Criticism generative of literature's ability to transcend the vagaries of socio-historical circumstances signified instead how literature, like all language, betrayed its own latent *inability* to express a singular, coherent meaning. In *Deconstruction and Criticism* Hartman and Hillis Miller subjected Wordsworth's writings, otherwise the paradigm of Romantic vision, to deconstruction, while Derrida and de Man took aim at Shelley's unfinished manuscript, *The Triumph of Life*, as ' exemplary' of Romanticism's radical indeterminacy and temporality. Despite its undeniable critical power and subsequent effect on Romantic criticism, deconstruction was accused of being as apolitical and ahistorical as New Criticism because of its nearly exclusive focus on textual analysis. It is not without some irony that *Deconstruction and Criticism* appeared in the same year as *Natural Supernaturalism*, a coincidence that symbolizes a radical critical divide of the later twentieth century, the battleground of a culture war over the critical hegemony of the humanities, especially in the North American academy.

Yet arguably deconstruction, proceeding in the spirit of poststructuralism's desire to demystify the ideological, social and political strategies of any 'great tradition' of literature or thought, was merely facing up to more unsettling factors that had gone into that tradition's making. If deconstruction suggested a traumatic break with and undoing of the New Criticism, it was also a 'linguistic turn' of a different kind, this one with an increased attention to the structures and meanings of language as heterogeneous and in flux rather than universal. In Abrams' work, and especially in essays like Bloom's 'The Internalization of Quest-Romance' (1969) and Geoffrey Hartman's 'Romantic Consciousness and Self-Consciousness' (1970), one already got a sense that the Romantic turn inward in order to make sense of an increasingly complex external world was, at least implicitly, an anxious as well as a transformative gesture, both a retreat and necessary protection from the outside. This was partly to re-invoke the traps of solitude and solipsism of which Arnold had accused the Romantics in the first place, except that Hartman and Bloom sensed the darker valence of Romantic vision, an unconscious as well as a conscious critical *agon* that Bloom outlines in *The Anxiety of Influence* (1975), which radicalized Walter Jackson Bate's 1970 *The Burden of the Past*[25] (and thus took aim at Harvard's domination of Romantic criticism mid-century) by reading literary tradition as psychodrama, a vast struggle by emerging writers both to escape and to transcend the achievement of past writers. One of the most important studies to emerge in the wake of deconstruction's influence, Tilottama Rajan's *Dark Interpreter* (1980)[26], captured this indeterminacy as Romanticism's sense of 'restless self-examination' (25). By re-invoking the 'self' in Romanticism, a move that distinctly situated her work post-post-structuralism, yet by suggesting the overdetermined and unresolved as well cogently self-defining aspects of its identity, Rajan's study signals in Romantic studies this self's more complex relationship to the world of its making, and by which it is made in turn, a harbinger of other changes taking place in Romantic criticism.

New Historicism, Feminism, Postcolonialism

In the 1960s and 1970s the critical methodology of Victorian studies, guided by the example of Raymond Williams's *Culture and Society: 1780–1950* (1957)[27] and E. P. Thompson's *The Making of the English Working Classes* (1966)[28], was shifting from formalist analysis to Marxist cultural history. This approach interrogated the ideological assumptions of liberal humanism, particularly how its cultural order, central to the nation's education agenda, promulgated an abstract (and implicitly elitist) sense of the 'best that has been thought and said' in history. What history? Whose history? For instance, how had the working class been at once disciplined and effaced by such paradigms? This turn to history, informed by a Marxist analysis of ideology as a means of historical conditioning and mystification, made sense in the wake of the social disillusionments and deprivations of post-WWII Britain, which had helped to win the war but at the final cost of the nation's domestic prosperity and global influence. Williams' focus was on the seminal effect of the Industrial Revolution in promoting certain notions of 'culture' that orchestrated and thus managed changes in economic, social, and political life. Rather than the object of textual or aesthetic study, then, which tended to de-historicize and de-politicize literature's effect, literature became for Williams part of a broader cultural articulation. Yet within this process, Romanticism became a mere prelude to a broader Victorian civilizing program, rather than a moment of political, economic and social engagement profoundly determining what the Victorians were then in turn able to make of literature.

Marilyn Butler's *Jane Austen and the War of Ideas* (1975)[29] made two essential responses to this sidestepped Romanticism. First, by reconsidering the historical significance of Austen's novels, which were previously treated as a high aesthetic achievement separate from the historical context of their making and mostly left out of the Romantic canon, Butler asked us to rethink what we thought of as 'Romantic'. Second, she re-addressed the far more vibrant, embattled and diverse political context of Romantic writing itself than had hitherto been considered. Butler's subsequent *Romantics, Rebels and Reactionaries* (1982)[30] extended this analysis to a broader cast of Romantic writers – Godwin, Burke, Radcliffe, Scott and Edgeworth, among others. Moreover, by extending Romanticism's historical range back to 1760, Butler reversed the tendency to condense its achievement to the canon of six male poets and to the limited timeframe of 1789 or 1798 to the 1820s. She placed special emphasis on the galvanizing effects of 1790s politics, and in general addressed how literature was forged from, and reflected back to its readers, a heterogeneous historical and political context: the American and French Revolutions, the Napoleonic Wars and a host of social, economic and cultural factors. Rather than search for a coherent Romantic identity – which in the past required overlooking Romanticism's volatile history – Butler painted a rather more nuanced view of Romantic identity as being at once revolutionary and reactionary, Whig and Tory, radical and conservative. This historical identity, to borrow Rajan's phrase again, restlessly self-examining itself and thus historically aware of its own generation, was one that knew itself to be contradictory and various. That is to say, Butler, like Rajan, demonstrated how Romanticism's search for itself was its defining socio-historical and aesthetic quality, rather than a sign of an implicit failure for which Victorian or post-Victorian critics needed to compensate.

Back in North America, a similar turn to history, exemplified in early modern studies by the work of Stephen Greenblatt, was signalled by Jerome McGann's *The Romantic Ideology* (1983)[31]. Greenblatt had redeployed deconstruction's hermeneutic of suspicion from its somewhat exclusive focus on texts themselves in order to read history-as-text, or history through its texts, especially at a moment in the advent of modernity when the issue of 'representation', in all senses of this word, was becoming central to human endeavour and thought. Put another way, New Historicism took deconstruction's 'linguistic turn' to heart to read language as both historically determined and determining. In this way McGann followed Greenblatt's model of suspecting all modes of historical representation (and thus reading historical documents as intentional rather than determinate structures of meaning, in the mode of poststructuralism) by taking issue with criticism's unreflective assumption of Romanticism's self-representations as the only way to read Romantic literature. For McGann such assumptions were entrenched in the central texts of both the English and German Romantic traditions, specifically those that addressed poetry's expression of a higher cultural-cum-spiritual power (i.e. one that removed literature above politics, unlike the novel). Although McGann considered Wordsworth, Coleridge, and Shelley in depth, it was thus his return to Byron that registered most (McGann is arguably the most important modern editor of Byron's works). Byron's ironic voice, questionable morality and contentious politics marked him as significantly different from his contemporaries, which is why he did not fit prevailing models of the Romantic ethos, like that of Abrams.

Hence, as McGann's study suggests, Byron becomes symptomatic of all those writers, like those Butler takes up, who were profoundly influential in shaping Romanticism's literary, critical and political imagination, yet had been set aside according to, once again, a specific ideology that had become ossified throughout the history of Romantic criticism. McGann's argument for the exchange between texts and contexts resembled Butler's approach, but was more New Historical and more overtly polemical. McGann's work was itself reacting to deconstruction and the polemicism of responses to it. At least by the time of Butler's work, this influence had largely bypassed the British academy, which tended to favour the kinds of empiricist and historical validations offered by something like the materialist practice of Williams's cultural history, and thus tended to suspect the often overtly theoretical and speculative cast of much North American Romantic criticism. (To this end, Butler does not so much revise as reclaim history, albeit to powerful effect.) Ironically, McGann underplayed the very hermeneutics of suspicion that made his own criticism possible, though by taking aim at deconstruction's supposedly apolitical and ahistorical temperament, he marks how the project of historical reclamation *and* revision was only just getting underway.

Arguably the single greatest impact on this revisionary process in Romantic criticism has been feminism. Contemporary feminist theory had been gaining ground at least since Simone de Beauvoir's *The Second Sex* (1949)[32], and emerged with powerful cultural force in the 1960s and 1970s. Written in the wake of this 'revolution', Elaine Showalter's *A Room of Their Own* (1977)[33] and Sandra M. Gilbert and Susan Gubar's *The Madwoman in the Attic* (1979)[34] demonstrated how neither the personal or the political, sexuality or textuality, could be separated from one another. Such changes had been a long time coming, at least since Mary Wollstonecraft's *A Vindication of the Rights of Woman* (1792), arguably the ur-text of feminism itself. Of course, how Wollstonecraft had been immediately vilified by reading her personal life in terms of her radical political, gender and sexual beliefs set the subsequent pattern for reducing women's writing to women's bodies (not to mention for forgetting Wollstonecraft in histories of women's writing). Women could only refract experience through their feelings or personal observations, without, like their male counterparts, an ability to transcend the personal into the universal. In *A Room of One's Own* (1929), from which Showalter derives her title, Virginia Woolf had turned the tables on such views in the early twentieth century by locating the observation of the world as the basis of a profound rearticulation of experience of which women need not be ashamed (after all, observation itself was, at least since Francis Bacon in the sixteenth century, the hallmark of the scientific revolution that produced the enlightenment and its aftermaths in the first place). But it was not until the political and social upheavals of post-WWII North America and Europe that feminism emerged as a critical force urging the reconsideration of all prevailing paradigms – a profound refusal to accept 'the given'. Concurrent with this renascence began the reclamation of women writers, or writers previously minoritized (and thus implicitly 'feminized'), by the (now not-so-)great tradition of largely white, male writers.

Showalter addressed only Victorian and post-Victorian women novelists, and Gilbert and Gubar start with only Austen and Mary Shelley from the Romantic period before moving on to the Victorians. Like the silenced and colonized figure of Bertha Mason in Bronte's *Jane Eyre*, from which Gilbert and Gubar derive their title, the effect, however unintentional, was to ghettoize Victorian from Romantic women writers. Combining feminist and Marxist theory, Mary Poovey's *The Proper Lady and the Woman Writer* (1984)[35] redresses this gap by examining how Mary Wollstonecraft, Mary Shelley and Jane Austen adapted their creative power to the late eighteenth- and early nineteenth-century paradigm of feminine propriety. Taking up Romantic poetic tradition, Marlon Ross' *The Contours of Masculine Desire* (1989)[36] then examines the role gender played in the writing, reading, publishing and reviewing of the Romantic period. Against literature's otherwise masculinist endeavour, Ross deploys a feminine poetic tradition that extends back to 1730 and forward to address how such genderings have determined current public tastes. Anne Mellor's *Romanticism and Gender* (1993)[37] distinguishes 'masculine' and 'feminine' Romanticisms, but in doing so exemplifies an implicit 're-essentialization' of gender categories. Nonetheless, all three articulate a cross-dressing, revisionary social and cultural history that instituted at last the reclamation of women Romantic writers. This reclamation remains unabated in Romantic criticism, and has produced re-examinations of the broader role sexuality played, and how sexuality played out, in the Romantic period, such as Eve Kosoksy Sedgewick's *Between Men* (1985)[38] and Andrew Elfenbein's *Romantic Genius: The Prehistory of a Homosexual Role* (1999)[39].

The focus on reclaiming lost aspects of British culture at home begs the question of what further exclusions this culture perpetrated. That Bertha Mason, Rochester's Creole wife, is transported back from the British colonies and locked in an attic, is nearly entirely effaced from Bronte's novel means that class and gender are not the only crucibles of an earlier criticism. In Romantic writing, the sudden appearance of a Malay at De Quincey's English cottage door in *Confessions of an English Opium-Eater* stages the Empire's stark confrontation with its own colonial – and colonized – other. Such encounters are focal points for the critical analyses of postcolonial studies, which examine subjects and subjectivities dispossessed by imperial power and imagination, just as Marxism examines class imbalances and feminism examines gender inequities. Postcolonialism takes its cue from such influential works as Edward Said's *Orientalism* (1978)[40], Gayatri Spivak's *In Other Worlds* (1987)[41] or Homi K. Bhabha's *The Location of Culture* (1994)[42], which examine the racial and ethnic biases of Western thought for its academic and sociopolitical inability to entertain the political, historical and economic mobility of culture(s), and so to give voice to those silenced by such ethnocentrism.

British Romanticism is a particularly fertile ground for such analyses because the Romantic period falls in the indeterminate and radically shifting historical ground between the first and second British Empires, which we outlined in chapter one. If Marxist- or feminist-influenced Romantic criticism explores the complex networks of discursive power that expressed and sustained Britain's national and domestic stability, postcolonialism expands this study to include not only race and ethnicity but also to suggest the broader global scope of British influence and how Romantic literature and culture at once expressed and challenged the ideological sway of this influence. Nigel Leask's *British Romantic Writers and the East: Anxieties of Empire* (1992)[43], for instance, examines Romantic responses to the East as the site of the Empire's anxious negotiation of its own national and domestic identity. Saree Makdisi's *Romantic Imperialism: Universal Empire and the Culture of Modernity* (1998)[44] argues how all aspects of the Empire, not only British, wrote both home to British subjects and among its colonial subjects as a complex negotiation of global identity not unlike our current emergent global modernity. Such works are only beginning to give us a sense of the fraught terrain of Romantic-era culture and history, and of the way in which the hegemonic discursive power of all regimes – economic, political, social, cultural – depends intimately and problematically on those forces it subdues and by which it is constantly challenged.

Cultural Studies and Beyond

The above survey by no means does full justice to the full scope of the development of Romantic criticism since the early nineteenth century. Nor can we survey fully the critical landscape that has resulted from such an evolution, though the remaining chapters in this guide map many of its essential reference points. The shifts in Romantic criticism since the 1960s and 1970s have been, as we suggested above, monumental. The evolution of cultural materialist and (new) historicist practice, in the wake of deconstruction and poststructuralism, has produced a diverse array of cross-fertilized critical methodologies that, like the 'linguistic turn' of the 1970s, can now be called the 'cultural turn' of our current critical situation. Such a turn began some time ago under the influence of the Birmingham School of Cultural Studies, in turn influenced by the work of Raymond Williams, or the Frankfurt School of Critical Studies (which is not to suggest the two have always been in dialogue with one another). Nonetheless, this cultural turn is making ever clearer to us the rich diversity of Romantic literature, thought and culture. Indeed, the very idea of a modern information economy that emerged in the eighteenth century and underwent such profound changes in the Romantic era has produced a kind of archive fever to reclaim as much of Romanticism's past as we can possibly document. Not only the expansion of the Romantic canon but the ever-expanding inclusion of all aspects of Romantic culture are now subject to our critical scrutiny: literature, animals, theatre programs, shopping, inventions, telepathy – the list seems endless. This increasingly detailed, descriptively dense picture of the Romantic idiom signals the importance of historical and material practice within Romantic criticism itself by situating all Romantic subjects' engagement in the social networks and cultural politics of Romantic everyday life.

One of the most significant works to emerge in the wake of New Historicism in Romantic criticism was Jon Klancher's *The Making of English Reading Audiences, 1790–1832* (1987)[45]. Klancher's study signalled a shift to a more multi-valenced historical examination of Romantic public life based on who wielded access to its various networks of communication, print culture in all its forms signifying a central matrix for this communication. Influenced by the work of the Frankfurt School theorist Jürgen Habermas, such work reads the social and cultural politics of Romantic everyday life as the dialogue between a private sphere of personal, communal or familial communication and a public sphere of 'official' discourses. Neither takes precedence over the other. Instead, both wage at once an antagonistic and productive negotiation for discursive power, exemplified in such recent studies as Kevin Gilmartin's *Print Politics: The Press and Radical Opposition in Early Nineteenth-Century England* (1997)[46] and William St Clair's *The Reading Nation in the Romantic Period* (2007)[47]. As Romantic critics gain a sense of, and access to, an ever-widening archive of Romantic print culture (magazines, newspapers, reviews, etc.), as this culture becomes more accessible through the digitization of published and previously unpublished print resources, we realize that our examination of Romanticism's influence, so exhaustively and variously covered over the past two centuries, has only just begun. One important result of this cultural materialism has been Ecocriticism, which reads Romanticism's supposedly philosophical or aesthetic view of nature, not as a retreat from the world of 'real' concern, but rather as an intense sociopolitical engagement with the fate of the planet. Jonathan Bate's *Romantic Ecology: Wordsworth and the Environmental Tradition* (1991)[48] and James McKusick's *Green Writing: Romanticism and Ecology* (2000)[49] mapped out in Romantic poetry the emerging paradigm for modern ecology and ecological understanding. Timothy Morton's *Ecology Without Nature: Rethinking Environmental Aesthetics* (2007)[50] challenges such work by suggesting that it relies, once again, on a Romantic ideology *of* nature, one that abstracts it as an essentially reparative or nurturing force. Only by understanding Romanticism's profound respect for a nature at once benign and 'red in tooth and claw', to borrow Tennyson's phrase, will we be able actively to move forward to solve the problems confronting the environment.

A final word about the professionalization of Romantic criticism. The second half of the twentieth century, partly as a fulfilment of the intellectual and cultural promise of liberal humanism, witnessed the institutionalization of Romantic Studies as a separate field of study in English and Humanities undergraduate and graduate programs. This identity has been supported through the scholarly influence of journals such as *Studies in Romanticism, The Wordsworth Circle, Romantic Circles, European Romantic Review* in North America and *Romanticism* in the United Kingdom, or through online journals such as *Romantic Circles, Literature Compass* (which devotes a separate section to Romantic Studies), or *Romanticism and Victorianism on the Net*, whose reach is global. The professional profile of Romantic Studies has been further extended through scholarly groups like the Keats-Shelley Association in North America (which publishes the *Keats-Shelley Journal*) or the Wordsworth-Coleridge Association (affiliated with *The Wordsworth Circle*) in the United Kingdom, or through larger academic organizations like the North American Society for the Study of Romanticism and the British Association of Romantic Studies. The emergence of the latter in particular has signalled the broadly international reach of Romantic Studies: both host annual or biannual conferences, are affiliated with journals that publish annual conference issues (NASSR with *ERR*, BARS with *Romanticism*) and frequently host allied organized sessions at other international conferences such as the Modern Language Association. Increasingly these organizations are establishing ties with other Romantics organizations in Italy, Germany and Japan, among other countries. Such connections are the inevitable and productive result of our increasingly diversified picture of Romanticism's multi-national contexts: the fact that it emerged in different locations in different ways and at different times. We have thus also only just begun to appreciate Romantic's international, global history as a way of reflecting upon our own increasingly globalized present.

That the above journals and organizations bring together both past, present and emerging critical methodologies in Romantic Studies makes them a sometimes vexed academic terrain, often mistakenly associating various too-theoretical or too-historical scholarships with various national (and nationalist) locales. Such struggles coincide with on-going debate about the historical, national and cultural parameters of Romanticism itself. The more broadly we define Romanticism and the Romantic period, the more we risk watering down the distinctive character of Romantic Studies. With increasing economic and social pressures on the very universities and colleges within which Romantic Studies came to institutional prominence, some see the writing on the wall for Romantic Studies. Some say this is as it should be: such cultural designations are too hegemonic and restrictive. Others bemoan this possible future: Romantic Studies having developed such a historically and theoretically diverse body of scholarly knowledge, it would be a tragedy to lose the very sense of cultural 'discrimination' that makes the further enrichment of this corpus possible. Either way, we *can* say with some certainty that such struggles, anxieties and possibilities remain profoundly reminiscent of the same period to which they address themselves. How will Romantic criticism evolve into the twenty-first century? Answering this question requires a crystal ball, though we can be certain, as Shelley reminded us, that Romanticism itself will continue to cast its shadows upon us from this future.

See also: Case Studies in Reading Critical Texts; Canonicity

Notes

1 Wordsworth, William, Preface to *Lyrical Ballads*,
2 De Quincey, Thomas, *Confessions of an English Opium-Eater*, ed. Joel Faflak, Peterborough: Broadview Press, 2009.
3 Shelley, Percy Bysshe, 'A Defence of Poetry', in *Shelley's Poetry and Prose*, 2nd ed., eds Donald H. Reiman and Neil Fraistat, New York: Norton, 2002, pp. 509–538.
4 Browning, Robert, 'Essay on Shelley', *The Poems, Volume I*, ed. John Pettigrew, supp. and comp. Thomas J. Collins. New York: Penguin, 1981, pp. ??.
5 Carlyle, Thomas, *Sartor Resartus*, eds Kerry McSweeney and Peter Sabor, London: Oxford University Press, 1987.
6 Arnold, Matthew, 'The Function of Criticism at the Present Time', in *Poetry and Criticism of Matthew Arnold*, ed. A. Dwight Culler, Boston: Houghton Mifflin, 1961, pp. 237–58.
7 Fox, William Johnson, Review of *Poems, Chiefly Lyrical [1830]*, in *Tennyson: The Critical Heritage*, ed. John D. Jump, London: Routledge & Kegan Paul, 1967, pp. 20–24.
7 Hallam, A. H., *Review of Poems, Chiefly Lyrical [1830]*, in *Tennyson: The Critical Heritage*, pp. 42–43.
8 Bagehot, Walter, 'Wordsworth, Tennyson, and Browning; or, Pure, Ornate, and Grotesque Art in English Poetry', in *The Collected Works of Walter Bagehot*, ed. Norman St. John-Stevas, 8 vols., Cambridge, MA.: Harvard Univ. Press, 1965, Vol. 2, pp. 365–67.
9 Arnold, Matthew, *Culture and Anarchy*, ed. Jane Garnett, London: Oxford University Press, 2006.
10 Lovejoy, Arthur O., 'On the Discrimination of Romanticisms', *Publications of the Modern Language Association* 39 (1924), 229–53.
11 Eliot, T. S., from *The Use of Poetry and the Use of Criticism* (1933), in *Selected Prose of T. S. Eliot*, ed. Frank Kermode, London: Faber and Faber, 1975, pp. 79–96.
11 Hulme, T. E., 'Romanticism and Classicism', *The Collected Writings of T. E. Hulme*, ed. Karen Csengeri, Oxford: Clarendon Press, 1994, pp. 59–73.
12 Leavis, F. R., *The Great Tradition*, London: Chatto and Windus, 1948.
13 Brooks, Cleanth, *The Well Wrought Urn: Studies in the Structure of Poetry*, New York: Harcourt, Brace, 1947.
14 Wasserman, Earl, *The Subtler Language: Critical Readings of Neoclassic and Romantic Poems*, Baltimore: Johns Hopkins University Press, 1959.
15 Wasserman, Earl, *Shelley: A Critical Reading*, Baltimore: Johns Hopkins University Press, 1971.

16 Bush, Douglas, *Mythology and the Romantic Tradition in English Poetry*, Cambridge, MA: Harvard University Press, 1937.

17 Bodkin, Maud, *Archetypal Patterns in Poetry: Psychological Studies of Imagination*, London: Oxford University Press, 1934.

18 Frye, Northrop, *Fearful Symmetry: A Study of William Blake*, Princeton: Princeton University Press, 1947.

19 Frye, Northrop, *The Anatomy of Criticism: Four Essays*, Princeton: Princeton University Press, 1957.

20 Bate, Walter Jackson, *From Classic to Romantic: Premises of Taste in Eighteenth-Century England*, New York: Harper, 1970.

21 Babbitt, Irving, *Rousseau and Romanticism*, New York: Houghton Mifflin, 1919.

22 Bowra, C. M., *The Romantic Imagination*, Cambridge, MA: Harvard University Press, 1949.

23 Bloom, Harold, et al, *Deconstruction and Criticism*, New York: Continuum, 1979.

24 Abrams, M. H., *Natural Supernaturalism: Tradition and Revolution in Romantic Literature*, New York: Norton, 1971.

25 Bate, Walter Jackson, *The Burden of the Past and the English Poet*, Cambridge, MA: Belknap Press, 1970.

25 Hartman, Geoffrey H., 'Romanticism and Anti-Self-Consciousness', in *Beyond Formalism: Literary Essays 1958–1970*, New Haven: Yale University Press, 1970, pp. 298–310.

26 Rajan, Tilottama, *Dark Interpreter: The Discourse of Romanticism*. Ithaca: Cornell University Press, 1980.

27 Williams, Raymond, *Culture and Society: Coleridge to Orwell*, London: The Hogarth Press, 1987.

28 Thompson, E. P., *The Making of the English Working Classes*, New York: Vintage, 1966.

29 Butler, Marilyn, *Jane Austen and the War of Ideas*, Oxford: Clarendon Press, 1975.

30 Butler, Marilyn, *Romantics, Rebels, and Reactionaries: English Literature and Its Background, 1760–1830*, New York: Oxford University Press, 1981.

31 McGann, Jerome, *The Romantic Ideology: A Critical Investigation*, Chicago: University of Chicago Press, 1983.

32 De Beauvoir, Simone, *The Second Sex*, trans. Constance Borde, ed. Sheila Malovany-Chevallier, New York: Alfred A. Knopf, 2010.

33 Showalter, Elaine, *A Literature of Their Own: British Woman Novelists from Brönte to Lessing*, Princeton: Princeton University Press, 1977.

34 Gilbert, Sandra M. and Gubar, Susan, *The Madwoman in the Attic: The Woman Writer and the Nineteenth-Century Literary Imagination*, New Haven: Yale University Press, 1979.

35 Poovey, Mary, *The Proper Lady and the Woman Writer: Ideology as Style in the Works of Mary Wollstonecraft, Mary Shelley, and Jane Austen*, Chicago: Chicago University Press, 1984.

36 Ross, Marlon, *The Contours of Masculine Desire: Romanticism and the Rise of Women's Poetry*, New York: Oxford University Press, 1989.

37 Mellor, Anne K., *Gender and Romanticism*, London: Routledge, 1993.

38 Sedgwick, Eve Kofosky, *Between Men: English Literature and Male Homosocial Desire*, New York: Columbia University Press, 1985.

39 Elfenbein, Andrew, Romantic Genius: *The Prehistory of a Homosexual Role*, New York: Columbia University Press, 1999.

40 Said, Edward W., *Orientalism*, New York: Pantheon, 1978.

41 Spivak, Gayatri Chakravorty, *In Other Worlds: Essays in Cultural Politics*, New York: Methuen, 1987.

42 Bhabha, Homi K., *The Location of Culture*, New York: Routledge, 1994.

43 Leask, Nigel, *British Romantic Writers and the East: Anxieties of Empire*, Cambridge: Cambridge University Press, 1992.

44 Makdisi, Saree, *Romantic Imperialism: Universal Empire and the Culture of Modernity*, Cambridge: Cambridge University Press, 1998.

45 Klancher, Jon, *The Making of English Reading Audiences, 1790–1832*, Madison: University of Wisconsin Press, 1987.

46 Gilmartin, Kevin, *Print Politics: The Press and Radical Opposition in Early Nineteenth-Century England*, Cambridge: Cambridge University Press, 1997.

47 St Clair, William, *The Reading Nation in the Romantic Period*, Cambridge: Cambridge University Press, 2007.

48 Bate, Jonathan, *Romantic Ecology: Wordsworth and the Environmentalist Tradition*, New York: Routledge, 1991.

49 McKusick, James, *Green Writing: Romanticism and Ecology*, New York: St. Martin's Press, 2000.

50 Morton, Timothy, *Ecology Without Nature: Rethinking Environmental Aesthetics*, Harvard: Harvard University Press, 2007.

7 Canonicity

Simon Kövesi

Chapter Overview

Booklists, Must-reads, Classics and Canons: Man-made Literature

It might not seem worth pointing out that the study of literature is entirely man-made. Yet so naturalized and pervasive do certain texts, authors, literary movements and literary subjects become that sometimes we have to make a special effort to remind ourselves that books do not grow on trees. Objects of widespread cultural fascination are only around because of us and the critical legacies of our forebears. Rarely, if ever, are works of literature regarded as 'classics' *now* because they were treated instantly on publication as 'works for all time'. More often, texts achieve an elevated status because subsequent generations decided to return to them again and again, and often for differing purposes, for separate qualities the text is seen to deliver. This chapter considers some of the forces that shaped the process of canon formation in the Romantic period (and the critical texts that contributed to that process), but it also examines the notion of 'canonicity' itself more broadly and invites students to consider and possibly challenge some of the critical assumptions that might have shaped their own learning experience as undergraduates.

As a means of encountering *critically* the question of canon formation, and of challenging the notion that a 'classic' has always been a 'classic', consider the reception and sales which John Keats and Percy Shelley experienced while still alive. Regardless of the fact that many of their literary friends thought they were brilliant talents, both sparked mostly venomous rejection in the reviewing press and indifference in terms of the market. While they were alive and publishing poetry, they seemed as unlikely to succeed as anyone else; indeed by most measures, they were markedly unsuccessful. Posthumously however, in the late Victorian period, both became boy-gods, perfect poetic creatures of sensuousness and purity of feeling. Shelley, effectively kicked out of University College, Oxford, for publishing a pamphlet called *The Necessity of Atheism* (1811), was eventually re-accommodated into the late-Victorian establishment. This accommodation is signalled most gloriously by the memorial statue of 1893 which embodies the poet as a washed-up supine corpse, alabaster white and unthreatening in his coldly de-politicized detumescence. The statue still lies in the college which turfed him out in 1811, and its flaccid form ignores how important Shelley's upright, hot political work became for the reformist and Chartist movements in the 1830s and beyond. Like many Romantics, Keats and Shelley took comfort in the idea that though they might be largely ignored by their peers, succeeding generations might make their work 'eternal' – by which they meant their work would continue to be read, and begin to wield influence. Unlike most Romantic poets whose eventual lot was obscurity, this pair turned out to be right to trust in posthumous fame. Eventually, their poetry was as lucky after their deaths as it was unlucky in life.

The texts that literary history and its engines of critical enquiry choose to focus upon and study – and the motivation driving those choices – follow broad patterns of human behaviour and interest: belief, desire, aspiration, politics, experience and, inevitably, prejudice. When it comes to the activation of that study and commentary in print, relations necessarily open up between literary and academic practice and publishers in the capital-driven world of business. Every book-based text we read (including this one) has, at some point in its history, a material relation not just to lives of the authors, but also to money, to markets and to cultural, political and industrial power. Any publication is the product of a whole host of latent extrinsic forces, many of which bear no direct relation to the writer's intentions, nor are they in anyway under the control of, the original writer. All published texts are social.

Thus if we conceive of a fixed 'canon' of approved texts, of the 'great works', or the 'classics', we do so because this is an edifice wrought by man (and historically, *male man*kind more often than not). Literary study and critical commentary are inherently shaped and implemented by – and through – people and their institutions of considerable power: institutions of education, libraries, booksellers, publishers, reviewers, school curriculum managers, film and television production companies, churches and political establishments. All will have some influence on the books in print, publications you gain access to, the texts you are pressured or 'required' to read, and so on. This is never clearer than in education, where your teachers, tutors, lecturers will all choose a set of texts for you to read: experts will guide you along a chosen path of literary excellence, which has to be bookended by practicality and the time-limits of a term, semester or academic year. But should we all study the same things?

No matter what their political persuasion, critics can be very prescriptive about what we should and should not read – indeed, some consider it their job to do so (you should ask your tutors and lecturers why a certain text was chosen to be on your Romanticism course: the response will always be interesting.) Creative writers can be just as prescriptive. Here is an extract from the preface to Charles Burton's long poem of 1823 – a sort of state-of-the-poetic-nation address – which clearly places itself in a tradition of poems which discuss and frame the literary pantheon in calling itself *The Bardiad*: 'The object of the "Dunciad,"' says Burton 'was to satirize *dullness*; that of the "Bardiad" is to commemorate genius, and to stigmatize its awful aberrations.' (Burton, 1823, pp. xii–xiii; Burton's emphasis). Burton exemplifies the problems confronting the poet, critic or academic wishing to represent, characterize or anthologize the literary world:

> Many, especially modern, Poets, will not be found in the following sketches. This, however, does not arise from invidious distinction; but from the fact that, of many authors, brilliant in talent, and superior in merit, numbers must ever remain disregarded; and that the estimate of their deservings would be too hazardous, at least, for the present. The *apotheosis* of a character is the work of a century; and even the estimate of genius should pass seven times through the furnace of criticism, before it can appear without dross and alloy. (Burton, 1823, pp. iv–v; Burton's emphasis)

Evidently Burton does not feel so firm in his judgements of his contemporaries: of the past, by contrast, he feels pretty certain. There will be exclusions for practical reasons – 'numbers must ever remain disregarded', says Burton; there are so many writers out there, who could possibly discuss them all? This is a pragmatic question that contemporary anthologizers of the Romantic period (and designers of your undergraduate curriculum) always face: how it is answered has a huge influence on the canon, and on what students study at university.

Readers of this book are unlikely to be familiar with Burton. His poem did not get picked up in many places, and he was all but ignored by the 'furnace of criticism' even though this poem went through two quick editions: in other words, though his work sold well, Burton never made it into the canon of established texts and subsequent generations of poets and critics simply did not pick him up. But Burton's choices are nevertheless interesting because they attest to a system of literary value which the builders of the twentieth-century canon of Romantic male poets, for example, clearly did *not* buy into; Burton excoriates Shelley and Byron, two poets who were to become central to the romantic canon in later years, and in so doing Burton celebrates the objectivity of his own judgement. 'The author' writes Burton of himself, 'knows that he stands upon the platform of Truth and Virtue' (Burton, p. v) and it is from his very solid platform of 'Truth and Virtue', that he writes confidently of our now canonical poets Byron, first, then Percy Shelley:

> Sad prostituted Genius! fit, alone,
> In some foul planet to erect his throne,
> Such as He best describes; some orb of fire,
> Where all, but beams of wretchedness, expire;
> The burning wreck of some demolish'd sphere,
> A *'wand'ring hell'* that wheels it's high career.
> His Alpine genius, towering, – varied, – bold, –
> *Sublime* in Fancy, as in Virtue *cold*,
> Like a fell Avalanche, comes wasting down
> On Piety's warm plain. Still worse the frown
> Of kindred Shelley on fair Mercy's reign.
> O! *righteous* GOD! how *long* wilt thou refrain?
>
>   Angel of verse! assert thy *sacred* cause!
> Maintain thy good, thy venerable laws!
> Summon thy *chaste*, thy *well-affected* train,
> And bid them sing of Piety again!
> In vain shall then the too-voluptuous Muse,
> With syren melodies, her victims choose;
> Or Byron laud his deeds of crimson dye,
> Sing meretricious love and chivalry;
> Or baser Shelley, on the gates of hell,
> With reckless vaunt impinge his sceptic shell.
>   (Burton, 1823, pp. 48–50)

Not only does Burton not want anyone to read either of these 'prostituted' talents ever again, he enjoys imagining them being punished in the orthodox hell that neither of them fully believed in. As with many of his contemporaries, the pious orthodox Christian in Burton wrestles with his poet-critic's appreciation of literary 'genius': small wonder then that he implicitly re-stages the conflicts in *Manfred* between the orthodox Abbot and the wilful brilliance of the self-determining Manfred. But unlike the close of Byron's play where Manfred neither gets dragged to hell nor allows the influence (nor the existence) of orthodox spirituality, in Burton's world of Christian moral certainties, the pair of atheistical poet anti-heroes are condemned, for eternity. And Burton – a graduate of the universities of Glasgow, Oxford and Cambridge, and, by 1823, an Anglican Minister based in Manchester – clearly approves.

In determining which writers we should read and which should be condemned to hell – in other words, in building a canon of brilliant writers and excluding others – Burton was following not only Alexander Pope's *Dunciad* (various versions published between 1728 and 1743), but Pope's biggest fan in the Romantic period, Byron himself. Many Romantic writers were as prescriptive as Burton and made it quite clear what they thought valuable, and what they did not: but their values and tastes diverged markedly from Burton's. Here, then, we encounter the instability of Romantic canonicity in its earliest stages. Byron's first major poem *English Bards and Scotch Reviewers* (1809) formed an excoriating attack on many of his poetic peers: it also listed those poets who he felt should be paid more attention. He came to regret much of this youthful arrogance, and his early attempt to steer and formulate critical taste: as William St Clair puts it, by 1812 'he realised he had been unfair to many writers who were now his friends' (St Clair, 2004, p. 163). But *English Bards* should not be dismissed as a work of hot-blooded juvenilia: it has serious intentions in that the author is evidently concerned that so much of what passes for poetry in his day is simply not worthwhile, and not worthy of Byron's sense of 'tradition'. Wordsworth – who came to be one of Byron's favourite whipping boys in later poems – does a similar thing in the Preface to the second edition of the *Lyrical Ballads* (1800). In castigating literature which appeals to gross sensuality, he is trying to re-form the literary taste of his day such that his *own* chosen path is rendered more valuable precisely because it is distinct from what Wordsworth sees as hack-writing and conventional, formulaic dross.

After the Romantic period, many others tried to form and guide literary taste, and thus the canon, in a similar fashion. For example, we might turn to John Ruskin (1819–1900), a hugely influential critic of art and culture. The following passage is typical of a highly confident Victorian mode of judging what is, and what is not, the 'best' literature to read. Students beware:

> The worst danger by far, to which a solitary student is exposed, is that of liking things that he should not. It is not so much his difficulties, as his tastes, which he must set himself to conquer...the more you can restrain your serious reading to reflective or lyric poetry, history, and natural history, avoiding fiction and the drama, the healthier your

mind will become. Of modern poetry keep to Scott, Wordsworth, Keats, Crabbe, Tennyson, the two Brownings, Lowell, Longfellow, and Coventry Patmore, whose 'Angel in the House' is a most finished piece of writing, and the sweetest analysis we possess of quiet modern domestic feeling; while Mrs. Browning's 'Aurora Leigh' is, as far as I know, the greatest poem which the century has produced in any language. Cast Coleridge at once aside, as sickly and useless; and Shelley, as shallow and verbose; Byron, until your taste is fully formed, and you are able to discern the magnificence in him from the wrong. Never read bad or common poetry, nor write any poetry yourself; there is, perhaps, rather too much than too little in the world already. (Ruskin, 1858, pp. 221 and 232)

In 1858, Ruskin delivers a 'safe' English-speaking canon of 'modern poetry'. It is mostly, but not exclusively, male. Dismissing novels and plays entirely, Ruskin maintains the Romantic period's elevated regard for poetry above all other written forms because it will lead to a 'healthier mind' in the student. Ruskin internationalizes his list with the American poets James Russell Lowell and Henry Wadsworth Longfellow, and while Walter Scott, Wordsworth (William – not Dorothy) and Keats are safe, Coleridge, Shelley (Percy – not Mary) and Byron are pretty much to be avoided. We could consider the wealth of exclusions here: the myriad poets of the Romantic period not mentioned and the numerous novelists and dramatists too. But there is not really any qualitative analysis to engage with: like so many builders of 'taste', Ruskin offers no tangible evidence in support of his bold, bald, assertions. The student is to rely on the superior intellect of Ruskin: this assertive critical mode does not expect questions or resistance. If readers' personal 'taste' baulks at the plate they are being served, well then it is their job to 'conquer' that puerile reaction. Ruskin's critical mode, moreover, effaces its implication in the material class-based and imperialist politics of the moment as is apparent when we consider the relation between canon-formation and nation-building.

Canons Defending the Borders: National Bards

Literary traditions tend to be grouped around national cultures, and the loose affiliation between nations and their languages. So, we talk of the 'British Romantic Canon' if we want to include Scottish, Welsh and Irish writers of the period – if in other words we want to maintain a colonial sense of a unified kingdom. Likewise we might talk of separate English, Scottish, Welsh and Irish Romantic canons. But in so doing, we might be assisting in the maintenance or construction of a secure sense of national identity for each of these groupings. We might be contributing to a literary national purpose, forged out of mutually sympathetic treatment of iconic writers. We might like that, or we might not.

Let's briefly consider Shakespeare. In the English-speaking world, it is often assumed that every child should know a little Shakespeare: it's a 'natural' part of their education, right? Well, history suggests, not at all. In fact, it was the Romantic period that saw the idolization of Shakespeare as the English national bard. As Richard W. Schoch points out, so prevalent were celebrations of Shakespeare by the 1830s that literary critics were bemoaning 'Shakespeare Clubs and Shakespeare Jubilees' as they were demeaning his legacy (Schoch, 2002, p. 75). By the end of the Romantic period, Shakespeare was endemic. Some of our most canonical Romantic writers – Keats, Coleridge, William Hazlitt, Charles Lamb and Thomas De Quincey among them – assisted in elevating Shakespeare to that position (see Bate, 1992). Schoch points out that 'David Garrick's 1769 Stratford Jubilee [was] the founding moment of institutionalized Bardolatry' (Schoch, 2002, p. 6): in subsequent decades, the Romantic writers who followed Garrick's lead concretized that canonisation process. Péter Dávidházi has even suggested this process took the ritualistic and formal pattern of the establishment of a religious cult: Shakespeare became a god, his complete works in every aspirational home sat snugly next to the Bible. Dávidházi warns us however that 'the danger of a critical self-paralysis caused by unconditional reverence should not be ignored or underestimated' (Dávidházi, 1998, p. 199).

Let us turn our attention further north: can we imagine a Scotland without the Romantic-period poet Robert Burns? Why is Burns at the crux of the national saltire – why for some does he still define and delineate a certain 'essence' of Scottishness, globally (if not in Scotland itself)? Burns is a naturalized part of the Scottish landscape; his poems even grace Scottish paper money. His words (the most well known of them) seem to be as quintessentially, emblematically, stereotypically (some might say as reductively) Scottish as purple heather, thistles and whisky. In Gerard Carruthers' words, there now exists 'a pervasive Scottish mythology of the demotic national character of which the ploughman poet seems to be both its best exemplar and most erudite expresser' (Carruthers, 2009, p. 2). But, how did that happen? What is it about Burns that makes Scottish critics return to him again and again, that positions him at the centre of national identity, at least for some? What forces institutionalized as an annual national ritual – Burns' Night – celebrated on or near the poet's birthday not just in mother Scotland, but as far and wide as the Scottish diaspora has taken 'The Bard'? Burns is no longer any old, dead poet: his status and his function take a definite article: and 'The Bard' in Scotland is paralleled by 'The Bard' in England. The cultural status of both is so solid that neither even needs to be named. Resistance has been mounted to the elevation of both – notably with George Bernard Shaw's conception of 'bardolatry':

out-and-out worship of Shakespeare's perfection which completely lacks any critical consideration. While interesting, Shaw's Promethean resistance to the god-tyrant of Stratford-upon-Avon was ineffectual in the long-term; indeed, it might have even stimulated the likes of Harold Bloom and Jonathan Bate to re-assert their versions of Shakespeare's 'invention of the human' and 'genius' respectively (Bloom, 1998; Bate, 1997).

Burns is still only a minor player in English Romantic teaching, for the political and national reasons outlined by Robert Crawford as follows:

> Burns's glory as a political poet lies in a democratic impulse subtly inflected in ways that are republican and Scottish nationalist. This makes him awkward for a British establishment which has constantly tried to tame him. (Crawford, 2009, p. 406).

But if Burns is 'awkward' for the British, in Scotland his status as 'the patriot bard' (Hogg, 2009) can have 'awkward' consequences also; dissenting criticism about the official version of Burns can result in outrage, nasty phone calls and scratched cars (see Carruthers, 2008). Burns in Scotland, Shakespeare in England: their canonical value is inextricably linked to the construction of national identity in various forms. Postcolonial, Marxist and other critics of recent decades (see chapters four and six above, for instance) have interrogated such categories as 'nation' or 'national culture' and criticized the naturalized national status of certain canonical writers as a way of unpicking and exposing the latent national pride of the critics who leap to defend that same status.

It is therefore apparent that what we study and how we study it are practices in many ways formed for us by latent historical and ideological currents – or at least this would be entirely true, were we not made *aware* that this is case. Hopefully, once we *are* made aware of the nature of the construction of the subject of literature – and start seeing it as a modifiable building rather than an immoveable mountain – we can begin making interventions into it, which might lead to its reformation and reconstitution. This dynamic process involving revision, extension, rejection and opposition, is absolutely fundamental to the subject as it evolves now. And that is why it is important for all readers of all slices of literary history – including the one called 'Romantic' – to be aware of the making of the established order of texts, to be aware of 'canonicity'.

On Not Reading

Essentially, in the study of literature as in all walks of life, none of us has to accept what has been selected and formed for us by preceding generations. If a teacher informs a student that she or he simply must, as an undergraduate student of Romanticism, have read a particular Wordsworth poem – let's say 'Daffodils' – the student might want to know not just about 'Daffodils', but also why it is possible for anyone to assume that any text is a *necessary read* in the context of any particular discipline. It is important to realise that these same small, quizzical responses to normalizing, essentializing assumptions about what is 'best', 'valuable' or 'central' in literary history every now and then come together to form opposition to established orders of textual valuation. These opposition forces, when politically organized and socially coalesced, can become hugely significant critical movements. Such small resistances have accumulated, in various shapes and over the last few decades, into movements which have dramatically altered the nature and shape of many things, including the study of the Romantic period. Such movements have coalesced around issues of class, gender, race and sexuality in particular, and have changed the way many of us regard literature and critical practice. Indeed, these movements have actually altered the literary history of the period itself: history now consists of different textual materials, and is engaged with previously ignored historical and cultural contexts. It appears that far from being a fixed truth, history changes all the time. Put more simply, the stories we tell ourselves about the past constantly change structure and focus.

Canon Building: the Pragmatic Necessity of Unnatural Selection

Even with a literary period as short as the one we know as 'Romantic', the sheer volume of materials we might now call 'textual', produced between 1780 and 1832, is immense: to adopt a favourite Romantic metaphor, it is a mountain range so huge and magically uncharted that it would be enough to fill anyone with sublime awe and not a little terror! The simple fact is – much though we might like to give the impression that we have done so – no one person can read everything written in the period. 'Who reads must choose, since there is literally not enough time to read everything, even if one does nothing but read' as Harold Bloom puts it in his extended affirmation of the necessity of maintaining a Canon of great texts (Bloom, 1995, p. 15). Every one of us has to decide what to read from this period, to select certain things above others, and of course, where we are free of censorship and have access to good libraries (virtual or real), we are all free to make those choices.

Harold Bloom claims that the pursuit of aesthetic pleasure in literature is 'an individual rather than a societal concern' (Bloom, 1995, p. 16). But the aesthetic is not only fostered by the lone reader's encounter with a singular text written by a lone author. And an individual's 'free choice' is always delimited by the fact that reading is an innately social business: we like our reading to be guided (and gilded) by education, by experts (like Bloom), by ordering and organizing narratives that bring texts together, or keep them apart. Some texts embody so much cultural kudos to a particular social peer group that we might feel impelled to read them if we then (perhaps only in our minds) wish have access to that peer group. I remember thinking Dostoevsky's work equated with a psychologically complex strand of nebulous, esoteric sophisticated maturity, so when I was nineteen I flaunted my copies of Dostoevsky as much as I could (I am still not sure what sort of peer group I was pretending to be a part of, through, in reading *The Idiot*). Aside from the incredible intrinsic benefit of reading Dostoevsky at such a formative age – it extrinsically made me feel good to have ticked him off an imagined classics list. Perhaps that same snobbish display of cultural superiority still informs my reading to a degree – it is hard to tell. But if I look at my books now, how many of them did I choose to read without being influenced at some stage by the opinion or recommendation of someone else? Do any of the books I have read appear on my shelves without being driven here by some sort of network of relation and association to an approving body of other people? In truth it is hard to unpick the prejudices and social pressures which have informed reading choices, from personal taste and a more objective valuation. For the Italian twentieth-century novelist and critic, Italo Calvino, the most worthwhile literary discovery of 'classic' literature has to exist outside of any schooling:

> School is obliged to provide you with the tools to enable you to make your own choice; but the only choices which count are those which you take after or outside any schooling.
> It is only during unenforced reading that you will come across the book which will become 'your' book. (Calvino, 1991, p. 6)

At important stages our reading of the Romantic period will be structured for us in more explicit and directed ways – by teachers and lecturers, by book lists, by publishers' lists, by libraries, by new cultural revisions of and returns to old texts (in films, in articles, in books, in pictures), by friends' suggestions and recommendations – even by people raising an eyebrow at what we don't yet know. No one has ever read their way into the Romantic period (or any other period) outside of a socializing mechanism of some kind: this is not insidious at all – we are social creatures, and reading is a social act even when we are on our own with a book – but the social dimension of reading shows up the pervasive and pragmatically necessary nature of selection, of classification and of the making of 'classic' literature.

Pragmatically, we need other people to make selections for us, because we cannot read all the literary texts available to us; but also, we all want to read the 'best' of literary history, the classy ones, the classics, and not the detritus, not the dull, conventional, derivative ones which were ignored and perhaps should remain ignored – but the exciting ones which (somehow) defined and changed their period – or else continue to be somehow relevant or valuable to us now. Life is short, and literary history is long and massive – and its dark corners replete with poor writing. We simply must rely on others to do some of our choosing for us, to give some precedence and preferment to some texts over and above other texts. At times a fierce critic of canonical hegemony, Henry Louis Gates Jr. sees a comforting communal purpose in the function of the canon:

> I suppose the literary canon is, in no very grand sense, the commonplace book of our shared culture, in which we have written down the texts and titles that we want to remember, that had some special meaning for us. How else did those of us who teach literature fall in love with our subject than through our own commonplace books, in which we inscribed, secretly and privately, as we might do in a diary, those passages of books that named for us what we had so long deeply felt, but could not say? (Louis Gates, 1992, p. 21)

Even if a 'common' reliance on others' choices is pragmatically necessary, and fostered through individual 'love' as Louis Gates rhapsodically has it here, it doesn't necessarily follow that the list of essential 'classics' has to remain fixed for all time. What one generation thinks should be ignored, or should remain on the shelf, another might think is central: what we value in literary texts and how we value them changes. Diverse though they may be, our values are also produced socially, and are determined by our historical contexts. Some people of course think that some values are eternal: but history tells us that is not the case. Humanity changes, its literary practice changes, and what we value in literature of the past also changes. Logically enough, what we value in and from a text will not be the same as our forebears: while the countless texts which form the Romantic period will now always remain the same (apart from discoveries of long lost works), it is the ones we choose to focus upon – those books we choose to pull down from the shelf, in other words – which collectively will determine how we understand that period. And in that pursuit of fresh understanding is delivered the reforming of the period, the changing and unsettling of the old order of things, and the establishment of the new – which will in turn become old (and tyrannical) and will need resistance and revision. As our Romantic period is one which saw revolution and change on epic scales, and saw challenge, argument and debate open up on all fronts, and brought into question all manner of moral 'certainties', and is a period forged in the heat of debate and critical enquiry, it is perfectly appropriate that we should initiate and seek out revolutionary rejection of critical truisms again and again.

Shooting the Canon

It might be that when someone regards an author as being 'eternal', 'for all time', 'timeless' and so on, they reveal that they have a fixed or essentialist notion not of literature, but of human values – indeed of humanity itself: in order for any text to be valuable forever, we logically have to consider certain elements of humanity to be immutable, intransigently and quintessentially at the centre of what it is that makes us human. If you think a work of literature should *always* be regarded as a classic, as essential reading, then actually you are loosening your argument away from any sense of history, any under-standing of the evolution and development of taste, value, ethics and art. Far from being a signal of an engagement with social complexity, the idea of a permanent canon is extreme in that it requires a complete uncoupling of aesthetic judgement from historical circumstance – not only the historical situatedness of the work of literature, but also the historical situation of the judge of that same canonicity. But the historical map tells us that our sense of value, as with our versions of tradition, does in fact change over time, all the time: it is not constant, nor agreed upon by everyone, now or in the past. Karl Kroeber helps us transform this complexity into a positive force:

> Awareness of the past's self-contradictions frees us from blind acceptance of the customary, so that we may innovate by means of what tradition has kept capable of resurrection by denying. Learning through such deconstructive reconstruction gives us the ground for reconceiving our own immediate situation, liberating ourselves from submission to both external and internalized unexamined preconceptions, freeing us to relate to the past in new ways. Whereupon, if we are successful, the old text that was our starting point may begin to radiate freshly inspiring ideas and perceptions. (Kroeber, 1994, p. 125)

We might therefore regard the canon with at least a degree of suspicion because it suggests fixity where there is none, an eternal pre-determination of literary quality where the goalposts and measures of such qualities in fact shift and merge, disappear and re-appear, like footprints in watery sand. Even in one individual's lived experience, a text that seemed to soar above all others perhaps even for a long period of time through repeated re-readings, might, on a revisit after a long period of absence (and so in different historical and psychological circumstances) seem to that same individual flat and silly. And so it is with the canon: it changes and must be seen to change and to be challenged because we also always change – not always for the better – but ineluctably. Much though we might want it to comfort us and give us the security in the transcendence of eternal writing, the canon is not secure at all, because it is made in our image: and our human image and our self-impression of that image change constantly, as we sift backwards and forwards and recover previously lost artefacts of culture, while letting go our clasp on others. Some of us might want humanity's literary traces carved into the rock of academic certainty, but such critical security seems as evanescent as Keats' name writ on water.

Case Study: Should we Read Pro-Slavery Poetry?

The position adopted by this essay is relativist, rather than absolutist, in that I have been *relating* not only texts to history, but am also suggesting that the valuation and appreciation of literary texts can never be eternal – that appreciation and valuation exist *relative* to their historical situation. That is to say, critical systems of valuation do change: and this must mean that the value (and the quality) of a text, can and must change over time. Many critics would disagree vehemently: John M. Ellis, for example, thinks that this sort of thinking means that the study of literature has lost its purpose entirely. Ellis firmly believes that classics are classic because they articulate things about humanity which *are* eternal, and that the proper valuation of works of literature can and must be a-historical and 'for all time': 'race-gender-class' focused criticism, as he calls it, damages literature by depressing the riches and diversities of literature (John M. Ellis, 1997, pp. 33–59) in the pursuit of narrow political issues.

Let us end this chapter on Romantic canonicity with questions, following a poetic extract which is neither canonical, nor indeed very 'nice' – in that it will hopefully ruffle the feathers of those readers who are pretty sure that slavery was a bad thing. This extract from a longer poem was written by a Liverpudlian labouring-class shoemaker. In this extract, excavated and recovered from obscurity by editor Tim Burke (Burke, 2003, p. 143 *ff.*), poet John Walker defends a trade on which his home town of Liverpool was dependent:

> With hopes of gain and just ambition led,
> In all directions see the vessels spread.
> But chief this town it claims the Afric trade,
> The merchant's toil this amply has repaid;

Some sweep the Guinea coast their ships to slave,
And negro convicts from destruction save,
With honest traffic and advent'rous toil,
Transplants them in a civilized soil,
Where knowledge dawns on the chaotic mind,
And tastes the joys of human life refin'd.
Now Christ's religion they may hear and learn,
Which savage ignorance could ne'er discern.
Who knows but Heaven is paving out the way,
Divine instruction thither to convey?
To barb'rous climes where gospel-light ne'er dawn'd,
His sacred word, with power he can command,
And from these emigrants means to collect,
The scatter'd remnants of his own elect.
Instructed hence in civil social life,
The chaste connections of a virtuous wife,
Numbers by servitude themselves commend,
Are bless'd with British freedom in the end.
Those pamper'd here who at the carriage swing,
Enjoy more pleasures than an Afric king.
Some partial ills attend a gen'ral good,
Such the Slave-trade, when rightly understood;
Whate'er men's motives, int'rests, views or ends,
God's providence the whole superintends.
You whose warm zeal before your reason runs,
And with feign'd wrongs the public ear now stuns,
Who loud remonstrance 'gainst the Afric trade,
Pretending Jesus' footsteps thus you tread.
Did he emancipate the Jewish nation,
And doom the Romans for their usurpation?
No regal powers to Israel did restore,
But left the tribes enthrall'd to Roman power;
Will you to more humanity pretend,
Than him emphatic still'd the sinner's friend?
Humanity is now the pop'lar cry,
Some years ago 'twas Wilkes and liberty;
Yet so inconstant is the public voice,
That soon must die – succeeds another choice.
Humanity tho' pleasing is the name,
To folly turns when stretched to the extreme,
This naked principle would fondly save,
The victims doom'd the injur'd laws do crave;

Allow its claims no culprit then would swing,
No safety then for subject or the king,
If law and justice lose their useful sting.
No punishment, delinquents hence would scare
Discipline 'mongst our troops and ships of war,
Proud of its triumphs with fallacious guise,
It melts the bosom, drowns the weeping eyes;
Like optic glasses fitted to deceive,
We grasp the object but we nothing have.
To trace this subject to its fountain head,
When the first happy pair their god obey'd,
Rightful dominion o'er the earth they swayed
Sin made its festal entrance on the stage,
Since men and beasts in mutual strife engage;
Th' oppressors and oppress'd alternate reign,
As time and place the circumstance ordain.
Hence slav'ry then is the effect of Sin,
Can only end with what it did begin;
While men are sinners some must slav'ry bear,
And the broad badge of fallen nature wear;
All men are slaves here in this mortal life,
The husband slaves for children and his wife.
Pleasures, amusements, dress and equipage,
Enslave the triflers of this present age,
The poor to th' rich, the rich unto the king,
And these are captives to some other thing.
The Jewish law, at least the moral part,
Is surely binding on each British heart;
And slavery then was deemed a legal trade,
When God himself was lawgiver and head.
To love our neighbour to ourselves is right,
Our charity intends a bolder flight.
We've beat the French and Dons by land and sea,
And now we'll beat them with pure piety.
Suppose the government the slaves should free,
The native consequences will surely be,
Ruin at home, for Slav'ry will remain,
And swell the revenues of France and Spain.
Merchants, tars, shipwrights, some with fam'lies great,
To distant climes compell'd to emigrate;
The trade exil'd what must mechanics do,
But close the banish'd fugitive pursue.

But if the trade illegal could be prov'd,
Yet Liverpolia stands but half reprov'd,
Her annual profits gen'rously apply'd,
Might turn the scale of justice on her side.
Thro' Britain's isle with weary'd steps I've trod,
And observations on each place bestow'd;
But Liverpool stands in the first degree,
For public spirit and bright charity.
Let none too rash condemn the Afric trade,
Till once the subject they have duly weighed;
Tho' Moors are purchas'd from their native shore,
And sold for slaves, were they not so before?
'Tis prov'd their state is better'd, – not made worse,
Then slav'ry is a blessing, not a curse.
Oh, might the Muse, her suffrages subjoin,
To those who've thanked lord Penrhyn and Gascoyne,
Who stood so staunch to prop the Afric trade,
When Wilberforce its condemnation read.

(Walker, 1789, pp. 150–2)

Questions of Canonicity and Value: the Case of John Walker

- Can you map the logic of Walker's defence of the slave trade?
- What ethical concepts and actions does Walker value?
- What is the style of this poem? Could you ascribe to it any stylistic or poetic features and habits of 'Romanticism' more broadly?
- How might Walker's social status as a 'journeyman shoemaker' (Tim Burke, 2003, p. 143) affect your reading of the poem?
- How do Walker's values differ from other writers in the Romantic period?
- How do Walker's values differ from your own?
- How might we 'value' Walker's text: is it of aesthetic, poetical, social, historical, mercantile interest?
- Should a text which supports the slave trade be taught and studied at university?
- Should we let John Walker into our canon of Romantic texts, or should we keep him out?

Notes

Bate, Jonathan, ed., 1992. *The Romantics on Shakespeare*. London: Penguin.
Bate, Jonathan, 1997. *The Genius of Shakespeare*. London: Picador.

Bloom, Harold, 1995. *The Western Canon: The Books and Schools of the Ages*. London and Basingstoke: Papermac.

Bloom, Harold, 1998. *Shakespeare: the Invention of the Human*. New York: Riverhead Books.

Tim Burke, ed., 2002. *Eighteenth-Century English Labouring-Class Poets 1700–1800*. Vol. III, 1780–1800. London: Pickering and Chatto, 2002.

Burton, Charles, 1823. *The Bardiad: A Poem*. Second Edition. London: Longman, Hurst, Rees, Orme and Brown.

Calvino, Italo, 1991. Why Read the Classics?. In *Why Read the Classics?* translated by Martin McLaughlin, 1999. London: Vintage.

Carruthers, Gerard, 2008. Happy Birthday Robert Burns. *The Drouth*, 30 (Winter 2008), pp. 78–83.

Carruthers, Gerard, 2009. Introduction to *The Edinburgh Companion to Robert Burns*. Edinburgh: Edinburgh University Press, 2009.

Crawford, Robert, 2009. *The Bard: Robert Burns, A Biography*. London: Jonathan Cape.

Dávidházi, Péter, 1998. *The Romantic Cult of Shakespeare: Literary Reception in Anthropological Perspective*. Basingstoke: Macmillan.

Ellis, John M., 1997. *Literature Lost: Social Agendas and the Corruption of the Humanities*. New Haven and London: Yale University Press.

Hogg, Patrick Scott, 2009. *Robert Burns: The Patriot Bard*. Edinburgh: Mainstream.

Kroeber, Karl, 1994. *Ecological Literary Criticism: Romantic Imagining and the Biology of Mind*. New York: Columbia University Press.

Ruskin, John, 1858. Things to be Studied. Appendix to *The Elements of Drawing*. New York: Wiley and Halsted.

Schoch, Richard W., 2002. *Not Shakespeare: Bardolatry and Burlesque in the Nineteenth Century*. Cambridge: Cambridge University Press.

St Clair, William. 2004. *The Reading Nation in the Romantic Period*. Cambridge: Cambridge University Press.

Walker, John, 1789. *A Descriptive Poem on the Town and Trade of Liverpool*. Liverpool: Henry Hodgson. In Tim Burke, 2002, ed., *Eighteenth-Century English Labouring-Class Poets 1700–1800*. Vol. III, 1780–1800. London: Pickering and Chatto, 2002, pp. 150–2.

Sexuality and Gender

Elizabeth Fay

In recent studies of subjectivity and identity the historical relation between sex as a biological state and gender as a social identity has come under scrutiny. Feminist theory, beginning with early distinctions between 'woman' and 'women' has led us to understand that gender can either be highly conventionalized or an adaptation of the personal to the social, and researchers have discovered that historically gender could even be transitional or could traverse categories, but sex has been held to be a given except in certain cases of biological ambiguity. (Famously, even before Simone de Beauvoir's theorization of the distinction between the historical and the conceptual woman in *The Second Sex*, Mary Wollstonecraft had already trod this ground in the *Vindication of the Rights of Woman* (1792). It is becoming increasingly clear that such ambiguity is precisely the point, and that archival evidence points to the ways in which the social, imaginary and institutional need have crafted an increasingly bimorphic conception of both sexuality and gender to meet the demands of an increasingly reified commercial liberalism.

Furthermore, Gay and Gender Studies have explored the terrain of masculinity and the problematic distinction of 'patriarchy' and 'deviance.' The recent work on masculinities has led us to recognize that eighteenth-century and Romantic period men discovered for themselves ways to inhabit social meanings of maleness that provided identities stretching what we think of as normative, particularly in the new urban masculinities such as the dandy, the Corinthian, the Jacobin. Women during the eighteenth century had more flexibility in fashioning their social identities than they did slightly later. as mercantile prosperity transformed their usefulness as domestic labour and administrators into that of status markers. Yet even so during the Romantic period there was room for the creation of new identities such as the female Jacobin, the Romantic friend, the respectable actress or poet, the reformer, as well as the courtesan and less acceptable Cyprian.

Dror Wahrman argues that in a bounded timeframe between the Renaissance and the end of the eighteenth century in Britain, the interpretation of gender shifted in a recognizable pattern across cultural forms. In the beginning of this period gender transgression was associated with dress, behaviour and appearance, and its deviance from heterosexual norms was not perceived to be politically charged or socially disruptive. Likewise other aspects of human diversity such as race or human/beast distinctions were considered social rather than biologically essential traits. By the end of the century, gender, race and other 'categories of difference' were collapsed into sex so that the body, its appearance, attitudes and behaviour had to be continuous with its sex, race and humanity. Difference was now understood to be biological, readable on the body, the essence of identity.

During the Romantic period, as sexuality began to coalesce into more tightly dimorphic definitions, gender still allowed for play in how those definitions could be adapted to a subjective and social sense of selfhood. In short, gender was performative. Despite current arguments that there is no real distinction between sex and gender, that both are social constructs and historically and culturally constituted, I will treat these as mutually flexible categories during the Romantic period while retaining for gender greater creative possibility for identity construction than for sexuality. Status and rank were important contributors to what I view as different constraints on gender and sex, as were positioning within the nuclear and extended patriarchal family, positioning within the community and positioning within one's social circle. I will consider both historical figures and literary characters in describing the differential between sex and gender, and in illustrating the performative nature of self- and social definition as these related to the categories, gradations and extensions of male/female and masculine/feminine. Leaving aside for the moment the question of biological sex, which was however certainly as fraught in the Romantic period as it is today in terms of the non-coincidence and permutations possible between primary sexual characteristics and the sexual identity assumed with the acquisition of secondary characteristics in puberty, I will address first the question of gender because it can override or rescript that of sex. I will then discuss historical and literary examples of gendered categories, and their disruption by sexual deviations from presumed norms.

In any discussion of sexuality or gender, the tendency is to begin with the female as the marked category, the male assuming the role of unmarked or normative. Women in the Romantic period had a sliding scale of femininities they could assume depending on class, urban or rural location, proclivities and opportunities. At one end is the hyperfeminine, at the other the damaged woman, and in the middle is the respectable married woman. These categories rely on two things: sexual activity and reputation. The hyperfeminine woman may or may not be married and her identification as hyperfeminine relies on her attraction for men in relation to their respectability rather than the degree of their desire. Two examples of women who were universally acknowledged as hyperfeminine, and although married not quite respectable, were

Georgiana Duchess of Devonshire, and Mary Robinson (who modelled herself in part on the Duchess her patron), the third example being, of course, Marie Antoinette. Women who were hyperfeminine and respectable tended to be fictional heroines modelled on Richardson's Clarissa.

The respectable married woman in the middle of the scale might best be represented by Mrs. Morland, Catherine's mother in *Northanger Abbey* (1818). Such a woman attends to her social, domestic and maternal duties without questioning her role in the patriarchal order, yet without conceding her self-respect in the completion of those duties. In this definition, *Pride and Prejudice*'s Charlotte Lucas cannot occupy the same space in the scale once she is Mrs Collins, despite her outward respectability, since she must humiliate herself in order to mollify both her social-climbing husband and his conceited patron. At the lowest position in the scale are the women who have, usually for economic reasons and/or due to social vulnerability, been sexually active prior to or instead of marriage and are therefore damaged both in terms of status and respectability. Those without economic resources were the subject of many lyric poems about deserted or wandering mad women such as Martha Ray in Wordsworth's 1798 'The Thorn', but the historical women were those who frequented the streets of urban centres as prostitutes, an idealized version being Ann in De Quincey's *Confessions of an English Opium-Eater* (1821). The tendency of literary depictions of such women to be sympathetic indicates a general view, despite the real vulgarity of bawdy houses and taverns populating the more dangerous quarters of London in which young Bucks, ramblers and other intrepid men ventured.

This scale intersects with the ratio of woman-to-marital status in which a woman's virginity and marital eligibility affect her social identity, and indeed her subjective status (Irigaray, 174, n.3; Rendell, 15). Whereas the married woman is no longer available and thus discounted, and the eligible virgin is the locus of masculine desire and marital scheming, the spinster and the crone are not quite female and have lost some part of their humanity, and the sexually active unmarried woman is closer to the category of bestial or subhuman (a category to which racially different men and women could be relegated). Thus the functions of respectability and marriageability according to patriarchal and class determinants interfere at every level with a woman's place on the scale of possible identities. Moreover, one's place and identity are clearly mobile and permeable: marriage or non-marriage changes one's position just as sexual indiscretion and socio-political or economic downfall can move one into the demi-monde or to the lowest end of the scale.

What complicates a simple scale along the lines of respectability are socio-political movements or fashions such as free love; evasions of normative customs such as elopement or travel; adultery mutually practised in a marital relation (as in the Duke and Duchess of Devonshire's marriage); the elevation of a mistress to wife (as in the case of Emma Hamilton, first mistress and then wife of the diplomat Sir William Hamilton). Some careers for women carried with them their own complicative risk: actresses, dancers and other entrants into the public arena were considered figuratively and possibly literally to be offering their bodies for sale, to be always already demireps despite their actual experience, understood to be awaiting backstage clients in the green room. Dorothy Jordan and Mary Robinson were lucky to be royal mistresses as the result of successful stage careers, although both discovered that royal desire did not provide economic security once desire faded. Actresses and performers were a lower class version of the courtesan, a woman such as Harriette Wilson whose status as professional yet elite mistress provided her with a degree of control and choice in her relations, as opposed to those women who, like Jordan and Robinson, were chosen.

We have here then a series of possibilities and mutations arranged along a *y*-axis of respectability, the axis coded by a sliding scale of class where downward mobility was far easier than upward mobility precisely because of women's social vulnerability to the crisis of sexual reputation. Nevertheless, British culture had historically been distinguished by the possibility of inter-marriage between the classes, and upward social mobility was possible both financially, as when two members of the same class marry such as Mr. Bingley and Jane Bennet in *Pride and Prejudice* (1813) – or more arguably, Mr. Darcy and Elizabeth Bennet – and class-wise, as when Sir William Hamilton made the daughter of a blacksmith his wife. If the *crise de sexe*, as we might term it, is peculiar to women transhistorically and is predicated on the conception of 'woman' that anchors notions of gender and femininity, the Romantic retained some of the plasticity of categorical boundaries available earlier. This flexibility revealed itself in the performative aspects of gender and identity during the period that accorded with the sense of commercial and cultural inventiveness that characterized the age.

Similarly a *y*-axis of possible gender roles existed for men, although the sliding scale operated to a far lesser degree since sex only affected respect-ability in terms of same sex relations, illegitimacy, or adventuring (heiress hunting). The largest danger for male respectability was not sexual, as for women, but criminality: the hint of wrongdoing could harm a man's reputation as much as sexual slander could harm a woman's. Because crimi-nality does not affect gender, except in the case of sodomy, I will leave that variant aside here. The gender positions available to men ranged from the ultra-masculine, as in the patrician, to the Whig liberal, and sentimental or paternal Burkean figure, to the libertine. Within that range there were, among others, the dandy, the Corinthian, the Buck, the army officer who bought his commission, the naval officer who rose by merit and the political radical.

For both women and men, then, a sliding scale of social and sexual identities not only existed, but could be transitional, and offered both danger and possibility. The opportunity to gain control over the direction of one's life and for social advancement was countered by the unreliability experienced by both men and women of dependency on family members or patrons, and the very real possibilities of a downward slide into bankruptcy, the demi-monde, flight from creditors, or spinsterhood for women and an impoverished old age. Engaging with and prospering from the flexibility of this scale required the ability to imagine oneself into a role and to perform that role well. This might mean the transformation of Charlotte Lucas into Mrs Collins, to cite *Pride and Prejudice* again, or it might mean Mary Robinson's many careers: naive wife, poet of sensibility, Drury Lane actress, royal mistress, Foxite Whig, political poet, fashion leader, celebrity, novelist and demirep. Indeed, how one played with the scale provided the period with its most characteristic types, perhaps best exemplified by the dandy, who might be himself a mere caricature or who might be a 'true original' such as Beau Brummel, the performance artist whose wit as much as his style were his line of credit, earning him a place (a transient one, however) in the Prince of Wales' cadre.

Nevertheless we must remember that infused into such scales were differentials such as age, class, status, race, disability, criminality and the taint of possible wrongdoing. Within a family, for instance, the difference between the eldest son and other sons, between the eldest daughter and other daughters and between elder and infant children made an important social distinction and could spell dependency or independence. Particularly in wealthy or landed families, primogeniture created a real class difference, since the second and remaining sons stood to inherit little in relation to the eldest son, while daughters normally could expect little relative to their brothers, and that little became their husbands' on marriage unless a protective father arranged otherwise in his will or the marriage contract. Illegitimate daughters could expect little, although illegitimate sons sometimes inherited. Social mobility could be achieved when a near relation was adopted by a childless or son-less couple, as when Edward, Jane Austen's second brother, was adopted by his wealthy uncle and aunt, Thomas and Catherine Knight. Cadet branches of the family, descended from younger sons, were in inferior relation to the main branch that retained the family seat and fortune. Merchants might rise into the titled gentry through recognition from the crown and could further enhance their family rank through the careful marriage of children. Servants, labourers and others below the middling classes might also have some opportunities for advancement, as in the case of Emma Hamilton or Margaret Simpson, a farmer's daughter with whom Thomas De Quincey had already had one child before he married her in Grasmere. Less rare was the case of William Blake, son of a hosier, and Josiah Wedgwood, son of a potter, neither of them elder sons; as men, they were somewhat more easily able to achieve their artistic and entrepreneurial potential through hard work and social networks. Women who also laboured to achieve their potential were more circumscribed in the kinds of labour they could pursue, but poets such as Charlotte Smith and artisans such as Mary Ann Bell, whose fashionable shop in Upper King Street was frequented by the elite, and whose magazine *La Belle Assemblée* was also a financial success (McKendrick 48, 72), were able to rise to prominence as well.

If modern identity theory, drawing from the fields of anthropology, sociology and psychology, concerns the ways that individuals experience themselves in different relational situations and change the personae they project accordingly, identity as performance pushes that theory a step further by suggesting that such adjustments can be more conscious, more studied and prepared, and in short closer to the actor's preparation for a role. If a day labourer must act subserviently to his supervisor, he presents a more equitable face to his fellow workers albeit within a social hierarchy established within that circle and, if married, will likely present a superior face to his wife and children at the end of the day. Analogously, in the Romantic era people experienced these relational shifts as part of daily life, although more rigorously enforced since status and rank played such an important role in social distinction. But during this volatile period in which radical thought, revolution in France, emergent feminism and liberalism combined to support and promote reform movements such as abolition, and to lay the ground for reforms in child labour laws, poor relief and the franchise, the capacity to play with identity projection also increased. One could become a particular identity, or could put on a face for a particular purpose. The lawyer Walter Scott made himself into the Laird of Abbotsford, using the historical imagination he developed in his poems and then his historical novels to create for himself a noble identity (authenticated when he was made baronet), and an implied lineage projecting from his estate near Melrose Abbey and the medieval arms and armour he displayed there, acquired through his interest in antiquarianism. Yet this noble identity was threatened by bankruptcy when Scott's printing business came close to collapsing when he was fifty-four, a time of life when solvency could spell a secure old age or disaster.

The Prince of Wales provides an example of the play possible between authentic nobility and projected personae. A dandy, a Foxite Whig, a conservative Tory, an art collector, a libertine, a gourmand, the prince varied between playing the decadent aristocrat and the metropolitan rambler, the politician and the London socialite, art connoisseur and the bourgeois consumer. He plunged enthusiastically into his roles, whether he was playing the Brummelian dandy or a member of the Fox circle, an ardent lover (weeping copiously over love notes and buying mistresses costly jewels) or a midnight rambler (evicting an unprotesting husband to hold an assignation with the wife). A sensualist, the prince enjoyed costume, designing outfits and interior décor, orchestrating banquets and entertainments, commissioning jewelry and paintings (acquiring over 450 for Carlton House by the end of the Regency), as well as drinking, eating, balls and less salubrious pastimes. He had numerous mistresses and enjoyed liaisons with lower class women before, during and after his disastrous state marriage to Princess Caroline, who claims he showed up for their wedding drunk. His debts for his extravagant habits of consumption were so enormous that Parliament had to pay off his creditors several times (£161,000 in 1787, and then an annual sum to meet his debt in 1795 of £630,000) (Smith, 92–7).

Even for the Regent, whose lifestyle was leading him to a bankruptcy that even the state had difficulty resolving, there was no stability on the gender scale. His love of ornament and pink satin had to be offset by a nominal heading of the 10th Regiment of Light Dragoons; his self-indulgent appetites (he was very fond of beef: in 1816, Carlton House went through 5264 pounds of meat a month, mostly beef, in addition to poultry, fish and seafood, pork and sausage – he had become an ardent member of the anti-French Beef-steak Society) countered by his exquisite taste in art (Murray, 184). His fashionable Whiggism when Prince of Wales was an easy identity to exchange for the conservative politician once he no longer felt the need to rebel publicly against his father's staunch Toryism; conservatism strengthened his positioning for the monarchy during his father's illness, and aided his relationship with Parliament.

At the same time, George discovered that projecting himself as heir to the seat of patriarchal power pitted him against the perceived liberalism of his estranged wife, Caroline, who was able to win support from the masses when he sought to divorce her. George's position on the gender scale was not as precarious as that of his wife or sisters, all vulnerable (some legitimately so) to charges of promiscuity, but he was not fully protected by his royal status either. Known to have sexual appetites as large as his appetite as a gourmand, George was frequently the subject of political caricatures on greed and vulgarity. In 1813 Leigh Hunt wrote in a journal article about him that although the prince could be a charming man, 'delightful, blissful, wise, pleasurable, honourable, virtuous, true and immortal', he was 'also a violator of his word, a libertine, over head and ears in disgrace, a despiser of domestic ties, the companion of gamblers and demireps' (collected in 'The Book of Days': *A Miscellany of Popular Antiquities*, 1832).

Those most at risk to the discrediting of their identity performances were not women but men: the charge of sodomy was a punishable one, and homosexuals who were unlucky enough to be discovered could lose everything, as the aesthete and suspected paedophile William Beckford did, or could be hanged, as happened to less wealthy victims of the sodomy laws: in 1726 three men were hanged at Tyburn for this capital offence; in 1810 several men were arrested at a London tavern reputed to be a homosexual meeting place, then pilloried and savaged by the mob. Beckford, the wealthy heir of a plantation owner (he inherited a million pounds at age 10), was famous for his huge fake Gothic home, Fonthill Abbey. But the abbey was built after he returned from a period of exile: despite his marriage to Lady Margaret Gordon, he was forced to flee (she accompanied him, however) when rumours circulated of his affair with William Courtenay, son of Viscount Courtenay.

Another famous exile was Lord Byron, whose decision to leave England arose not from his bisexuality but from his social disgrace in being divorced by his wife. Nevertheless, he had to be extremely cautious in arrangements for his homosexual affairs, using code (usually classical Greek) when referring to them. Byron's first volume of poetry was devoted to his early love, the Cambridge chorister John Edlestone, whom he memorializes after his death in the 'Thyrza' poems of 1811–1812, although for publication he codes Edlestone there as female. His friend in later years, Percy Bysshe Shelley – perhaps as a response to Byron's questionable sexual allegiances – referred to homosexuality in 'Discourse on the Manners of the Ancient Greeks Relative to the Subject of Love' (1818), as something that, while accepted among the ancients, was 'inconceivable to the imagination of a modern European.'

Fashionable figures who played with the fine line between male-sanctioned society and male-only identification, like Beau Brummel, could become magnets of social attention. Brummel's career began as a gazetteer to a Coronetcy in the Tenth Light Dragoons. At that time its colonel was the thirty-something Prince of Wales. The Prince liked having himself surrounded by handsome men, and Brummel qualified. His promotion was thus assured, but he soon returned to civilian life, giving small but exquisite dinners, and building a reputation for elegance and elitism. His reputation was built on his strictness of dress and hygiene, especially his teeth which he brushed to extreme whiteness with twigs, the elegance of his manners and his witticisms.

Women had a less easy time of it, but there were ways to play with gender prevarication. Although sapphism or 'Sapphic love' was a disreputable charge, it was not significantly different from other charges of promiscuity and sexual excess; French radicals used it to discredit Marie Antoinette along with other charges of sexual misconduct, but lesbianism as such was not a completely recognized practice. What was both recognized and accepted was the practice of 'Romantic friendship', in which two women set up house together. Since the abundance of women unable to marry due to lack of a dowry, unable to work in respectable and sufficiently remunerative jobs and unable to find a comfortable position with family members meant a strain on the social order, the solution of women living together – such as Jane Austen did with her mother, sister and good friend after her father died – was not unknown. When women unrelated by family chose to live together and had sufficient social status and funds to make their household interesting, like the so-called 'Ladies of Llangollen', Sarah Ponsonby and Lady Eleanor Butler, who eloped to Wales and constructed a Gothic cottage for themselves, they became a fixture on the tour circuit. Their solution was not unlike that of Horace Walpole who similarly disguised his homosexuality by relocating to a more rural location beyond London and constructing a Gothic fantasy for himself, Strawberry Hill, which also became an object for tourists. It is not coincidental that in the three cases of Beckford, Walpole, and Ponsonby and Butler, the Gothic was the architectural order of choice: in certain circles the Gothic was associated with sensuality, political opposition and aberrant identity.

Some women were able to play with the theatrical convention of breeches roles in which young women played cross-dressed parts in the tradition of Shakespeare's Portia, where the play's denouement depends on the gender confusion and revelation centered on the heroine. Mary Robinson was famous for her breeches parts, and the fact that the Prince of Wales asked her to come dressed in such a costume to one of their midnight assignations makes clear the sexual draw of a costume that revealed the outlines of a woman's legs. Others such as Lady Caroline Lamb also made use of a breeches costume to play with gender confusion so as to heighten their femininity, but some did so in order to pass as men (or in the probable case of Lord Byron, used the confusion between women dressed as young men and young men dressed so as to appear to be women in breeches, to disguise a homosexual assignation). One such woman who is known to have used a male identity is Mary Shelley's friend, Diana Dods, who passed as David Lyndsay in order to be published; Lyndsay was known for his *Dramas of the Ancient World* (1822) as well as short stories and poetry. But Dods also used another male identity, Walter Sholto Douglas, posing as the husband of Mary Shelley's close friend Isabella Robinson Douglas. The line between posing and passing, and experiencing subjectivity, however fraught, is a fractured one; although Dods (herself illegitimate by birth) married the flirtatious Robinson to camouflage her out-of-wedlock pregnancy and child, Dods spent several years passing as a man. The multiple disguises surrounding this couple apparently appealed to Shelley, but also reproduce the tensions and fractures inherent in identity creation and performance.

Other women resistant to a normative heterosexual role had to be more secretive; the highly educated Anne Lister, for instance, was of a privileged class and perhaps her residence in West Yorkshire rather than London limited the range of her gender play more than if she could have used the disguises available in the metropolis such as masquerade balls and costume for outings in Pall Mall, or the convenient dark corners of theatres or Vauxhall and Ranelagh Gardens. However she did manage her own estates, working outdoors to supervise her male workers, and actively developing the natural resources of her property. We know of her Sapphic leanings because of diaries she kept in code of her liaisons with other women, only recently deciphered, but she successfully participated in local society as a pillar of propriety.

If Sapphism, sodomy and gender play were variants of heteronormative roles for women and men, roles that played with the extremes of femininity and masculinity were also ways to extend the possibilities of heteronormativity through identity performance. The ultra feminine role that bent the rules of respectability might be that of the courtesan. Harriette Wilson was a well-known example, her exquisite taste, manners and education putting her in direct contrast to the Cyprian, or demirep marked by poor taste in dress and vulgarity of manner. ('Cyprian' refers to the island of Cyprus famous for the worship of Venus; other sexually suggestive slang words such as paphian and Sapphic were similarly employed to exploit and/or disguise the erotic subtext of such terms). The Corinthian was not analogous to the courtesan sexually, since she supported (marketed) herself through marriage-like alliances with wealthy men, while the Corinthian was sexually aggressive towards women, but he was analogous in using his role as a Corinthian (the aristocrat who attends Gentleman Jackson's Boxing Club in Bond Street, or pursues other sports) to extend his masculinity. Whereas the courtesan did so by associating with men of higher class than herself, the Corinthian did so through association with the lower-class athleticism of celebrity boxers, jockeys and other examples of muscular sport closely associated with betting, gambling and competition.

The mainstay of gender performance as dictated by sexual identity during the Romantic period, however, was largely heterosexual. The intense focus on the marriage market in Romantic period novels reveals how heavily grounded in that market the social economy was, with families negotiating cash settlements as well as land. The public entertainments available during the London season, in St James's and throughout Britain, were acknowledged market opportunities as much as leisure pursuits. But the third category of women that disrupts the neat seller/property binary illustrated in the virgin/mother binary, the prostitute, undoes the neat division between owner and object because the prostitute sells her own body, becoming in the process both seller and commodity, active subject and subject of the sale. Similarly the professional courtesan and the more amateurish mistress are outside the virgin/mother possibilities, although the mistress has a better chance of becoming a wife, and likewise codes the financial support and gifts received from her lover in domestic terms. Such relationships can be contractual, as in Mary Robinson's famous settlement with the Prince of Wales, or Maria Fitzherbert's insistence that she was truly married to the prince despite the illegitimacy posed by her Catholic faith.

The mistress is in some ways an imaginative construct, reinventing herself when necessary, and freed to do so through her mobility outside the marriage market. But she is also a threat to the patriarchal system because of this mobility and because of her intervention in the market economy. For this reason Mary Robinson held a precarious place in London society, both fashionable and always potentially risible. Indeed, she always walked a delicate line, for if mistresses (with their close association with Cyprians) might be supposed to have poor taste in clothes, that is, clothing that was excessive by being extravagant both visually and financially), and were expected to be excessively revealing of their bodily 'wares' (as Robinson was often depicted as being), then her bid for respectability, especially as an author, was always hanging in the balance. But Robinson made a reputation out of dressing her body, her clothes so becoming to her appearance – whether the fashions she brought back from the court of Marie Antionette or fashions of her own invention – that specific items and accessories were imitated and named after her such as the 'Perdita' hat. Her purposeful engagements of the most renowned society painters for her portraits shows her acumen in dressing her body to portray varied identities, none of which alone could contain her, and all of which countered the vicious depictions of her body in anti-Foxite caricatures.

Yet bi-directionalism between public and private meant not just a certain play between inhabiting particular roles and types (the dandy, the Corinthian, the woman of fashion, the Bluestocking and other new urban masculinities and femininities, as well as older ones such as the courtier, the rake, the salon hostess, and the courtesan) and individual expression. It also meant an effort to discover self-identity through performance, to act oneself out. This could become a caricature, as in the case of Beau Brummell but even more so in his copycat admirers such as George Lionel Dawson Damer, a younger son of the Earl of Portarlington who frequented the fashionable club Whites. Or it could mean discovering one's more desirable self, who one truly wants to become, through performing a part well.

This, of course, is the mainstay of women's novels, where the heroine who performs well ends by marrying the hero. But in Austen's novels this conception is made more explicit: her heroines are made to be more self-conscious about the effect of their chosen role or that of others on identity. Thus Elinor in *Sense and Sensibility* (1811) realizes that her own hewing to propriety could mean a disastrous outcome for her own chances of marriage, but much earlier than this she is aware that her sister Marianne's self-dramatizing is self-destructive and detrimental for those connected to her. Once Marianne begins to act 'herself' after her dangerous illness, the rest of the family's fortunes can begin to resolve themselves as characters adhere to or shift their performances of identity.

In the end, Romantic-period sexuality and gender was in the process of coalescing into the more normative forms identified with the Victorians, but was still in the transitive period of experiment, play and idiosyncrasy rather than character type, socio-normative submission, and strict formalism. One could perform a number of identities, choosing the self that best suited the occasion, or one could adhere to a specific sense of identity that could nevertheless be a complete invention. Although insincerity or counterfeit character was insupportable if not accompanied by wealth, money accompanied by inclusion in a social network with associations of rank could make artificed character completely acceptable. Much of the Romantic ethos had to do with performing authenticity, creating the conditions of sincerity and authorizing individual genius. Performing identity, which necessarily took place through sex and gender, was part and parcel of this experiment with becoming. The Romantic period was the laboratory of the modern self, its willingness to experiment with the theatre of the social its trial by fire. In the end, Romantic performativity paved the way for Modernism and Modern identity. Our own attitudes toward gender play and sexual identity have their origins in Romanticism and its liberal attitudes toward the making of the self.

See also: Changes in Critical responses and Approaches; Case Studies in Reading Critical Texts

Notes

Bennett, Betty T., *Mary Diana Dods, a Gentleman and a Scholar*. New York: William Morrow, 1991.

Crompton, Louis, *Byron and Greek Love: Homophobia in 19th-Century England*, Berkeley: University of California Press, 1985.

Derry, John W., *The Regency Crisis and the Whigs*. Cambridge: Cambridge University Press, 1963.

Faderman, Lillian, *Surpassing the Love of Men: Romantic Friendship and Love between Women from the Renaissance to the Present*. New York: William Morrow, 1981.

Fothergill, Brian, *Beckford of Fonthill*. 1979. Rpt. Dublin: Nonsuch Publishing, 2005.

Fulford, Tim, *Romanticism and Masculinity: Gender, Politics and Poetics in the Writings of Burke, Coleridge, Cobbett, Wordsworth, De Quincey and Hazlitt*. Basingstoke, England: Macmillan, 1999.

Goldsmith, Jason, 'Celebrity and the Spectacle of Nation.' *Romanticism and Celebrity Culture, 1750–1850*. Ed. Tom Mole. New York: Cambridge University Press, 2009, pp. 21–40.

Irigaray, Luce, 'Love Between Us,' in *Who Comes After the Subject?* Eds Eduardo Cadava, et al. New York: Routledge, 1991.

Irigaray, Luce, 'Women, the Sacred and Money,' *Paragraph* vol. 8 (1986): pp. 6–17.

Labbe, Jacqueline M., *Charlotte Smith: Romanticism, Poetry and the Culture of Gender*. Manchester, England: Manchester UP, 2003

Lister, Anne, *I Know My Own Heart: The Diaries of Anne Lister 1791–1840*. Helena Whitbread, ed. New York: New York University Press; 1992.

Livingston, Ira, 'The "No-Trump Bid" on Romanticism and Gender'. *Essays and Studies*: 51. (1998), pp. 161–73.

McKendrick, Neil, Plumb, J. H., and Brewer, John, eds., *The Birth of a Consumer Society: The Commericialization of Eighteenth-Century England*. London: Europa Publications, 1982.

Murray, Venetia, *An Elegant Madness: High Society in Regency England*. Harmondsworth: Penguin Books, 1998.

Rendell, Jane, *The Pursuit of Pleasure: Gender, Space and Architecture in Regency London*. London: Continuum, 2002.

9 Race and Ethnicity

Carol Bolton

The British Romantic period saw a huge expansion in colonial settlement, followed in many territories by the replacement of small-scale ad hoc ventures with imperialist economic, legal and administrative structures. Greater British intervention in countries all over the world, as well as more direct engagement with their populations, led to a heightened awareness of the differences between ethnic and racial groupings to make sense of colonial policy. As well as examining what race meant in practical engagements with new territories, this historical period drew on earlier Enlightenment philosophy and empirical studies of the development of different races (which were themselves influenced by classical ideas). It is difficult to define the term 'race', due to the multiplicity of forms in which British ideas about it appear; for instance, historical accounts, travel narratives, missionary tracts, philosophical and political discourse, as well as imaginative works, such as poetry and novels. At this time, race was also increasingly constructed as a biological classification based on natural hereditary traits, such as skin and hair colour, stature and cranial size. All these multifarious representations of race and ethnicity contribute to a conceptual framework that posits the superiority and inferiority of human social groups. This framework shapes the way in which people think about themselves and act towards other societies, and the late eighteenth- and early nineteenth-century period of contact with the people of

Africa, India and the Middle and Far East was crucial in contributing to this. So, race can be defined as a social construction, produced through human relations over time, and serving an ideological function. The social construct-edness of race has to be understood through specific historical, cultural and political contexts, which are examined here.

This chapter, therefore, explores the ways in which theories about race and ethnicity manifested themselves in the Romantic period. Though the European and indeed the British contexts for framing ideas of difference are significant ones – between locations such as north and south, or the regional distinctions of Scotland, Ireland, England and Wales – this account focuses on the wider geographical perspective. This is because the existing concepts of inclusion or exclusion that shaped identity, whether national, racial or ethnic, were becoming increasingly complicated by Britain's engagement with new territories. This occurred through commercial trade, exploration and colonial expansion, and a brief explanation of this context, and notable events within it that relate to issues of race and ethnicity, is provided here. Racial distinctions made by eighteenth-century philosophers are examined as part of this contex-tualisation. This is followed by a comprehensive discussion of individual and important social and ideological developments and their impact, such as the slavery debate, the influence of 'orientalism' and the scientific impetus for racial classification that emerged at this time. Throughout the chapter, literary representations of race and ethnicity will be referred to that demonstrate the cultural proliferation of these attitudes within Britain. To conclude, I will briefly discuss the changing critical landscape of literary studies over the last thirty years, in which this dimension of Romantic literature has been increas-ingly scrutinized.

The Historical Context

It is unlikely that there was ever a time in history when Britain did not trade with other nations around the globe, and in the eighteenth century sugar came from the West Indies, tea from India, and tobacco from America. Increasingly, trade with China created a British demand for silks, porcelain and wall hangings in the fashionable 'chinoiserie' style, as it became known, even influencing the interior design of the Royal Pavilion in Brighton by John Nash (1815–1822). So the products of other countries, and the cultural influ-ences of other societies, have always contributed greatly to British tastes and trends through commercial engagement with them. During the eighteenth century Britain embarked on a mercantilist programme to develop trade and markets further afield, combined with a vigorous expansionist policy in which exploration of foreign territories went hand in hand with colonial settlement. Britain's transformation, from a role of economic and colonial intervention to twentieth-century world power, largely occurred in the Romantic period. At the end of the Napoleonic wars in 1815, Britain had consolidated, or gained, possessions in India, the West Indies, Canada, South Africa and Australia, and by 1820 it controlled a quarter of the world's population. The commercial development of these territories corresponded with the dissemination of social, cultural and religious beliefs, through the legal, administrative and linguistic structures used to support them.

Between 1780 and 1830, Britain's colonial territories ranged from white settler colonies and dependencies (in Canada, the West Indies, South Africa and Australia) governed by British colonial administrators, and trading outposts run by small numbers of British officials (such as British India, which was originally a territory of the East India Company). Other regions that Britain engaged with were the Islamic countries of the Middle and Far East, as well as the Turkish and Greek territories of the Mediterranean. Though Britons had always been travellers, explorers and settlers in new territories, wider engagement with a huge, disparate, imperial population led to a greater impetus to understand and describe them. So alongside the economic output and products of these territories abroad, Britain 'imported' ideas about them. For instance, voyages to the South Pacific by Captain Cook, expeditions across Canada by Alexander Mackenzie and Samuel Hearne, and missionary justifications of attempts to 'civilize' native populations in India, were consumed by a curious British public. This led to the dissemination of literary, historical and scientific modes of discourse to categorize native populations, often by those who sought to control them. However, the information that emerged from these encounters was often partial or subjective, because it was intended to justify the imperial project.

The frequently unreliable, indiscriminate reports of foreign social behaviour, or cultural and religious rites, led to the creation of racial stereotypes and (in today's terms) racist descriptions. Such representations were disseminated through other forms of literature popular with British readers, such as novels and poetry, as well as contemporary art and theatre. These texts often promoted metropolitan moral values over cultural difference, and recommended their own social model as an example to other nations. During the Romantic period, attempts to legitimize British political and cultural domination also led to theoretical hypotheses of a racial hierarchy that placed white Europeans in pole position. Nevertheless, it is also possible to distinguish resistance to such beliefs in works that privilege indigenous cultural heterodoxy, so disturbing coherent projections of British colonial policy on its possessions. These texts contain ambiguous responses to Britain's role overseas because exactly at the moment that its influence abroad was expanding, many British citizens appeared to desire a more responsible engagement with other territories of the world. This is evident, for instance, in British debates about the loss of the American Colonies (after their Declaration of Independence in 1776), the propriety of continuing the slave trade (as the abolitionist movement gathered momentum in the 1770s) and the best methods for ruling India (after 1788, when the British governor was arraigned for corruption).

Eighteenth-Century Racial Theory

With the increase in European knowledge of global territories, eighteenth-century philosophers such as Immanuel Kant, Johann Gottfried Herder and David Hume all engaged with the topic of race to find causal relations for the differences between human groups throughout the world. Using historical precedent, geographical and climatic distinctions, as well as descriptions of social manners and behaviour, their studies contributed to the branch of anthropology known as ethnology. A common idea that had gained valency among racial theorists since Greek antiquity was that distinctions between humans could be made on whether they were 'civilized' or 'savage'. In the Enlightenment period (or 'Age of Reason') white northern Europeans were distinguished as rational and civilized beings, while the opposite character-istics of unreason and savagery were applied to non-white people. In this way a hierarchy of difference became endemic that bestowed superiority on certain nations based on their colour. Such distinctions supported the colonial appropriation of territories through stadialist theory. This was the belief that man progresses towards civilization by increasingly sophisticated stages in his development. It originated from anthropological evidence that primitive (or 'savage') men were hunters first, who progressed to a higher level of civilization (the 'barbarian' stage) by living in settled societies based on a pastoralist economy. According to this theory, humans develop to a yet more civilized level once they engage in farming, commerce and manufacturing. Within such an ideological framework, nomadic societies, hunter-gatherers or those who cultivate land in a way that Europeans do not recognize forfeit their claim to it. Although this idea originally applied to European 'savage' cultures, such as the Scots or German tribes, it travelled transatlantically to justify the appropriation of Native American land.

Ideas about savagery were inherited from the classical writings of Tacitus, who perceived the tough Germanic natives as an example of 'hard primi-tivism'. This social model was contrasted with the 'soft primitivism' of a lost 'Golden Age' of innocence, ease and plenty. These categories were assessed through environmental factors, such as terrain or climate, which in their comfort or harshness were said to have imbued certain races with essential characteristics. In this theory, for instance, the Tahitians were perceived as 'soft primitives', and the natives of Tierra del Fuego, the Maoris and the

Australian aborigines, as 'hard primitives'. The positive representation of certain native characteristics led to the largely fictional creation of the 'noble savage', an ideal figure endowed by European observers with admirable physical and moral attributes. However, towards the end of the eighteenth century, missionary accounts of native populations in the South Pacific and India found repugnant ideas of natural virtue in what they perceived to be pagan savages. These reports of superstition and depravity that were sent home to British readers justified their conversion to Christianity.

Though the Enlightenment period was one in which scientific ideas gained ground, established Christian beliefs were retained in theories of racial difference, with the divinely ordained 'Great Chain of Being' still employed as a conceptual framework. In this hierarchical structure, every form of existence was assigned a unique status, with angels above human beings, and various examples of fauna and flora in descending positions on the scale. In the seventeenth century, in order to find a missing link between humans and primates, it was proposed that the non-European 'savage' should occupy the position between Caucasians and the lower inhabitants of this rational and moral evolutionary ladder. Later scientific interventions, specifically from the fields of cultural anthropology and biology, were based on such theories and extended racial categories further, as discussed below.

The African Slave Trade

From the start, the racial distinctions applied by Enlightenment theorists structured the African slave trade. The most simplistically applied dichotomy of difference ordered that white people (believing in their greater rational capabilities) were slave-owning and that black people were enslaved. This was because, while slavery was prevalent in many forms of human society before Europeans engaged in the African trade, the religious or tribal differences historically used to distinguish between master and slave were extended to race. Britain became involved in the transatlantic trade between its domestic seaports, the west coast of Africa and America and the Caribbean, in the sixteenth century. The scale of this commercial enterprise was unprecedented, seeing the estimated capture and abduction of as many as 11 million Africans, with their enforced transportation to the colonial plantations of another continent (Walvin, 2001: viii).

During the Romantic period, opposition to the British slave trade gained more and more influence. In 1772, when James Somerset – an American plantation slave who had travelled to London with his owner – was freed by the Mansfield Judgement, a popular idea emerged that no one could be a slave while on English soil. Such a belief was tied up in national concepts of liberty and equality, but the moral distinction between the British legal position on slave-ownership and colonial practices soon drew greater scrutiny. In this way the issue of slavery itself, as well as the brutality endemic in a commercial enterprise that treated humans as trade goods, became central in public discourse. This led to the formation of the Abolition Society in London in 1787. Supported in its endeavours by William Wilberforce, the parliamentarian champion of anti-slavery, government discussion and action eventually followed. After several defeated parliamentary bills in the 1790s and early 1800s, the slave trade was brought to an end in 1807, with the complete abolition of slavery in the British Empire by 1834, although plantation slaves served a term of apprenticeship for several years after this date before achieving full emancipation.

So the years between 1772 and 1834 were crucial in the emergence of a new, more humanitarian-oriented society in Britain. The political strategies that reformers used in support of abolition were reinforced by social action, in the form of extra-parliamentary campaigns and 'anti-saccharine' societies. In fact what makes this debate so distinctive is the huge amount of popular support it attracted, which was harnessed to bring about political change. This has led modern commentators to see the Romantic period as progressive in its moral individualism. However, the emergence of the abolitionist movement meant that more and more texts in defence of slavery were also produced. And despite the moral, legal, economic and religious arguments introduced on both sides of the debate, differences in colour, rationality and intellectual ability between blacks and whites were frequently alluded to.

On the pro-slavery side of the debate, economic and nationalist arguments against abolition – invoking the financial detriment to West Indian planters, or the dire consequences for Britain's economy and its future as a European power – were often intermingled with justifications based on racial difference. Many theorists stated that slavery was prevalent in Africa prior to British involvement, and that Africans were savages or heathens incapable of rational thought and moral feeling and therefore unfit for freedom. For instance, Edward Long's *History of Jamaica* (1774) argued that Africans were innately inferior due to their blackness, their lack of intellect, and their savagery. Equally racist reasons for prizing African workers, based on evaluations of their physical strength, labouring ability and resistance to tropical diseases were given less priority. Long's book presented a polygenetic account of race, positing Africans as a separate species from Europeans, and claiming that their inferiority predetermined their servility. Pro-slavery writers also argued that enslaving Africans benefited them, by exposing them to the civilizing effects of Christian doctrine and European social and cultural influences.

To make the opposite case, pro-abolitionist writers drew on more positive representations of Africans in their natural environment. For instance, Mungo Park's *Travels in the Interior of Africa* (1799) counteracted pro-slavery texts of the period in presenting West Africans as peaceful, industrious members of a complex society, rather than as warlike savages. Park's work relates to a strand of writing, such as Anthony Benezet's *Historical Account of Guinea* (1771) and Carl Bernhard Wadstrom's *Essay on Colonization* (1794–5), which assumed the full humanity and improvability of Africans. The African experience, through the slave narrative, also supported the anti-slavery cause and became a popular literary genre during the Romantic period. Several ex-slaves who had survived the West Indian plantations, such as Ottabah Cugoano and Mary Prince, wrote about their ordeals, often under the aegis of white abolitionist 'ghostwriters' who encouraged them to publish their stories. Such accounts usually described African life in ideal terms and concentrated on the brutal treatment of the narrators and their fellow slaves once captured and transported to the colonies. The polemical intention of such works was to promote African slaves as figures of sensibility in order to engage British empathy, and therefore action, in support of abolition.

Many British literary figures also supported the anti-slavery campaign, with Samuel Taylor Coleridge, Robert Southey, William Wordsworth, Hannah More and Ann Yearsley all writing poems on the subject. Their humanitarian but often sentimental stand against the enslavement of their fellow humans publicized the harsh treatment of individual slaves to arouse indignation in their readers. However such representations also created an idea of Africans as passive victims within the system of slavery, in need of white abolitionists to act on their behalf. Other imaginative depictions of slaves presented them carrying out murderous retribution on their oppressors. Africans, therefore, were perceived as either violent (relating to ingrained ideas of savagery), or lacking agency and unable to effect change themselves without white assistance, so contributing to racial stereotypes positing black inferiority. Eurocentric assumptions of superiority at this time were further encouraged by Christian perceptions of white as the colour of spiritual life, infantilizing Africans by perceiving them as figures of pity in their state of slavery and needing help to emerge from their darkness.

Orientalism

Africa was not the only region to shape perceptions of racial difference. A major geographical area that Britons engaged with, initially through trade, was known as the 'Orient'. An unspecific eastern locus, it had imaginative and ideological connotations that went far beyond any real dimensions. In practical terms, the eastern nations that Britain was in contact with were in the Mediterranean (such as Turkey), the Middle East, India and the Far East. Much of the engagement with these territories was through trade with the British East India Company, and after 1813 through the colonial government in India. During the Romantic period, Britain was keen to develop more sources of raw materials, and the East India Company in Bengal ensured a supply of cotton, silk, indigo, tea and saltpetre to European consumers, so providing an important source of revenue. Along with the luxury goods of the east for which Europeans developed a taste, they also became fascinated by written accounts of this region. Ideas about the 'Orient' were largely transmitted through fictional works such as the *Arabian Nights* (1704–1717), where readers could learn of a land of magic and miracles, luxury and opulence, governed by harem sensuality and oriental despotism. This framed expectations of oriental life and customs generally, and for most of the eighteenth century European writers made little attempt to depict eastern culture and society realistically. It was the perception of the east as an exciting, exotic location for scenes of adventure and sexual liberty that ensured the huge commercial success of literary works such as Byron's *Turkish Tales* (1813–16).

However the Romantic period also saw the influence of orientalist scholars such as Constantin Volney and William Jones, and the latter's translations of Arabian poetry and Indian sacred texts inspired Southey, Coleridge, Byron, Shelley and Thomas Moore to create their own oriental poetry. Jones' interest in comparative philology and his historical and geographical investigations also increased knowledge of the subcontinent and respect for its culture. Unlike contemporary perceptions of Africa by European commentators, that it was void of recognizable human systems of knowledge, Asia was perceived as an ancient and immense cultural repository; so much so that Thomas De Quincey, in his *Confessions of an English Opium Eater* (1821), found the vastness and antiquity of Asia overwhelming and fearful. His nightmare vision of this continent, with its disparate parade of creatures and gods threatening to physically overwhelm him, represents his anxiety that contact with the east will swamp the youthful culture of Europe in its ancient, arcane ritualism. Such perceptions support the view of the critic Edward Said, in *Orientalism* (1978), that ideological influences connect orientalist works to the expansion of Britain's empire.

British imperial interest in India manifested itself in political debate and journalism at home, based on negative reports of financial corruption and nepotism within its government. Combined with accounts (often from missionary sources) of Hinduism as a superstitious or pagan religion that was underpinned by rituals such as child sacrifice and *sati*, this led to calls for greater control of the region and its population. For instance, the abhorrence of Hindu practices in literary representations such as Southey's narrative poem the *Curse of Kehama* (1810), as well as the mistaken perception of it as a polytheistic faith, supported the policy of the Anglicist lobby for control of India through British education and Christian conversion. However, Southey's fascination for his Indian subject matter also creates ambiguity in his text, and the fact that his enthusiasm for its mythological dimensions was criticized by readers in his own time shows the contradictory nature of western representations. Nevertheless, as with Africa, cultural, religious and racial difference was used to defend imperial practice in all forms of discourse. The perceptions of native populations as devious, tricky, or 'inscrutable' were based on unequal power relationships between Europeans and those they sought to govern (as recent 'Subaltern Studies' demonstrate). They created the 'oriental' figure as an often conflicting composite 'Other' to reflect the inferior or alien qualities that the west wanted to impose on it. This dichotomized taxonomy of difference was further legitimized through scientific racial theories.

Scientific Racism

The basis for Romantic-period racial theory came from Enlightenment natural historians Carl von Linné (or Linnaeus), in his work *Systema Naturae* (1748), and Georges Buffon in his study, *Histoire Naturelle* (1749). Among other classifications of natural history these writers divided human beings into racial groups. Before their proposition that the term 'race' should have a new set of contexts, this word had been used to mean 'tribe' or 'nation' in its historical application of descent. However for Linnaeus and Buffon the word came to mean 'variety', based on physical appearance rather than lineage. Though Linnaeus did not subscribe to all the concepts regarding the 'Great Chain of Being', he did believe in a set hierarchy of organisms, and placed man in the order of primates with other mammals. However, he thought the characteristic that distinguished men from apes was the former's ability to use reason. Linnaeus found the variations that existed within the genus *Homo sapiens* to be a result of different cultures and climates, and that the four main categories were: *Americanus* (supposedly red-skinned and prone to anger, though observing cultural traditions); *Asiaticus* (yellow-skinned, melancholy and opinionated); *Africanus* (black, cunning, passive and impulsive); *Europeaus* (white, clever, inventive and governed by laws). The last category, the most rational and 'civilized' of mankind, was obviously the superior type in his view.

These racial hierarchies, and their corresponding ethnic stereotypes, developed further in the Romantic period through Eurocentric scientific methods. Expeditions claiming territory for Britain also facilitated racial classification, as explorers were instructed to observe and collect natural phenomena, including native skulls. Comparative anatomy was used to explain important differences between humans as well as animals, and natural historians were able to classify people into racial groups through the use of this physical evidence. A central proponent of this method for explaining racial difference was the German scientist, Johann Friedrich

Blumenbach, who amassed a large collection of human skulls and through crude empirical method speculated on the causes of variety. His attempt to differentiate between the races of man, based on their anatomical proportions, in *On the Natural Variety of Mankind* (1795) directly contributed to modern racist categories. A contemporary of Blumenbach's, the Dutch anatomist Pieter Camper, was also a skull collector. His studies contributed to a hierarchical classification, with black people at the bottom of the racial scale (just above those of apes) in his work, *On the Connexion between the Science of Anatomy and the Arts of Painting* (1794). His use of 'facial angles' to measure physical dimensions of each race, established an aesthetic hierarchy of human beauty, with Europeans at the top. The ideal physical standards were those of classical Greece, and the further human racial traits were from that notion of perfection, the less Caucasian they were. Numerous authors began to publish books to prove that Europeans were at the top of the racial hierarchy they believed in. European superiority was supported by reports of native beliefs, customs and manners, so that the physical descriptions of races were influenced by character assessments that often embodied a moral judgement. For instance, the French naturalist Georges Cuvier argued that cranial capacity, or brain size, meant that black people were inferior in intellect. His anatomical studies of the dead body of Sarah Baartman (known as the 'Hottentot Venus') contributed to contemporary moral opinions based on Linnaeus's assessment that African women were shameless. While Baartman was alive, she had been put on show in Britain and France to demonstrate her distance from white normative physical features. After her death in 1815, Cuvier's dissection of her body identified her prominent buttocks and labia as evidence of excessive black sexuality. Such professions, combined with Cuvier's belief in a limited intellectual capacity, presented Africans as closer to animals than humans.

Among such ideas of difference circulated the belief, evident in Charles White's *Account of the Regular Gradation of Man* (1799), that black people were not simply a different, lesser race, but a distinct species (which justified their enslavement). Before the development of evolutionary theories in the mid-nineteenth century, there were two primary belief systems for explaining the origins of mankind. The first was monogenism, in which all people were supposed to have originated from Adam and Eve, though some races had degenerated from that ideal more than others. This was a belief held by Blumenbach, who stated that the original colour of mankind was white, with differences in skin colour being due to climatic influences. Other nineteenth-century speculations about colour difference cited leprosy and syphilis as causes of skin darkness. The second, alternative theory of human origin, held by polygenists such as White, refuted the biblical story. They looked to biological and anatomical hypotheses to argue that because they were of a different species, black people were subject to domination by superior

Europeans. Such theorists even refuted the evidence of miscegenation to claim that the 'cross-species' offspring of black and white parents were sterile, despite their fertility corroborating African humanity.

Racial theories were often framed by distinctions between black and white people at either end of a colour spectrum, though Kant had posited Native Americans at the bottom of his own hierarchical scale, in *On the Different Races of Man* (1775). Changing approaches to physical evidence and fluctuating value judgements adapted such theories, and comparative systems became increasingly racist as the nineteenth century progressed. Other candidates for lower positions within systems of racial taxonomy were the Irish (Celtic) and Jewish, and Said maintains that 'orientals' were also constructed as degenerate members of a racial hierarchy (1995: 206). He goes on to state that binary oppositions, between European subject and 'Other', races deemed advanced or backward, and nations that are governed or dominated, have always framed western perceptions of the east. More recent critics question these solid distinctions, as well as the replication of such overarching terms that homogenise differences within them. Nevertheless, 'oriental' races were viewed in a framework of biological determinism that presented them as frozen, static and incapable of change. This is also true of the other taxonomical categories constructed during the Romantic period, which contributed directly to the racial eugenics of the late nineteenth-century.

Critical Interventions

Despite the reservations that have been applied to Said's critical work, it was ground-breaking in examining the role of European literary discourses in the ideology of empire, and the contribution of such writings to racial 'othering'. Another important early work within this field was Frantz Fanon's *Black Skins, White Masks* (1952), which analyzes colonial systems to explain how those subjugated within them internalize their racist distinctions. Since the 1980s a large diverse group of literary critics, historians and cultural theorists have explored the impact of colonial expansion, imperialist discourse and racial ideology on the Romantic period, by incorporating a wide range of approaches. The influence of 'new historicism' on Romantic literature has broken down perceptions of it as an aesthetic movement limited to a few canonical male writers and broadened the categories of writings and authors included under this overarching title. Critical works such as Marilyn Butler's *Romantics, Rebels and Reactionaries* (1981) and Jerome McGann's *The Romantic Ideology* (1983) were in the vanguard of historical and political readings that placed greater emphasis on issues of class, gender and race.

Such socio-political approaches have also been influenced by studies in the field of postcolonialism. Arguments that literature, as a cultural form, replicates or supports the unequal power relations within society to promote hegemony have been extended to systems of colonial administration by critics such as Gauri Viswanathan, in *Masks of Conquest* (1989). While it can always be argued that writing within any culture makes it complicit in the imperial project because it is likely to employ the dominant linguistic structures and cultural attitudes of the governing metropolitan centre, this negates the critical voices that existed within the period. And, though Sonia Hofkosh and Alan Richardson, in *Romanticism, Race and Imperial Culture* (1996), maintain that Romantic literature inherently promotes colonialist and racist attitudes, this has been challenged by critics within the 'Subaltern Studies' group. Using Gramscian ideas to critique traditional Marxist approaches to structures of power, members of this group, such as Ranajit Guha and Gayatri Chakravorty Spivak, attempt to consider the voices of those who are left unrecorded or excluded within colonial structures.

In considering colonialist writing, JanMohammed's idea of 'Manichean allegory' is useful for understanding the power differentials within its representations. Like Said, JanMohammed considers how cultural and colonial oppositional categories are applied to race. The distinctions between dominant and subordinate groups are thereby shown to employ other dichotomies, overlaid on them by the colonizer, who equates white and black with good and evil, or civilization and savagery, to maintain superiority. However, such rigid ideas of alterity (or otherness) have been increasingly questioned, especially by Homi K. Bhabha. His work highlights the ambivalence of colonial discourse to show the fragility of hegemonic constructions and the illusory nature of binary distinctions between the positions of colonizer and colonized, or white racial categories and others. The critical analysis of Romantic texts in the light of this methodology – by John Barrell and Nigel Leask, for instance – has revealed similar ambiguities and contradictions within them, rather than projecting a solid vision of racial or ethnic difference.

Writings that reflect nationalist or colonialist positions have been examined in recent critical approaches to understand their place in creating racial and ethnic stereotypes, including the imaginative writings that absorbed, promoted or sometimes challenged these ideas. While, the European (and particularly French) context has always been significant in defining ideas of British identity, as Linda Colley's *Britons: Forging the Nation, 1707–1832* (1992) demonstrates, other theorists believe Britain's colonial engagement is just as crucial. Mary Louise Pratt's study of travel-writing, *Imperial Eyes* (1992), examines the ways in which European explorers impose a totalizing, imperial vision on the world for their readers. Saree Makdisi's *Romantic Imperialism* (1998) reappraises canonical works to show that distinctive ideas of race and nationalism emerged from the colonial context to create a cultural movement. The varied critical perspectives in *Romanticism and Colonialism: Writing and*

Empire, 1780–1830 are nevertheless analogous in demonstrating how later rigid distinctions of imperialism were problematized at this time, with 'a paradigm shift in race theory and in the ways "race" was related to nationality and culture' also occurring (Fulford and Kitson, 1998: 20).

Recent critical engagements with the Romantic period interrogate the solid distinctions within colonialist or racist hegemonies, or provide examples of the empire 'writing back' in works of resistance and dissent. They also seek to represent those on the imperial margins, in terms of geography and experience. In the wake of such interventions, Romantic theorists continue to make these 'voices' available, as in Peter Kitson's and Debbie Lee's *Slavery, Abolition and Emancipation: Writings in the British Romantic Period* (1999), or in critical studies of their cultural impact, such as *Discourses of Slavery and Abolition: Britain and its Colonies, 1760–1838* (2004). As the range of approaches, topics and texts increases awareness of the diversity and heterogeneity of Romantic-period discourse, the racial and ethnic stereotypes that were constructed at this time also continue to be challenged by a more complex, and accurate, view of Britain's imperial population.

See also: Case Studies in Reading Critical texts; Changes in Critical Responses and Approaches

Notes

Barrell, J. (1991), *The Infection of Thomas De Quincey: A Psychopathology of Imperialism.* New Haven and London: Yale University Press.

Bhaba, H. K. (1994), *The Location of Culture.* London and New York: Routledge.

Coleman, D. (2005), *Romantic Colonization and British Anti-Slavery.* Cambridge: Cambridge University Press.

Franklin, M., ed. (2006), *Romantic Representations of British India.* London and New York: Routledge.

Fulford, T., and Kitson, Peter J., eds. (1998), *Romanticism and Colonialism: Writing and Empire: 1780–1830.* Cambridge: Cambridge University Press.

JanMohamed, A. R. (1989), 'The Economy of Manichean Allegory: The Function of Racial Difference in Colonialist Literature', in Henry Louis Gates Jr (ed.)'*Race'*, *Writing and Difference.* Chicago and London: Chicago University Press, pp. 78–106.

Kitson, P. and Lee, D., eds, (1999), *Slavery, Abolition and Emancipation: Writings in the British Romantic Period*, 8 vols, London: Pickering and Chatto.

Leask, N. (1992), *British Romantic Writers and the East: Anxieties of Empire.* Cambridge: Cambridge University Press.

Makdisi, S. (1998), *Romantic Imperialism: Universal Empire and the Culture of Modernity.* Cambridge: Cambridge University Press.

Pratt, M. L. (1992), *Imperial Eyes, Travel Writing and Transculturation.* London and New York: Routledge.

Richardson, A., and Hofkosh, S. (1996), *Romanticism, Race and Imperial Culture, 1780–1834.* Bloomington, Ind: Indiana University Press.

Said, E. W. (1978, rev. 1995), *Orientalism: Western Conceptions of the Orient*. Harmondsworth: Penguin.

Said, E. W. (1994), *Culture and Imperialism*. London: Vintage.

Spivak, G. C. (1994), 'Can the Subaltern Speak?' in P. Williams and L. Chrisman (eds) *Colonial Discourse and Post-Colonial Theory*. London and New York: Longman.

Walvin, J. (2001), *Black Ivory: Slavery in the British Empire* (2nd edn). Oxford: Blackwell.

Mapping the Current Critical Landscape

Peter J. Kitson

Any student approaching the literature of the Romantic period is bound to be daunted by the sheer range and volume of critical materials which are currently available, including studies of individual poets, novelists and prose writers, general treatments of large themes, issues and genres, as well as a host of handbooks and companions. The object of this essay is to suggest and outline a few of the leading contemporary critical perspectives on the literature of the Romantic period in the current critical landscape, and identify what may prove to be the leading trends for the forthcoming years.

The first thing to address, however, is the issue of what defines the field of Romantic studies itself. One problem that people working in the field encounter is an uncertainty about how the object of study is to be defined. Such terms as 'Romantic literature', 'Romantic-period literature' (or 'writing'), 'Romanticism', the 'long eighteenth century', and even 'Georgian' are all used to describe or encompass the literature written during the period from c. 1780 to 1837 (when the reign of Queen Victoria begins). The main issue for scholars working in the field is that this period has come to be defined by the term 'Romantic' which relates more to a kind of writing, in both style and subject, than to a defined historical period, such as Victorian, Elizabethan, or the Medieval. 'Romantic' and 'Romanticism' are critical constructions and the terms were not used by the writers themselves to define their work. The terms signify an investment in imagination as a creative force, nature as a subject for poetry, and in the role of the poet as prophet and visionary. The difficulty with such terms is thus that they exclude a large variety of writing by those who do not subscribe to the 'Romantic' agenda, most famously, Jane Austen.

Many thus working in the period prefer to see themselves as working on late eighteenth- and early nineteenth-century literature, or in the period of the 'long eighteenth century' which covers the period from 1688 to 1832 and stresses political continuity rather than the upheaval of the Romantic revolutions. Hence current criticism of Romantic period literature is often contained within the longer historical timeframe of the long eighteenth century. Recently a number of studies have appeared arguing for the continuing importance of the influential cultural phenomenon of Sensibility, or the belief in the importance of the emotions and affections (especially sympathy and benevolence) in human relationships in the period, and suggesting that Sensibility is part of the same process of cultural revolution as Romanticism. A number of critics and scholars have focused on the crucial role Sensibility plays in all aspects of cultural life in the eighteenth century and its relationship to a growing and increasingly wealthy middle class, eager to consume all kinds of products, including novels, poetry and drama. Jerome McGann has claimed that Sensibility is a highly sophisticated literary tradition and an alternative to Romanticism, and Markman Ellis that the novel of Sensibility was a new literary form capable of addressing current issues such as consumerism and capitalism, as well as slavery and prostitution. In the eighteenth century the volume of trade between Britain and the world vastly expanded and luxury items such as tea, coffee, sugar, spices, silks, cotton and porcelain, among others, became increasingly predominant in Britain. Eighteenth-century society became more and more a consumer society with an expanding and increasingly affluent middle class intent on refining its culture and investing in cultural and leisure activities, such as reading and going to the theatre. Literary Sensibility was very much a part of this middle-class project to enhance its cultural standing and social importance by refining its morals and manners, and creating an aristocracy of feeling rather than of rank and status. The role of consumerism, trade with the colonies and the marketplace are now seen as more central to literary analysis of Romantic period literature than in the past, and Sensibility is a crucial term for that process.

The ideal of Sensibility was gendered feminine and allowed women to create a social area for themselves separate from the masculine sphere, a place of domesticity, beauty and moral sensitivity. Conversely, men were also affected by Sensibility, creating the sensitive and feeling male, epitomized by Henry Mackenzie's novel, *The Man of Feeling* of 1772, a man capable of sympathy, sociability, benevolence and excessive emotion. A number of critics have addressed the issue and continuities or oppositions between Sensibility and Romanticism and its relationship to the birth of contemporary consumer society. G. J. Barker-Benfield has stressed the relationship between Sensibility, feeling and the marketplace; Adela Pinch has also argued for the continuities between Sensibility and Romanticism, both of which are movements concerned with identifying the origins of our affection and emotions. Poets such as Charlotte Smith, in her highly influential *Elegiac Sonnets* of 1782, employed a highly emotional response to natural landscape, combined with a deep sense of personal melancholy very much in the mode of Sensibility. Percy Shelley, notably exclaims 'I fall upon the thorns of life! I bleed!' in his highly emotional 'Ode to the West Wind'. Of course, many Romantic period writers such as Coleridge and Byron, came to react against the excessive emotionalism of Sensibility. Most notably, Jane Austen critiqued Sensibility in the character of Marianne Dashwood in her novel *Sense and Sensibility* (1811). Marianne displays her Sensibility through enthusing about nature and literature, falling in love at first sight with the unreliable Mr Willoughby, and weeping hysterically when he leaves her. McGann and others have also pointed out that Sensibility, as a movement which stressed first impressions and an innate and intuitive sense of right and wrong, along with its notion, derived from conceptions of humanity (notably the eighteenth-century philosopher, Jean-Jacques Rousseau), that all human beings are essentially good, espoused a liberal and humanitiarian politics that became associated with the radicalism of the French Revolution in the 1790s and suffered from the subsequent conservative reaction to that event which swept Britain from around 1793 onwards, politicizing Sensibility as a potentially dangerous and suspect mode. Nevertheless, Sensibility's relationship to the Romantic Age with its associated ideas of sympathy and sentiment is a complex and intricate one, and one that critics are increasingly exploring.

While single author studies of the major Romantic period poets, such as Wordsworth, Coleridge, Blake, Byron, Keats and Shelley remain vibrant, more sustained attention has increasingly been given to women writers, labouring and working-class writers, and a host of non-canonical novelists and poets. Writers such as William Godwin, John Thelwall, Walter Scott, Joanna Baillie, Anna Barbauld, Robert Burns, Thomas Moore, Hannah More, Mary Robinson, Charlotte Smith, Ann Yearsley, Felicia Hemans, John Clare and many more have benefited since the early 1980s from this feminist and historicist scholarly activity. To an extent this is an attempt to recover the writing of the period itself. Although poetry was always the privileged genre of the period, more recently sustained and serious study of the Romantic period novel has occurred, and that historically most slighted of all Romantic genres, popular drama, has now become, or is becoming, a new and exciting area for serious study.

Surveying the recent critical endeavours of Romantic Period studies, there appear to be certain areas which are attracting new or renewed interest and are being transformed by recent criticism. Much current critical endeavour is focused on the recovery of texts and authors to the critical purview of scholars and readers. Once marginal figures are now being restored to the centre of the critical landscape by numerous scholars and critics. This work of historical recovery is on-going and the re-establishment of such non-canonical writers to the curriculum will leave a richer and more complex field of study. Central to this endeavour is the growth of digital Romanticism and the exponential rise in the electronic availability of previously difficult to obtain works by lesser-known, forgotten or excluded texts, especially by women writers. Notable resources include *Romantic Circles*, the Women Writers Project at

Brown University, and *The Blake Archive*. The Blake Archive is a pioneering attempt to present the texts of Blake's illuminated books in facsimile, enabling us to compare plates printed and coloured differently at different times in the poet's life. The images often exhibit a high level of difference, challenging the notion of any single, authoritative edition of Blake's writing and art. Such electronic archives and hypertexts will make available to the student and general reader a massive amount of primary and secondary critical material that was only accessible in the past in specialist archives and collections.

Since the 1980s critical attention moved away (but not completely) from the concern with the male canon of the 'Big Six' poets (Blake, Wordsworth, Coleridge, Keats, Byron and Shelley), to consider the wealth of writing, especially female, that makes up Romantic period literature. As part of this endeavour was an increased interest in the social and political events of the period, from the American and French Revolutions to the 1832 Reform Act. A series of historically minded critics, including Marilyn Butler, Jerome J. McGann, Alan Liu and Marjorie Levinson, known as 'new historicists', shone the spotlight on the social and political realities of Georgian Britain and accused the canonical Romantics, in particular Wordsworth and Coleridge, of turning their backs on humanity in favour of an idealized and mystical form of natural religion, typically practised by them in the English Lake District. In many ways, current criticism of the literature of the period has expanded and deepened this concern with the social and political by widening the focus of the critic to encompass within his or her purview a 'Global Romanticism' that describes both the geographical reach of their concerns but also the wide sweep of knowledge about the globe and the interrelationships between the two.

The Romantic period witnessed Britain's establishment as a major European imperial power and strengthened her trajectory towards becoming the global superpower of the nineteenth century. The process has been charted in many places, but Linda Colley's *Britons: Forging the Nation, 1707–1837* (1992) is one of the most influential accounts of the construction of British national identity in the period. Colley's argument is that Britons came to define themselves as 'Protestants struggling for survival against the world's foremost Catholic power', France (p. 5). Colley's impressive study of national identity, however, has been criticized for a too exclusive concern with continental and Catholic France as the 'Other' against which Britons came to define themselves. At the conclusion of the Seven Years War in 1763, Britain emerged as the leading colonial power in the West Indies, Canada and the Indian subcontinent. Additionally, her fleets were exploring the globe searching for new lands, such as the famed southern continent *terra australis incognita*, and new trade routes, such as the Northwest Passage over the Canadian Arctic. Britain was also the leading nation involved in the transatlantic slave trade, a legal trade in the British colonies up until 1807, when it was formally abolished there, though Britain retained her slave colonies in the West Indies. Britons were thus faced with a wide range of other nations, peoples, religions and customs to which they reacted in various ways, sometimes favourably, often aggressively, and which truly forged their sense of national identity. Since the turn to history in the 1980s, numerous and diverse scholars are now addressing the impact of Britain's rapidly burgeoning commercial empire on the literature and thought of the period, encompassing the role of slavery, race, colonialism and commerce. It is thus fair to say much recent writing about the period has derived from a perspective that is variously informed by historical considerations of colonialism, empire and slavery and post-colonial theoretical accounts of subject formation and construction. Such critics are concerned with the cultural effects of colonialism and imperialism as well as the legacies these forces have bequeathed to the contemporary world. The two main (though not the only) areas where this has been especially apparent are transatlantic slavery and the Oriental.

The Romantic Period in English literature coincided with the period when the British Atlantic slave trade was at its height. Between 1680 and 1783 more than two million African slaves were transported to the British colonies alone, and it is estimated that British ships were carrying over 50,000 slaves a year to the Americas between 1791 and 1800. Most of the slaves went to the sugar colonies, which were believed to account for a substantial portion of Britain's commercial prosperity. Jamaica alone produced 60,000 tons of sugar in 1791 rising to 100,000 tons in 1804, making the colony the biggest exporter of sugar in the world. Many Romantic-period writers were involved in the slave trade, slavery itself or the campaign for its abolition. The Gothic novelist Matthew Lewis inherited his father's plantations in Jamaica, and William Beckford's family were enormously wealthy as a result of their extensive Jamaican slave estates. Jane Austen's father was the trustee of an Antiguan slave estate and Charlotte Smith's father-in-law had West-Indian slave interests. Both Smith and Austen addressed the issue of slavery in their writings, though Austen is famously more oblique than Smith in her allusions to the subject in *Mansfield Park* (1814). Wordsworth and Coleridge met in Bristol at the house of the sugar merchant and plantation owner at St Nevis, John Pinney. Blake, Wordsworth, Coleridge, Robert Southey, John Thelwall, Anna Barbauld, Ann Yearsley, Mary Robinson and many others all addressed the subject of slavery in their writing.

Literary and cultural scholars of the Romantic period, with a few notable exceptions, have become interested in British colonial slavery and its abolition only rather recently. In the 1980s, and more particularly in the 1990s, the study of the literary and cultural forms of slavery and abolition began to emerge as a distinct area of specialism within literary studies. By the end of the 1990s, a growing number of critics had approached the subject from a wide range of perspectives. Vincent Carretta, Angelo Costanzo, Helena Woodward and Helen Thomas transformed our understanding of the slave narrative; Deirdre Coleman, Moira Ferguson and Felicity Nussbaum demonstrated the relationship between abolitionism and British women's writing; Markman Ellis showed that antislavery and sentimentalism were closely aligned, while Alan Richardson, Joan Baum, Brycchan Carey, Debbie Lee, Tim Fulford and Helen Thomas have all explored the multiform ways in which the concerns of the emerging Romantic movement interacted with the ideals of the abolition, and later, the emancipation campaigns. The sociologist Paul Gilroy influentially introduced the now widely recognized category of the 'Black Atlantic' into Romantic studies. Gilroy pushes the critical concern away from too narrow a consideration of Black people with enslavement to focus on the issue of the transatlantic Black diaspora and alternative modes of cultural production. One notable effect of this process has been the meteoric rise in literary status of the former slave and abolitionist, Olaudah Equiano, whose powerful narrative, *The Interesting Narrative of the Life of Olaudah Equiano* (1789) or *Gustav Vasso, The African,* is now taught and studied with equal status to the literature that has always held the most canonical status. This critical concern has led to a reappraisal and study of Black writers such as the poet Phillis Wheatley, Ignatius Sancho, Ottobah Cugoana, Mary Prince and many others.

The texts of the abolition movement, long confined to remote library archives, have also been made available to a wider readership as well. By 2000, a dozen anthologies of eighteenth- and nineteenth-century literature both by and about slaves in the British colonies have appeared; several editions of important African self-representations, such as those by Olaudah Equiano and Ignatius Sancho, had been issued. In recent years we have had a major biography of Oladauh Equiano by Vincent Carretta and a controversial discussion of slavery and literature by Marcus Wood. While authors such as Markman Ellis and Brycchan Carey stress the importance of Sensibility and a sympathetic engagement with human suffering, especially that of the brutalized, punished, imprisoned or tortured slave, Marcus Wood, in a series of powerful critiques of Romantic and other writing about slavery, argues that such writers simply failed to humanize the slave, largely because of the vicarious nature of an aesthetic of Sensibility which appropriates the slave's sufferings for the metropolitan domestic audience and its unease with the idea that the slave could attain his or her freedom through violent rebellion. Wood thus argues that eighteenth-century representations of African slaves tend to find pleasure in the experience of sympathising with the slave at the expense of the real human suffering he or she experiences, which remains unknowable.

These critics laid the groundwork for what, in the first decade of the twenty-first century, has become an important sub-field in the areas of eighteenth-century literature and the literatures of the Romantic era. It is no longer possible to teach or to research eighteenth- and early nineteenth-century literature without paying attention to issues of race and empire, and without recognizing Britain's participation in the trade in human beings. Having become established as an important sub-field of literary studies in the 1990s, the study of the literature of slavery and abolition is now seen as occupying a crucial place in the current critical landscape of the culture and thought of the Romantic period.

In recent years, Romantic-period criticism has thus been transformed by the application of critical approaches deriving from postcolonial critical perspectives. What we describe as the Romantic Movement coincided with the beginnings of a modern British Imperialism, which involved the governance and exploitation of increasingly large portions of the globe as the nineteenth century wore on. It also involved conflict with other imperial formations of the time, some expansive and others in decline; European empires such as the French and Russian, and non-European empires such as the Turkish Ottoman and the Qing Empire of China. Many Romantic period writers, the Wordsworths, De Quincey, Austen and so on, had family who were involved in Empire in one way or another, and it certainly impinged on their consciousness as a pressing fact of life.

Representation of other nations and peoples is familiar in Romantic period writing, especially that about the East or the Orient. In fact the cultural historian Raymond Schwab influentially described the Romantic age as the 'Oriental Renaissance', as the growing European fascination with, and discovery of, Eastern languages and literatures fuelled the interest of writers and their readers for Oriental subjects. Many writers, such as British East India Company legal expert, Sir William Jones, regarded the East as a source of imaginative and creative renewal; however what was once viewed as a sympathetic engagement with the East, or alternatively dismissed as escapism and exoticism, has recently come to be considered in a much more suspect, if not sinister light. Rather than studying the East to learn about and understand other cultures, a number of postcolonial scholars and critics have claimed that European engagement with the East, and especially with Islam, is instead simply a series of recurring negative stereotypes. It is alleged by such critics that Europeans use the East against which to define their own self-image as rational and modern. Although a substantial body of writing had already appeared on this subject, it was the Palestinian-American critic Edward Said's study *Orientalism* (1978) which defined the idea and scope of the critique for a new generation. Said claimed that the discipline of Orientalism, the academic study of the East as well as imaginative writing about the East, does not describe the East at all. Orientalism, he claims, is thus a 'western style for dominating, restructuring, and having authority over the orient. (3)' Said claimed that this political imperative was not just seen in the writings of contemporary travellers, diplomats, colonial administrators, linguists and historians but also in the work of imaginative writers and artists. Not only were novelists such as Kipling, Conrad, and Flaubert, whose subject was often the East, guilty of furthering the project of Orientalism and Empire, but also writers such as Jane Austen, Charles Dickens, Henry James and Thomas Hardy, whose works hardly mention such subjects, were similarly embroiled. Orientalism thus became a grand narrative that subsumed many forms of cultural and scholarly endeavour to represent and contain the East. The Orientalist creates the orient by assuming a European self that is rational, modern, technological, active, creative, masculine and in need of an irrational, despotic, sybaritic, passive, feminine, despotic and corrupt other to authenticate it.

Said's work has been both praised and criticized in equal measure and it stimulated an extensive, sophisticated and often bitter debate. Nigel Leask concurred with Said that imaginative literature about the East shared, unwittingly or otherwise, in the project of knowing and dominating the East but he argued that Romantic writing gave rise to anxieties as well as certainties about the European self. Said, he claimed, was right to make the link between imperialism and knowledge about the East, but wrong to see this as 'a closed system'. Leask argued, for instance, that in the Byron's Eastern Tales, such as *The Giaour* and *The Corsair*, the poet's 'gaze, fixed like many of his fellow countrymen on the collapsing fabric of the Ottoman Empire, also turned back reflectively on his own culture as the world's dominant colonial power, and the significance of his own complicity in that power as a poet of Orientalism' (1992, 4, 23).

Srinivas Aravamudan, in his book *Tropicopolitans: Colonialism and Agency, 1688–1804* (1999) further problematized Said's concern with Western Self and Oriental, redefining the eighteenth-century European colonial in the context of the 'Tropicopolitan'. Aravamudan's term is used as a way of negotiating 'the colonized subject who exists both as a fictive construct of colonial tropology and actual resident of tropical space, object of representation and agent of resistance'. 'Tropicopolitans' are thus fictional representations of real colonial subjects, yet they are also at the same time ideological constructions that can be put to different purposes. For Aravamudan, 'Tropicopolitans' reveal memories of traumas such as slavery and are as much concerned with opposing colonialism as being a part of its discourse (1999, 4, 5, 17, 18). Instead of the binaries of Said's Orientalism, Aravamudan prefers to situate writing about racial others in the context of a dynamic interaction of Islamic and European cultures. For Aravamudan the Orient has multiple uses, some utopian and others repressive. Most recent postcolonial criticism of Romantic poetry, therefore, has tended to reinforce Said's perspectives, albeit in a more complex way. Saree Makdisi, in his *Romantic Imperialism: Universal Empire and the Culture of Modernity* (1998), furthered and complicated Said's project by placing Western responses to the East in the context of modernization; the industrializing, rationalizing, secularizing technological project of European imperialism which, he argued, tends towards the emergence of a single and dominant world system, what we know as the process of 'globalization'. For Makdisi, Romanticism's obsession with the pre- and anti-modern marks it out as involved in a critique of modernization, whether in Wordsworth's 'spots of time,' Scott's Highlanders in *Waverley* or the oriental settings of Byron's *Turkish Tales*. Byron's Levant, he argues, functions not as a description of a real place but as an 'anti-modern Orient', defined and structured by its own sense of time; however, rather than functioning as resistance to European modernization, such constructions serve only to reinforce the very modernity against which they are defined and support not contradict the totalizing and globalizing processes of empire (1998, 1–22, 123).

Recently even Jane Austen, long-regarded as astute and ironic critic of the manners and mores of the English rural and provincial gentry, has not been immune to the postcolonial gaze. Said first directed our attention to Austen's postcolonial context by focusing on the important fact that Sir Thomas Bertram, the patriarch of *Mansfield Park* (1814), owns slave properties in Antigua. Crucially, he is called away in the course of the novel to deal with matters there and, in his absence, the interlopers Henry and Mary Crawford encourage the Bertram family to engage in inappropriate amateur theatricals. Austen's moral value system, as symbolized in the landed estate of Mansfield Park, is thus premised on the income that its owners derive from slave labour. Slavery is thus present in the novel both as a reality and a theme. Said claims that novelists such as Austen constructed an 'idea of England' within a critical distinction between 'home' and 'abroad'. He sees Austen's detail of Sir Thomas' Antiguan properties as highly significant and her refusal to explore its implications as telling. He situates her novel 'at the centre of an arc of interests and concerns spanning the hemisphere, two major seas and four continents' (101).

Said's discussion of *Mansfield Park* has sparked a fascinating and extensive debate about Austen's complicity with Empire and slavery. In 2002 Marcus Wood argued against Said that Austen's novel in fact presents a deliberate critique of the system of plantation slavery by means of allusion and irony. In his telling reading of the novel, Wood claims that the issue of the income from Antiguan slave estates exerts a 'constant pressure' on every character at Mansfield Park (305). Focusing on the discourse of 'improvement', Wood argues that Sir Thomas values Fanny Price much in the way that he regards his slaves, and assesses her worth accordingly. Especially convincing is Wood's reading of Sir Thomas' enthusiastic evaluation of Fanny's charms when he returns from Antigua to reassert his patriarchal authority over his family. Wood draws our attention to the similarity between Sir Thomas' enhanced appreciation of Fanny's physical attributes with that of the prospective buyer at a West Indian slave auction: 'Austen utilizes an economic language, and a language of ownership and improvement, which can incorporate and equate Fanny, the plantation, and the slaves in identical linguistic terms' (319).

The global context of Austen's work was further explored in the pioneering volume of essays, *The Post Colonial Jane Austen* (2000), edited by You-Me Park and Rajeswari Sunder Rajan, which further situated Austen's novels, and especially *Mansfield Park*, in the context of 'a geographically expansive world, the world that European travel, exploration, commerce, military adventure and imperialism brought into being and redefined in terms of colonial relations of domination, race, classed and gendered' (4). For the critics in that volume Austen's novels are more a part of a *'colonial discourse'* than an F. R. Leavis inspired 'great tradition' of English novelists. The contributors to this volume extend but also complicate Said's analysis of the novel, specifying with greater accuracy the historical moment to which the novel belongs in the longer history of British Imperialism and teasing out the complicated ironies and allusions which Austen fashions in her sophisticated fictions. Notably, as well as the issue of slavery, the novel also anticipates the growing involvement of Britain with the Qing Empire of China, in Fanny's reading of recent travel accounts of the Macartney Embassy to China. Nor is Austen the only Romantic-period writer to be subject to enquiries concerning race and slavery. Coleridge's most famous poem, 'The Rime of the Ancient Mariner', previously viewed as a poem about a voyage of spiritual rather than geographical discovery, is now placed in the frame of contemporary exploration and the slave trade. The poem can be read as a text about the postcolonial guilt experienced by the mariner incorporating details of the slave trade that the younger Coleridge knew so well from his days as a radical activist in Bristol, lecturing against the contemporary war with France as well as the Trade in slavers. Critics such as Debbie Lee and Marcus Wood have drawn our attention to the details of disease, the rotting oceans as indicators of the poem's clear contemporary concerns.

The gothic novel has also emerged as a fertile ground for postcolonial readings with its creation of boundaries and depictions of humanity and otherness. In Mary Shelley's *Frankenstein* (1818), the creature is now frequently regarded as representative of an otherness that includes race. Both Debbie Lee and H. L. Malchow, taking their cue from George Canning's 1824 comparison in a parliamentary debate of Frankenstein's creation to that of a prematurely emancipated slave, situate the creature as a rebellious slave. Similarly, Charlotte Dacre's *Zofloya; or, The Moor* (1806), with its depiction of a Machiavellian and charismatic black servant (who turns out to be the

Devil), has received much recent scholarly attention. This new pre-occupation in Gothic studies with issues of race, nation and empire can be seen in the collection of essays from 2003, *Empire and the Gothic: the Politics of a Genre*, edited by Andrew Smith and William Hughes.

If postcolonial approaches to Romantic literature have become more apparent and crucial in recent years because of our contemporary need to grapple with the vexed question of how human beings are to manage their various interactions in a postcolonial world, then critical approaches which stress environmental concerns are equally important. In response to the challenges posed to the world by a series of historical human interventions, such as climate change, global warming, diminished food stocks and disappearing rain forests, a number of critics have returned to Romantic nature poetry, with its concern with the inter-relationships between the natural world and human communities and its criticism of an unfettered commercial and industrial process, for clues and guidance as to how an alternative 'green' consciousness and practice might be imagined. Instead of the new historicists' depiction of Romantic nature poets, especially Wordsworth and Coleridge, as politically evasive and reactionary individuals who turned their backs on radical politics and contemporary events to commune with an idealised nature in the Lake District, eco-criticism gives us a Romantic canon re-invigorated with fresh insights and significances. The first major eco-critical study of the Romantic poets was Jonathan Bate's *Romantic Ecology: Wordsworth and the Environmental Tradition* (1991), which made a case for the significance of Wordsworth's poetry of nature for the present day. Bate's *Song of the Earth* (2000), also advocated what he called 'ecopoetics' and argues that the Romantic poets tried to re-imagine the relationship between human community and the natural environment. In 1994, Karl Kroeber's *Ecological Literary Criticism: Romantic Imagining and the Biology of Mind* also argued that the Romantic poets anticipated our current green and environmental concerns. Lawrence Buell's *The Environmental Imagination* (1995), though mainly focused on the American nature writers, such as Emerson and Thoreau, argued for the crucial importance of the natural environment in literary texts. James McKusick's *Green Writing: Romantic Imagining and the Biology of Mind* (2000) claimed that the writings of the English Romantics, especially Wordsworth, but also John Clare, were highly influential in providing the underpinnings of American Environmentalism.

Such Romantic ecological literary criticism has re-evaluated the writings of the Romantic nature poets, especially Wordsworth, whose depictions of rural communities as well as isolated figures wandering the landscape in such poems as 'Michael', 'The Ruined Cottage', and *The Prelude* can speak powerfully to our post-industrial society anxious to hang on to or regain its relationship with a disappearing landscape. Wordsworth and

Coleridge's collaboratively produced collection of 1798, *Lyrical Ballads*, deals with a lived-in natural environment which is under threat from a number of man-made forces. Coleridge's major contribution to that collection, his 'The Rime of the Ancient Mariner', as critics such as James McKusick have suggested, presents us with a destructive human intervention within the natural world, when the Mariner gratuitously and without thought, destroys a harmless wild creature, thus unleashing a series of punitive natural responses from a dynamic and holistic eco-system. Wordsworth's 'Tintern Abbey' similarly depicts the inter-relationship between humanity and nature, a nature under threat from encroaching pollution in the Wye Valley. As well as restoring Wordsworth and Coleridge to the centre stage of Romantic writing, eco-criticism has also celebrated the work of numerous other poets, especially the 'peasant poets' Robert Bloomfield, Ann Yearsley and John Clare. Such poets wrote from an experience of living within the rural community from the point of view of the local rural labourer. Clare, in particular, inveighs against the inroads made into the life of rural communities by the new forces of landscape 'improvement' and 'enclosure'. In his poem 'The Mores' Clare angrily decries how 'Inclosure came and trampled on the grave/Of labour's rights'. For Clare such forces are destroying communities with a symbiotic relationship with the natural environment and removing people's traditional rights.

Eco-criticism with its understanding of environmental concerns promises to remain a major presence in the twenty-first century. Indeed Timothy Morton's recent volume, *Ecology Without Nature: Rethinking Environmental Aesthetics* (2007), outlines the paradoxical notion that for us to establish a genuine ecological awareness, the idea of nature itself which sets up an opposition between the perceiving human and some object 'out there' needs to be relinquished and re-thought. If everything is really inter-related in a dynamic ecosystem, then the idea of nature as determined in the works of the Romantics and others can become a barrier to breaking through to a truly ecological way of thinking and acting and establishing an authentic environmentalism.

One further area which has expanded greatly in recent years and may well emerge as a leading area of criticism in Romantic period studies in the twenty-first century is that of drama. Often decried in the past as not worthy of the same serious study as poetry and the novel because of its melodramatic and popular nature, in recent years the genre has moved further towards the centre stage in terms of both research and teaching. Probably this is because drama, as a form, is inextricably involved in the kinds of negotiations that I have already outlined, those relating to gender, nation, class and race. Scholars and students of the Romantic period have come to understand the central importance of drama in the period, both as a cultural institution and leisure interest and as a source of important and relevant texts reflecting on the current concerns and issues in Romantic period Britain. New editions of the drama of the period are appearing, such as Peter Duthie's edition of Joanna Baillie's *Plays on the Passions* (2001) and Jeffrey N. Cox and Michael Gamer's *Broadview Anthology of Romantic Drama* (2003) which contains plays by Hannah Cowley, Elizabeth Inchbald, George Colman the Younger, Matthew Lewis and Joanna Baillie, as well as Coleridge, Shelley and Byron.

Scholars and critics of the period are also attempting to study the theatre as a social space as well as the dramatic texts that it produced. Gillian Russell's *The Theatre of War: Performance and Society, 1793–1815* (1995) argued that the theatre functioned as a political arena in the period and provided a series of dramatic metaphors for the conduct of the war. Two theatres, Covent Garden and Drury Lane, were licensed to produce 'legitimate drama' with spoken parts by the Licensing Acts of 1737 and were closely censored by the Lord Chamberlain's Examiner of Plays. Other theatres, known as the 'illegitimates', were allowed to stage lower forms of drama which were set to music, involving dance and sensational special effects. Jane Moody's *Illegitimate Theatre in London, 1770–1840* (2000) depicts the emergence of this illegitimate theatre and the cultural struggle between London's licensed or 'patent' playhouses and the newer minor theatres.

A number of critics have discussed the roles of women writers and performers in the period. Betsy Bolton's *Women, Nationalism, and the Romantic Stage* (2001) explores the ways in which these women, including Mary Robinson, Emma Hamilton, Hannah Cowley and Elizabeth Inchbald, used the theatre to intervene in the political debates of the 1780s and 90s, and most recently, Felicity Nussbaum's *Rival Queens: Actresses, Performance, and the Eighteenth-century British Theater* (2010) shows how female performers, such as Susannah Cibber, Anne Oldfield and Catherine Clive, were crucial to the success of the commercial theatres through their influence on the drama produced, as well as their defining of femininity for the wider world. Eighteenth-century actresses are important as the first modern subjects, actively shaping their public identities to make themselves into celebrated properties. Likewise critics such as David Worrall in a series of recent works, including *Harlequin Empire: Race Ethnicity and the Drama of the Popular Enlightenment* (2007), have explored the world and networks of the popular theatre and the representation of foreign cultures and ethnicities on the popular British stage from 1750 to 1840 and its harlequinades, melodrama, pantomimes and spectacles. In these theatres, he claims, discussions about natural and civil rights, voyage and discovery, and Britain's relationship with other cultures were relentlessly enacted.

Conclusion

Romantic period studies is a vibrant and developing field of enquiry which is constantly moving in new directions, employing new approaches and discussing areas of concern for the present day, such as the changing world environment and our relationships with the natural world. As well as the production of new texts and the rediscovery of neglected writers, the current critical landscape shows an increasing concern with a Transatlantic and a Global Romanticism, intrigued by the period's perceptions and understandings of other peoples and cultures of the world, especially in terms of religion, and the creative but also troubled relationship between East and West.

Notes

Aravamudan, Srinivas (1999) *Tropicopolitans: Colonialism and Agency, 1688–1804.* Durham, NC: Duke University Press.

Barker-Benifeld, G (1996) *The Culture of Sensibility: Sex and Society in Eighteenth-Century Britain.* Chicago: Chicago University Press.

Bate, Jonathan (1991) *Romantic Ecology: Wordsworth and the Environmentalist Tradition.* London and New York: Routledge.

—— (2000) *The Song of the Earth.* London: Picador.

Baum, Joan (1994) *Mind-Forg'd Manacles: Slavery and the English Romantic Poets.* North Haven, CT: Archon Books.

Bolton, Betsy (2001) *Women, Nationalism, and the Romantic Stage.* Cambridge: Cambridge University Press.

Buell, Lawrence (1995) *The Environmental Imagination: Thoreau, Nature Writing and the Formation of American Culture.* Cambridge, MA and London: Harvard University Press.

Carey, Brycchan (2005) *British Abolitionism and the Rhetoric of Sensibility: Writing, Sentiment and Slavery, 1760–1807.* London: Palgrave.

Carretta, Vincent (2005) *Equiano the African: Biography of a Self-made Man.* Athens: Georgia University Press.

Colley, Linda (1992) *Britons: Forging the Nation, 1707–1837.* New Haven: Yale University Press.

Ellis, Markman (1996) *The Politics of Sensibility.* Cambridge: Cambridge University Press.

Gilroy, Paul (1993) *The Black Atlantic: Modernity and Double Consciousness.* London: Verso.

Hughes, William and Smith, Andrew (eds) (2003) *Empire and the Gothic: The Politics of Genre.* London: Palgrave.

Kroeber, Karl (1994) *Ecological Literary Criticism: Romantic Imagining and the Biology of Mind.* New York: Columbia University Press.

Leask, Nigel, *British Romantic Writers and the East: Anxieties of Empire*, Cambridge University Press, 1992.

Lee, Debbie (2004) *Slavery and the Romantic Imagination.* Philadelphia: University of Pennsylvania Press.

Pinch, Adela (1996) *Strange Fits of Passion: Epistemologies of Emotion, Hume to Austen.* Stanford: Stanford University Press.

Makdisi, Saree (1998) *Romantic Imperialism: Universal Empire and the Culture of Modernity.* Cambridge: Cambridge University Press.

Malchow, H. L. (1996) *Gothic Images of Race in Nineteenth-Century Britain.* Stanford: Stanford University Press.

McKusick, James (2000) *Green Writing: Romantic Imagining and the Biology of Mind.* New York: Columbia University Press.

Moody, Jane (2000) *Illegitimate Theatre in London, 1770–1840.* Cambridge: Cambridge University Press.

Morton, Timothy (2007) *Ecology Without Nature: Rethinking Environmental Aesthetics.* Cambridge, MA and London: Harvard University Press.

Nussbaum, Felicity (2010) *Rival Queens: Actresses, Performance, and the Eighteenth-century British Theater.* Philadelphia: University of Pennsylvania Press.

Park, You-Me and Rajan, Rajeswari Sunder (eds) (2000) *The Postcolonial Jane Austen.* London: Routledge.

Russell, Gillian (1995) *The Theatre of War: Performance and Society, 1793–1815.* Oxford: Clarendon Press.

Said, Edward (1978) *Orientalism.* London: Pantheon Press.

—— (1991) *Culture and Imperialism.* London: Random House.

Wood, Marcus (2003) *Slavery, Empathy and Pornography.* Oxford: Oxford University Press.

Worrall, David (2007) *Harlequin Empire: Race Ethnicity and the Drama of the Popular Enlightenment.* London: Pickering and Chatto.

Glossary

Allegory: A story with two meanings that is capable of being understood on two or more levels: the primary, or surface level, and the secondary, figurative level. A famous example is John Bunyan's 1678 prose fiction *Pilgrim's Progress* which narrates the journey of its hero, Christian, through various landscapes (such as the Slough of Despond, Vanity Fair, Doubting castle) to the Celestial City. Christian's journey is a figurative account – an allegory – of Christian salvation

Augustanism (or Neo-Classicism): An artistic movement of the first part of the eighteenth century that sought to reproduce the literary, artistic and architectural styles of the 'classical' civilisations of ancient Rome and Greece. The term 'Augustan' was an allusion to the Roman emperor Caesar Augustas with whom Kings George I and II were compared. The Augustan literary style copied the highly ordered, well-proportioned verse forms of the Classical period. Romanticism in many ways reacted against the Augustan emphasis on reason and discipline in literary composition, though the poetry of Lord Byron often displays a strong affiliation with the Neo-Classical style (see his long satirical poem *Don Juan*).

Ballad: A narrative poem associated with oral traditions of folk-tale and folk-song. A ballad usually consists of four line stanzas with a simple, melodic rhyme scheme to facilitate oral or musical recitation. Several Romantic writers appropriated the ballad form in some of their most famous poems: for example, Coleridge's *The Ancient Mariner* and Keats' *La Belle Dame Sans Merci*.

Blank Verse: A form of poetry introduced to England in the mid-sixteenth century that is comprised of unrhymed lines usually of iambic pentameter (five stresses per line with the first stress falling on the second syllable of the line). It is a form used especially in dramatic, epic and reflective verse and it was employed extensively by the Romantic poets: see Wordsworth's *Prelude*; Coleridge's *Frost at Midnight*; Shelley's *Prometheus Unbound*.

Closet Drama: A play written to be read rather than performed, or one that would be very difficult to perform on the stage. Plays as different as Byron's dramatic poem *Manfred* (1817), Shelley's lyrical drama *Prometheus Unbound* (1820), or Beddoes' dramatic poem *The Bride's Tragedy* (1821) fall into this category. In the past the term has been used (rather too broadly) to designate the Romantics' resistance to, discomfort with, or incompetence at writing for the stage. The term thus also suggests an attempt to separate drama, a more respectable genre disposed toward the solitary act of reading a text (also associated with the Romantic reclamation of Shakespeare as the nation's pre-eminent dramatic artist, as opposed to dramaturge), from theatre, a more public event to which was often ascribed a dubious or problematic moral or mass cultural character. More recent criticism on Romantic theatre and drama, such as writing on Joanna Baillie's *Plays on the Passions* (1798), has expanded our understanding of how the Romantics used closet drama, however tentatively or reluctantly, to negotiate between private and public spheres via its exploration of a range of aesthetic, political, and philosophical issues.

Conversation Poem: A term that refers to a relatively small group of Romantic lyric poems by Coleridge (*The Eolian Harp, Frost at Midnight,* among others) in which a solitary speaker/poet addresses his experience and contemplation of his immediate reality to an absent interlocutor, thus establishing a philosophical dialogue or 'conversation' with this person. A precursor of the conversation poem is something like the 'conversation piece' in late seventeenth- and early eighteenth-century painting, which depicts groups of two or more friends or family members in a state of informal interaction. Its spirit is thus social and democratic, though Coleridge's poems ostensibly belie this impetus. Like closet drama, the conversation poem thus suggests a traditional way of thinking about the Romantic 'turn inward' from increasingly complex social, political, and historical issues. Yet also like the closet drama, it characterizes a broader Romantic concern with, and anxiety about, how poetry negotiates between the public and private spheres, between the interior space of one's thoughts and the exterior world of social action and interaction. The conversational mode, that is to say, suggests the attempt of poetry to deal with the increasingly popular, often mass cultural phenomena of the novel and theatre.

Deconstruction: A mode of literary criticism emerging in the 1960s and 1970s most frequently associated with the work of French philosopher and theorist Jacques Derrida and the work of the Yale literary critic Paul de Man. The word deconstruction, both as critical practice and character of all writing, refers to elements of a text which indicate its tendency, consciously but especially unconsciously, to contest or reverse its own intentions. For Derrida this tendency is symptomatic of an instability within Western metaphysics, beginning with Plato, and its legitimation and privileging of the written word and its very truth claims. So, while deconstruction has since been often reduced merely to a textual practice or a quality of texts or to an exclusively philosophical or theoretical *ethos,* and thus misinterpreted as ahistorical or apolitical, its rather more powerful impetus was to unmask the historical and political effects elided by the Western authority and hegemony ascribed to texts and writing.

Epic: A long narrative poem in elevated style usually recounting the exploits of a hero or warrior and incorporating elements of history, myth and folk tale. Two notable instances of Epic at the beginning of the European literary tradition are Homer's *The Odyssey* and *The Iliad*. In the Romantic period, Shelley (*Alastor*) and Keats (*Hyperion*) adopted the Epic and Byron's satire *Don Juan* also contains elements of this form.

Irony: a mode of textual self-consciousness whereby a work reveals its status as literary, or fictive, and an author signals ambivalence towards what is being narrated and undermines its apparent seriousness. The term 'Romantic irony' is often used to refer to the literary self-consciousness, playfulness and often self-mockery that characterises certain Romantic works and that exposes the artificiality of the literary text as a textual composition.

Hermeneutics: The interpretation of a literary text, or the theory of interpretation of texts. In literature, the term often refers to the study of the way in which literary meaning is communicated in a text.

Intertextuality: This term originated in the 1960s with the French philosopher Julia Kristeva and it was developed later in the work of poststructuralist theorists such as Roland Barthes. It refers to the idea that all literary texts are connected to each other and to the texts that precede them, that texts are caught up in processes of quotation and citation such that it becomes difficult to sustain a notion of true literary originality: as Kristeva put it, a text is a 'mosaic of quotations' that signal its absorption and transformation of other materials.

Jacobin: A person associated with or sympathetic to the Jacobin cause in the French Revolution. The Jacobin Club (1789-1794) was the most important political society in France, named after the Dominican convent where its members met in Paris on Rue St. Jacques (which stems from the Latin *Jacobus*). In British literature the term is most commonly associated with radical writers of the 1790s and their various calls for social and political reform: William Godwin, Mary Hays, Thomas Holcroft, Elizabeth Inchbald, and Mary Wollstonecraft. What became known as the Jacobin novel is most frequently associated with these writers, but immediately thereafter, given British reaction against French political and military ambition, the word became a way of deriding, castigating, or denouncing anyone sympathetic to the revolutionary cause.

Lyric Poem: A short poem from between approximately fifteen to fifty lines that can take various forms in terms of rhyme scheme and metre (a lyric poem can take the form of an ode, for instance – see John Keats' *To Autumn*). It usually recounts the experiences of a single individual, often though not always the poet, and is concerned especially with the inner life and subjective responses of the speaker. Romantic-era poets John Clare and Robert Burns were accomplished in the form and all the Romantic poets employed the lyric to varying extents

Ode: A lengthy poem, formal in tone and complex in structure. The ode is serious in subject matter and is sometimes employed in celebration or commemoration of some famous figure or event: for example, Tennyson's *Ode on the death of the Duke of Wellington*. Poets in the Romantic period developed the meditative ode to explore specific Romantic themes, such as natural landscape, or the inner life of the poet: see Keats' *On Melancholy*, Shelley's *Ode to the West Wind*, for instance.

Orientalism: In broad terms the word orientalism refers to scholarship and writing that focus their understanding and interpretation of Eastern culture through the lens of Western or occidental thought. In more specific theoretical terms, exemplified by Edward Said's influential study *Orientalism* (1978), postcolonialism takes orientalism as the target of its critical practice by examining the extent to which the writings of Western academics and artists reflect a broader imperialist practice, the effect of which is to represent as 'other' or 'marginal' to Western identity Eastern influence, so as to defuse or efface this influence.

Parody: A piece of writing that seeks through exaggerated imitation to render a certain style or idea ridiculous. A famous instance of Romantic-era satire is Byron's *The Vision of Judgement*, a parody of Robert Southey's *A Vision of Judgement* which was itself written in response to Byron's satirising of Southey in *Don Juan*. Although the main objective of parody is usually derisive, it can have a didactic aim in seeking to expose the follies and vices of the wider culture.

Pastoral: Meaning 'pertaining to shepherds', a form of literature which eulogises rural life. Pastoral has its origins in ancient Greece and has a long history throughout the Western literary tradition, from the Greek and Roman poets Theocritus and Virgil, through the English poets Edmund Spenser (*The Shepheardes Calendar*, 1579), John Milton (*Lycidas*, 1637) and George Crabbe (*The Village*, 1783). British pastoral poets from the eighteenth century tended to eschew the idealisation of rural life that had characterised the genre previously. Both George Crabbe and William Wordsworth (see his poem *Michael*, 1800) portrayed the harsh realities of rural living especially as old ways of life broke down under the influence of urbanisation and industrialisation. Pastoral has also assumed other literary forms, such as drama, music and landscape painting.

Picturesque: A term from visual art and literature of the 1790s, formulated in William Gilpin's *Three Essays* (1792) or Richard Payne Knight's *An Analytical Inquiry into the Principles of Taste* (1805) and emerging from eighteenth-century writings on the beautiful and the sublime (Edmund Burke, Immanuel Kant) and earlier from seventeenth-century landscape painting (Lorraine, Poussin) to designate the aesthetic pleasure derived from natural scenes both remote and familiar, wild or tranquil, savage or idyllic. The picturesque can thus be said to merge the terror of sublimity with the balance and harmony of beauty to express the vital interest and variety of human responses to the natural world, whether in Wordsworth's locodescriptive verse, J. M. W. Turner's paintings, or various travel writings of the period

Postcolonialism: A field of theoretical and critical inquiry that emerged in the 1980s and 1990s to examine subjects dispossessed, supressed, or appropriated by any colonizing power. Postcolonial studies takes aim specifically at the imperializing effects of power associated with Western European (since the fifteenth century) and American (since the nineteenth century) global expansion. One of its recurrent targets of critique is the British Empire. Postcolonialism thus examines the apparatuses of power, both political and discursive, in order to critique their colonizing effects. The dissemination of orientalist writing by the West about the East (see above) is one focus of this critique. All these are clearly indicated under the Annotated Bibliography.

Poststructuralism: A broad mode of theoretical inquiry emerging in the 1960s with the writings of figures such as French psychoanalyst Jacques Lacan and French philosopher Jacques Derrida. Often treated synonymously with deconstruction, poststructuralism situated itself against structuralism as exemplified by anthropologist Claude Levi-Strauss or semiologist Roland Barthes (whose later work turned toward poststructuralism) in order to read their tracing of the larger organization of symbolic structures in the cultural practices of myth or ritual as what Lacan might call acts of fantasy or what Derrida might call acts of logocentric authority. To mark the time 'after' or 'post' structuralism was thus also to mark the instability of structuralist thought itself, and so to mark the 'post' poststructuralism of this initial structuralist controversy and its profound influence on critical thought and practice in the academy and beyond since the 1960s. Indeed, one of the most epochal effects of poststructuralism has been to rethink the disciplinary and some might say artificial divide between the academy and the 'outside world', which still others might say has led to a devaluation or relativization of all cultural values.

Regency: In British history the Regency proper refers to the timespan between 1811, when George III was declared unfit to rule because of mental incapacity and his son the Prince of Wales took over as Prince Regent, and 1820, when George III died and the Regent assumed the throne as George IV. More broadly the term can be traced back to the first Regency 'crisis' of 1788-89, when George III was momentarily declared unfit to rule. In the broadest cultural terms, the term Regency has at times been used to map generally onto the period between the French Revolution and the advent of the Victorian period in the 1830s, and thus as a term relatively synonymous with Romanticism itself. A somewhat more careful marking of this rather expansive definition, however, is to use the term Regency roughly to characterize the fashion, architecture, and style of early nineteenth-century British culture, especially the 1810s to 1830s.

Satire: a work in which the folly or vice of an individual, a group or an entire culture is derided or ridiculed. Satire has a long history in Europe reaching back to the ancient Roman satirists (Juvenal, Horace and Seneca) whose work influenced English Neo-Classical writers in the early-to-mid eighteenth century, notably Alexander Pope whose poems *The Rape of the Lock* and *The Dunciad*, for instance, ridiculed the vanity and superficiality of contemporary culture. Jonathon Swift's fiction and essays also constituted some of the most famous satires of this period: *Gulliver's Travels*; *A Tale of the Tub*, and *A Modest Proposal*. Although several Romantic poets occasionally wrote satire (Shelley's *The Masque of Anarchy*; Keats' *The Cap and the Bells*), satirical poetry in the Romantic period is associated principally with Byron: see especially *Don Juan* and *The Vision of Judgement*

Sensibility: A term that refers formally to the Age of Sensibility or roughly the later eighteenth century, typified by Laurence Sterne's *A Sentimental Journey* (1768) or Henry Mackenzie's *The Man of Feeling* (1771). More generally, sensibility designates in literature of the period one's passionate, emotional responses to the world and others, and so is also tied variously to sentiment (the unity of thought and feeling) and sympathy, both associated with the writings of Adam Smith, as in his *Theory of Moral Sentiments* (1759). Sensibility thus came to influence and typify Romantic literature of the 1790s and beyond, increasingly with some defensiveness about the association of Romanticism with the dangerous excesses of personal and social response and action, as exemplified by the influence of Rousseau's *Julie, or the New Heloise* (1761) or Goethe's *The Sorrows of Young Werther* (1774) on British writing. What were previously privileged as signs of refined sensibility thus came to stand, on one hand, for effeminate weakness and an inability to fulfill one's active place in the social sphere, and on the other a dangerous political motivation that threatened to undermine or emasculate proper British governance.

Sonnet: A short poem comprised of fourteen lines usually in iambic pentameter, but with considerable variations in rhyme-scheme. The three main variations of the sonnet form are: Petrarchan (after the Italian Francesco Petrarca); Spenserian (after the English poet Edmund Spenser), and Shakespearean. Originating in medieval Italy, the sonnet emerged in England in the sixteenth century and became a major literary form through the work of poets such as Spenser, John Donne, John Milton and, especially, Shakespeare. From the late-seventeenth through to the late-eighteenth century, the sonnet largely fell out of use until its revival during the Romantic period. William Wordsworth wrote several major sonnets, possibly his most famous being *Composed on Westminster Bridge, September 3, 1802.* The Romantic sonnet is usually a deeply meditative form of verse addressing and developing a specific intellectual idea or emotional response: see Keats' *On First Looking into Chapman's Homer*; Shelley's *Ozymandias*.

Travel Writing: A genre of historical, biographical and autobiographical, scientific, and especially literary writing that corresponds with the age of modern European global exploration and expansion inaugurated in the fifteenth century. In the Romantic period travel writing became especially important as a way for British citizens to experience a world increasingly under the domination of British colonial interests. Travel writing thus expressed the increasingly cosmopolitan and global nature of British national identity, whether to open others to an experience of this broader world or to train them about the benefits of imperial ambition and thus, once again, to misread or misinterpret the very culture this literature sought to express. For British authors, the genre of travel literature became one way to articulate their experience of domestic spaces (the walking tours described by writers associated with the Lake District, for instance), but more importantly their encounter with other lands, as in Mary Wollstonecraft's *Letters Written in Sweden, Norway, and Denmark* (1796), the fictional romance of Sydney Owenson's *The Missionary: An Indian Tale* (1811), or Mary and Percy Shelley's *History of a Six Weeks' Tour* (1817) – and so was extremely influential on all forms of Romantic writing, from Coleridge's *The Ancient Mariner*, to Mary Shelley's *Frankenstein*, to De Quincey's *Confessions of an English Opium-Eater*.

Annotated Bibliography

The list below is organized by topics so that students can easily locate their areas of interest. There is a wealth of single author studies that for reasons of space we have not been able to list, though some of these, because of their of broad thematic appeal, have been listed. Although we have attempted to be as representative as possible, the following list is necessarily selective. Students should take the following suggestions as starting points for their own interests, an introduction to the body of past and present criticism that exists beyond the entries below. The study of Romantic literature and culture has expanded considerably in the past thirty years and reflects an increasingly intersecting number of theoretical perspectives and disciplinary interests. Many of the following citations belong in more than one category, as you will be able to tell from their titles alone. A great part of the adventure of delving into this rich body of material is discovering, through the studies below, resonances between disciplines and critical approaches, especially as the fields of study we now take for granted were becoming defined and subsequently evolving in the Romantic period itself.

General Introductions to Romantic Literature and Culture

The following list reflects the development of Romantic studies from its emergence in the earlier twentieth century as a separate field of study still ambivalent about Romanticism (Lovejoy and Praz; and later, Bate, Bowra, Bush) to a mid-century New Critical concern with the complexities of close textual readings (Wasserman) or shortly thereafter a focus on the consciousness of Romantic vision and transcendence (Abrams, Bloom, Frye, Hartman). In reaction to the emphasis in these earlier criticisms on finding a coherent, organic Romantic identity, we can then chart the subsequent influence of deconstruction (Chase, de Man, Rajan) and a return to investigate the more complex and diverse historical and political contexts from which Romantic literature emerges (Butler, McGann). In the spirit of this re-thinking of Romantic history, subsequent texts explore the divide between Romanticism and Enlightenment thought (Brown), and thus reflect a concern to re-define Romanticism's historical and philosophical reach. The Beer, Johnston, and Pfau collections indicate the expansion of the Romantic canon and the productive opening up of Romantic studies to a variety of disciplinary and theoretical interests towards the end of the twentieth century. Here 'Romanticism' and the 'Romantic' emerge, less as coherent or easily defined critical identities than as modes of thinking about an increasingly diverse array of socio-historical phenomena, as reflected in the subsequent categories in this list. Duff's text re-contextualizes our increasingly heterogeneous understanding of Romantic thought and culture in terms of the genres that express them, while Elfenbein offers a social philology of the rise of English studies in Romanticism. In this way both texts reclaim critical purchase on the rather singular nature of the Romantic achievement.

Abrams, M. H., *Natural Supernaturalism: Tradition and Revolution in Romantic Literature*, New York: Norton, 1971.

Abrams, M. H. (ed.), *English Romantic Poets: Modern Essays in Criticism*, London: Oxford University Press, 1960.

Bate, Walter Jackson, *From Classic to Romantic: Premises of Taste in Eighteenth-Century England*, Cambridge, MA: Harvard University Press, 1946.

Beer, John (ed.), *Questioning Romanticism*, Baltimore: Johns Hopkins University Press, 1995.

Bloom, Harold, *The Visionary Company: A Reading of English Romantic Poetry*, Ithaca: Cornell University Press, 1971.

Bowra, C. M., *The Romantic Imagination*, Cambridge, MA: Harvard University Press, 1949.

Brown, Marshall, *Preromanticism*, Stanford: Stanford University Press, 1991.

Bush, Douglas, *Mythology and the Renaissance Tradition in English Poetry*, Cambridge, MA: Harvard University Press, 1937.

Butler, Marilyn, *Romantics, Rebels, and Reactionaries: English Romanticism and Its Background, 1760–1830*, Oxford: Oxford University Press, 1982.

Chase, Cynthia. *Decomposing Figures: Rhetorical Readings in the Romantic Tradition*. Baltimore: Johns Hopkins University Press, 1986.

de Man, Paul, *The Rhetoric of Romanticism*, New York: Columbia University Press, 1984.

Duff, David, *Romanticism and the Uses of Genre*, Oxford: Oxford University Press, 2009.

Elfenbein, Andrew, *Romanticism and the Rise of English*, Stanford: Stanford University Press, 2009.

Frye, Northrop, *A Study of English Romanticism*. Chicago: University of Chicago Press, 1968.

Hartman, Geoffrey H., 'Romanticism and Anti-Self-Consciousness', in *Beyond Formalism: Literary Essays 1958–1970*, New Haven: Yale University Press, 1970, pp. 298–310.

Johnston, Kenneth R. (ed.), *Romantic Revolutions*, Bloomington: Indiana University Press, 1990.

Jones, Steven E., *Satire and Romanticism*, New York: St. Martin's Press, 2000.

Lovejoy, Arthur O., 'On the Discrimination of Romanticisms', *Publications of the Modern Language Association* 39 (1924), pp. 229–53.

McGann, Jerome, *The Romantic Ideology: A Critical Investigation*, Chicago: University of Chicago Press, 1983.

Peckham, Morse, *Romanticism and Ideology*, Hanover: Wesleyan University Press, 1995.

Pfau, Thomas and Robert F. Gleckner (eds.), *Lessons of Romanticism: A Critical Companion*, Durham: Duke University Press, 1998.

Praz, Mario, *The Romantic Agony*, Angus Davison, trans., Oxford: Oxford University Press, 1933.

Rajan, Tilottama, *Dark Interpreter: The Discourse of Romanticism*. Ithaca: Cornell University Press, 1980.

Wasserman, Earl, *The Subtler Language: Critical Readings of Neoclassic and Romantic Poems*, Baltimore: Johns Hopkins University Press, 1959.

Class, Economics, Politics

The influence of a cultural materialist criticism typified by the groundbreaking studies of Thompson and Williams opened Romanticism to a sociopolitical exploration that takes up a variety of influences such as Karl Marx, Michel Foucault and any number of post-Marxist theorists. Accordingly this criticism addresses how Romantic literature both reflects and is shaped by the alloy between class, economics and politics, overlooked in the previous focus of criticism on Romanticism's aesthetic, formal, or philosophical identity. Barrell's study takes up the protean nature of the law. As these issues have become productively cross-fertilized in texts cited in other categories below, we urge you to look past this particular list to note its resonance across the field of Romantic studies in all categories listed below

See also: Gender and Sexuality; Gothic; Nationalism, Race, Colonialism, Empire; Narrative and the Novel; Poetry; Print Culture and Readership.

Barrell, John, *Imagining the King's Death: Figurative Treason, Fantasies of Regicide, 1793–1796*, Oxford: Oxford University Press, 2000.

Canuel, Mark, *Shadow of Death: Literature, Romanticism, and the Subject of Punishment*, Princeton: Princeton University Press, 2007.

Collings, David, *Monstrous Society: Reciprocity, Discipline, and the Political Uncanny, c. 1780–1848*, Lewisburg: Bucknell University Press, 2009.

Connell, Philip, *Romanticism, Economics, and the Question of Culture*, Oxford: Oxford University Press, 2002.

Favret, Mary, *War at a Distance: Romanticism and the Making of Modern Wartime*, Princeton: Princeton University Press, 2010.

Haywood, Ian, *Bloody Romanticism: Spectacular Violence and the Politics of Representation, 1776–1832*, Basingstoke: Palgrave Macmillan, 2006.

McCann, Andrew, *Cultural Politics in the 1790s: Literature, Radicalism and the Public Sphere*, Basingstoke: Palgrave Macmillan, 1999.

Rowlinson, Matthew, *Real Money and Romanticism*, Cambridge: Cambridge University Press, 2010.

Scrivener, Michael, *The Cosmopolitan Idea in the Age of Revolution and Reaction, 1776–1832*, London: Pickering and Chatto, 2007.

Shaw, Philip (ed.), *Romantic Wars: Studies in Culture and Conflict, 1793–1822*, Burlington: Ashgate, 2000.

Thompson, E. P., *The Making of the English Working Classes*, New York: Vintage, 1966.

Watson, John Richard, *Romanticism and War: A Study of British Romantic Period Writers and the Napoleonic Wars*, Basingstoke: Palgrave Macmillan, 2003.

Williams, Raymond, *Culture and Society: Coleridge to Orwell*, London: The Hogarth Press, 1987.

Worrall, David, *Radical Culture: Discourse, Resistance, Surveillance, 1790–1820*, Detroit: Wayne State University Press, 1992.

Drama and Theatre

One of the most vibrant fields in Romantic studies in recent decades has been the study of Romantic drama and theatre. Previously criticism viewed the Romantic writers as (largely failed) dabblers in drama, and so the genre was accorded marginal status. The reclamation of previously disregarded women writers (Bolton, Burroughs), along with a re-thinking and re-contextualization of what previously canonical writers were attempting to achieve by writing dramas (Burwick, Richardson), has opened the field to a broader cultural and critical study of Romantic drama's national and transnational influence (Carlson, Cox) and the often contentious political history of drama publication and theatre practice in the Romantic period (Moody, O'Quinn, Russell, Worrall). The O'Quinn/Moody anthology is perhaps the best introductory glimpse into our expanding knowledge of this diverse terrain

See also: Class, Economics, Politics; Gender and Sexuality; Nationalism, Race, Colonialism, Empire.

Bolton, Betsey, *Women, Nationalism, and the Romantic Stage: Theatre and Politics in Britain, 1780–1800*, Cambridge: Cambridge University Press, 2001.

Burroughs, Catherine B., *Closet Stages: Joanna Baillie and the Theatre Theory of British Romantic Women Writers*, Philadelphia: University of Pennsylvania Press, 1997.

Burwick, Frederick, *Illusion and the Drama: Critical Theory of the Enlightenment and Romantic Era*, University Park, PA: Pennsylvania State University Press, 1991.

Carlson, Julie A., *In the Theatre of Romanticism: Coleridge, Nationalism, Women*, Cambridge: Cambridge University Press, 1994.

Cox, Jeffrey N., *In the Shadows of Romance: Romantic Tragic Drama in Germany, England, and France*, Athens: Ohio University Press, 1987.

Moody, Jane, *Illegitimate Theatre in London, 1770–1840*, Cambridge: Cambridge University Press, 2000.

O'Quinn, Daniel, *Staging Governance: Theatrical Imperialism in London, 1770–1800*, Baltimore: Johns Hopkins University Press, 2005.

O'Quinn, Daniel and Jane Moody (eds), *The Cambridge Companion to British Theatre, 1730–1830*, Cambridge: Cambridge University Press, 2007.

Richardson, Alan, *A Mental Theatre: Poetic Drama and Consciousness in the Romantic Age*, University Park, PA: Pennsylvania State University Press, 1988.

Russell, Gillian, *The Theatres of War: Performance, Politics, and Society, 1793–1815*, Oxford: Clarendon Press, 1995.

Worrall, David, *Theatric Revolution: Drama, Censorship and Romantic Period Subcultures 1773–1832*, Oxford: Oxford University Press, 2006.

Ecology

Romantic ecocriticism takes up an increasing attention to and anxiety about the fate of the planet in the later twentieth century, especially focused in the rise of the environmental movement signalled in the 1960s with the publication of Rachel Carson's *Silent Spring*. This ecological concern has a broad reach across the Humanities and Social Sciences, as well as other fields, but has found a particular resonance in Romantic studies. The Romantic return to nature, previously understood in largely aesthetic or philosophical terms, has now prompted a rich and growing body of criticism that examines the historical, cultural and sociopolitical valence of Romantic responses to the environment as anticipating the modern environmental movement. Bate, Kroeber and McKusick are the starting points for this Romantic 'green criticism' or 'eco-criticism', which has expanded to include reflections on the field itself (Buell), on the colonial effect of Romantic notions of nature on other environments (Hutchings), and on Romantic notions of animal rights (Perkins). Morton's text turns Romantic ecology on its head by arguing that it entails a Romantic ideology *of* nature that misses nature itself, thus abstracting the very problems environmental criticism purports to solve.

See also: Imagination, Prophecy, the Sublime; Nationalism, Race, Colonialism, Empire; Romantic Theory and Criticism; Poetry

Bate, Jonathan, *Romantic Ecology: Wordsworth and the Environmentalist Tradition*, New York: Routledge, 1991.

—— *The Song of the Earth*. New York: Picador, 2000.

Buell, Laurence, *The Future of Environmental Criticism: Environmental Crisis and Literary Imagination*, Malden: Blackwell, 2005.

Hutchings, Kevin, *Romantic Ecologies and Colonial Cultures in the British Atlantic World, 1770–1850*, Montreal: McGill-Queen's University Press, 2009.

Kroeber, Karl, *Ecological Literary Criticism: Romantic Imagining and the Biology of Mind*, New York: Columbia University Press, 1994.

McKusick, James, *Green Writing: Romanticism and Ecology*, New York: St. Martin's Press, 2000.

Morton, Timothy, *Ecology Without Nature: Rethinking Environmental Aesthetics*, Harvard: Harvard University Press, 2007.

Perkins, David, *Romanticism and Animal Rights*, Cambridge: Cambridge University Press, 2003.

Gender and Sexuality

The expansion of the Romantic canon to include previously marginalized or entirely overlooked male or female writers coincides with a surge in writing on Romantic gender and sexuality. The result has been a re-thinking of the categories of 'masculine' and 'feminine', as revolutionary in Romantic studies as it was when writers like Wollstonecraft challenged the categories in the Romantic period itself. Arguably work on gender and sexuality reflects the single greatest influence propelling the growth of Romantic studies in the later decades of the twentieth century. Gilbert and Gubar, Poovey, Sedgwick, Ross, Jacobus and Mellor are among the ur-texts. Fay's feminist introduction to Romanticism, and three essay collections (Favret and Watson, Feldman and Kelley, Craciun and Lokke) represent how the field flourished in the 1990s and 2000s, along with studies by Elfenbein, Favret, Ferris, Fulford, Hofkosh and Todd. Later contextualizations (Behrendt, Kipp, Sha, Wolfson) suggest the productive cultural directions the field is taking. This list does not include the heroic work of numerous editors involved in historical reclamation of women writers as the standard editions upon which to build a future scholarship – Nora Crooke, Pamela Clemit, Betty Bennett and Stuart Curran, to name only a few. Despite the field's ongoing vitality, one also has to recognize that issues of gender and sexuality, like those of class, politics, economics or nationalism, have been thoroughly absorbed into the study of Romantic literature and culture. This does not make such categories irrelevant, but rather indicates how influential such notions have become.

Behrendt, Stephen C., *British Women Poets and the Romantic Writing Community*, Baltimore: Johns Hopkins University Press, 2009.

Craciun, Adriana and Kari Lokke (eds). *Rebellious Hearts: British Women Writers and the French Revolution*, Albany: State University of New York Press, 2001.

Elfenbein, Andrew, *Romantic Genius: The Prehistory of a Homosexual Role*, New York: Columbia University Press, 1999.

Favret, Mary, *Romantic Correspondence: Women, Politics, and the Fiction of Letters*, Cambridge: Cambridge University Press, 1993.

Favret, Mary and Nicola J. Watson (eds), *At the Limits of Romanticism: Essays in Cultural, Feminist, and Materialist Criticism*, Bloomington: Indiana University Press, 1994.

Fay, Elizabeth A., *A Feminist Introduction to Romanticism*, Malden: Blackwell, 1998.

Feldman, Paula R. and Theresa Kelley (eds), *Romantic Women Writers: Voices and Countervoices*, Hanover: University Press of New England, 1995.

Ferris, Ina, *The Achievement of Literary Authority: Gender, History, and the Waverley Novels*, Ithaca: Cornell University Press, 1991.

Fulford, Tim, *Romanticism and Masculinity: Gender, Politics, and Poetics in the*

Writings of Burke, Coleridge, Cobbett, Wordsworth, De Quincey, and Hazlitt, New York: St. Martin's Press, 1999.

Gilbert, Sandra and Susan Gubar, *The Madwoman in the Attic: The Woman Writer and the Nineteenth-Century Literary Imagination*, New Haven: Yale University Press, 1979.

Hofkosh, Sonia, *Sexual Politics and the Romantic Author*, Cambridge: Cambridge University Press, 1998.

Jacobus, Mary, *Romanticism, Writing, and Sexual Difference: Essays on* The Prelude, Oxford: Oxford University Press, 1989.

Kipp, Julie, *Romanticism, Maternity, and the Body Politic*, Cambridge: Cambridge University Press, 2003.

Mellor, Anne K., *Gender and Romanticism*, London: Routledge, 1993.

Poovey, Mary, *The Proper Lady and the Woman Writer: Ideology as Style in the Works of Mary Wollstonecraft, Mary Shelley, and Jane Austen*, Chicago: Chicago University Press, 1984.

Ross, Marlon B., *The Contours of Masculine Desire: Romanticism and the Rise of Women's Poetry*, New York: Oxford University Press, 1989.

Sedgwick, Eve Kosofsky, *Between Men: English Literature and Male Homosocial Desire*, New York: Columbia University Press, 1985.

Sha, Richard, *Perverse Romanticism: Aesthetics and Sexuality in Britain, 1750–1832*, Baltimore: Johns Hopkins University Press, 2009.

Todd, Janet, *Gender, Art, and Death*, New York: Continuum, 1993.

Wolfson, Susan, *Borderlines: The Shiftings of Gender in British Romanticism*, Stanford: Stanford University Press, 2006.

Gothic

Like drama and theatre, Gothic literature was previously seen as the poor cousin of more 'respectable' genres, like poetry, the novel or non-fiction prose, usually because of its less savoury association with issues of gender, sexuality, class and race. Over the past several decades the Gothic has emerged as both a paradigmatic Romantic genre as well as a discursive force crossing and transgressing generic, political and cultural boundaries in the Romantic period and beyond. Sedgwick and Baldick are foundational texts, Sedgwick by asking what 'coherence' Gothic conventions do and do not have, Baldick by examining the cultural power Mary Shelley's first novel exerted on the nineteenth-century imagination. Botting (*Making Monstrous*) and Castle read Gothic fiction as a force of prescient psychoanalytic critique. Later studies follow in this psychoanalytical vein (Bruhm, Punter), or expand it in a socio-political direction (Chaplin, Schmitt, Smith). Some studies emphasize the influence of the Gothic in specific genres (Gamer, Bruhm, Castle), whereas others explore a broader Gothic 'poetics' (Williams) or the Gothic's deeply 'counterfeit' process of identity-formation (Hogle). Excellent general introductions are Botting (*Gothic*) and Hogle's Companion.

See also: Gender and Sexuality; Class, Economics, Politics; Nationalism, Race, Colonialism, Empire; Narrative and the Novel

Baldick, Chris, *In Frankenstein's Shadow: Myth, Monstrosity and Nineteenth-Century Writing*, Oxford: Clarendon, 1987.

Botting, Fred, *Gothic*, New York: Routledge, 1996.

—— *Making Monstrous: Frankenstein, Criticism, Theory*, Manchester: Manchester University Press, 1991.

Bruhm, Steven, *Gothic Bodies: The Politics of Pain in Romantic Fiction*, Philadelphia: University of Pennsylvania Press, 1994.

Castle, Terry, *The Female Thermometer: Eighteenth-Century Culture and the Invention of the Uncanny*. Oxford: Oxford University Press, 1995.

Chaplin, Sue, *The Gothic and the Rule of Law, 1764–1820*, New York: Palgrave Macmillan, 2007.

Gamer, Michael, *Romanticism and the Gothic: Genre, Reception, and Canon Formation*, Cambridge: Cambridge University Press, 2000.

Hogle, Jerrold E. *The 'Undergrounds' of The Phantom of the Opera: Sublimation and the Gothic in Leroux's Novel and Its Progeny*. New York: St. Martin's Press, 2002.

Hogle, Jerrold E. (ed.), *The Cambridge Companion to Gothic Literature*, Cambridge: Cambridge University Press, 2002.

Punter, David, *Gothic Pathologies: The Text, the Body, and the Law*, New York: St. Martin's Press, 1998.

Schmitt, Cannon, *Alien Nation: Nineteenth-Century Gothic Fictions and English Nationality*, Philadelphia: University of Pennsylvania Press, 1997.

Sedgwick, Eve Kosofsky, *The Coherence of Gothic Conventions*, New York: Methuen, 1976.

Smith, Andrew, *Gothic Radicalism: Literature, Philosophy, and Psychoanalysis in the Nineteenth Century*, New York: St. Martin's Press, 2000.

Williams, Anne, *Art of Darkness: A Poetics of Gothic*, Chicago: University of Chicago Press, 1995.

History

Perhaps more than any other category, one can say that 'history' encompasses all of Romantic criticism, even those studies that typify the supposed ahistoricism of which various approaches like New Criticism or deconstruction have been accused. That said, we have limited the following list to texts that reflect both an on-going concern with charting the diverse cultural, social and political history of the Romantic period, particularly the 're-emergence' of history in New Historical study (Chandler, Levinson, Liu, McGann, Roe). The list also includes reflections on the rise of history and historical study in the period (Bann, Groom), as well as studies that reflect the period's anxieties about historical identity (Christensen, Siskin) or concerns about how history and literature are mutually re-forming (Rajan and Wright).

Bann, Stephen, *Romanticism and the Rise of History*, New York: Twayne, 1995.

Chandler, James, *England in 1819: The Politics of Literary Culture and the Case of Romantic Historicism*, Chicago: University of Chicago Press, 1998.

Christensen, Jerome, *Romanticism and the End of History*, Baltimore: Johns Hopkins University Press, 2000.

Fay, Elizabeth A., *Romantic Medievalism: History and the Romantic Literary Ideal*, New York: Palgrave Macmillan, 2002.

Groom, Nick, *The Making of Percy's Reliques*, Oxford: Oxford University Press, 1999.

Jarvis, Robin, *Romantic Writing and Pedestrian Travel*, New York: St. Martin's Press, 1997.

Levinson, Marjorie *et al.*, *Re-Thinking Historicism: Critical Readings in Romantic History*, New York: Blackwell, 1989.

Liu, Alan, *Wordsworth: The Sense of History*, Stanford: Stanford University Press, 1989.

McGann, Jerome, *The Beauty of Inflections: Literary Investigations in Historical Method and Theory*, Oxford: Clarendon Press, 1985.

Rajan, Tilottama and Julia M. Wright (eds), *Romanticism, History, and the Possibilities of Genre: Re-forming Literature, 1789–1837*, Cambridge: Cambridge University Press, 1998.

Roe, Nicholas (ed.), *Keats and History*, Cambridge: Cambridge University Press, 1995.

Siskin, Clifford. *The Historicity of Romantic Discourse*. New York: Oxford University Press, 1988.

Imagination, Prophecy, the Sublime

One might call these the three central issues of an earlier Romantic criticism, and thus of Romanticism itself, and so readers should consult many of the General Introductions listed above for their preoccupation with and detailed accounts of these issues. Some of the following texts tarry longer with an earlier tradition that championed the sublime properties the Romantic prophetic imagination (Barth, Engell, Paley). Others investigate these terms more ideologically and thus attend to the representational purchase Romanticism did, or did not, claim for the imagination and prophecy (Balfour, Goldsmith, Pyle). Related to the psychological valence of earlier critics of Romantic imagination such as Bloom or Hartman, later critics like Ferguson, Hertz, and Wieskel take up the figure of the Romantic sublime as a figure for examining this imagination's psychological complexity.

See also: General Introductions.

Balfour, Ian, *The Rhetoric of Romantic Prophecy*, Stanford: Stanford University Press, 2002.

Barth, Robert J., *Romanticism and Transcendence: Wordsworth, Coleridge, and the Religious Imagination*, Columbia: University of Missouri Press, 2003.

Engell, James, *The Creative Imagination: Enlightenment to Romanticism*, Cambridge, MA: Harvard University Press, 1981.

Ferguson, Frances, *Solitude and the Sublime: Romanticism and the Aesthetics of Individuation*, New York: Routledge, 1992.

Goldsmith, Steven, *Unbuilding Jerusalem: Apocalypse and Romantic Representation*, Ithaca: Cornell University Press, 1993.

Hertz, Neil, *The End of the Line: Essays on Psychoanalysis and the Sublime*, New York: Columbia University Press, 1985.

Paley, Morton D., *Apocalypse and Millennium in English Romantic Poetry*, Clarendon: Oxford University Press, 1999.

Pyle, Forest, *The Ideology of Imagination: Subject and Society in the Discourse of Romanticism*, Stanford: Stanford University Press, 2005.

Wieskel, Thomas, *The Romantic Sublime: Studies in the Structure and Psychology of Transcendence*, Baltimore: Johns Hopkins University Press, 1976.

Medicine, Science, Technology

Modern medicine and the disciplines of science in general emerged during the Romantic period, and both the cultural turn in Romantic criticism and its attention to the connection between literature and other disciplines has produced a rich and growing body of work on medicine and science. King-Hele on the influence of Erasmus Darwin on Romantic thought is an early instance of this work. The most recent history of Romantic science, and one of the best, is Holmes, and any study of Romantic medical science needs to start with the encyclopaedic writings of Roy Porter on the topic, of which we have listed only one. The Cunningham/Jardine, and later the Schaffer, Fulford/Lee/Kitson and Herringman collections are all excellent overviews of the state of the field. Herringman's monograph explores geology as the Romantic marker of a historical consciousness about which the Victorians would soon become especially anxious. Allard and Wallen offer differing theoretical perspectives on the impact of medicine and the medicalized body (and body politic) on Romantic thought and politics (Golinski approaches similar concerns via the discourse of Romantic chemistry), while Richardson relates the physiology of Romantic brain science to the emerging fields of what we now call psychology and cognitive science. Underwood explores the impact of scientific thought on Romantic political economy and Bewell examines how medical discourse informed British colonial practice. Others take up literature's preoccupation with vitality and life science at the centre of the time's philosophical and religions debates (Gigante, Richards, Ruston), and thus, like other texts on this list, productively elide previous divisions between the scientific and literary imaginations. Related is the exploration of a rising anxiety about the effects of technology (Jones).

See also: Nationalism, Race, Colonialism, Empire; Imagination, Prophecy, the Sublime; Psychology, Subjectivity, Identity; Narrative and the Novel; Poetry; Print Culture and Readership.

Allard, James, *Romanticism, Medicine, and the Poet's Body*, Aldershot: Ashgate, 2007.

Bewell, Alan, *Romanticism and Colonial Disease*, Baltimore: Johns Hopkins University Press, 1999.

Cunningham, Andrew and Nicholas Jardine, *Romanticism and the Sciences*, Cambridge: Cambridge University Press, 1990.

Fulford, Tim, Debbie Lee, and Peter J. Kitson (eds.), *Literature, Science, and Exploration in the Romantic Era: Bodies of Knowledge*, Cambridge: Cambridge University Press, 2004.

Gigante, Denise, *Life: Organic Form and Romanticism*, New Haven: Yale University Press, 2009.

Golinski, Jan, *Science as Public Culture: Chemistry and Enlightenment in Britain, 1760–1820*, Cambridge: Cambridge University Press, 1992.

Heringman, Noah (ed.), *Romantic Rocks: Aesthetic Geology*, Ithaca: Cornell University Press, 2004.

Heringman, Noah (ed.), *Romantic Science: The Literary Forms of Natural History*, Albany: State University of New York Press, 2003.

Holmes, Richard, *Age of Wonder: How the Romantic Generation Discovered the Beauty and Terror of Science*, London: UK General Books, 2008.

Jones, Steven E., *Against Technology: From the Luddites to Neo-Luddism*, New York: Routledge, 2006.

King-Hele, Desmond, *Erasmus Darwin and the Romantic Poets*, New York: St Martin's Press, 1986.

Porter, Roy, *The Greatest Benefit to Mankind: A Medical History of Humanity*, New York: W. W. Norton and Company, 1997.

Richards, Robert J., *The Romantic Conception of Life: Science and Philosophy in the Age of Goethe*, Chicago: University of Chicago Press, 2002.

Richardson, Alan, *British Romanticism and the Science of the Mind*, Cambridge: Cambridge University Press, 2001.

Ruston, Sharon, *Shelley and Vitality*, New York: Palgrave, 2005.

Shaffer, Elinor S. (ed.), *The Third Culture: Literature and Science*, Berlin and New York: W. De Gruyter, 1998.

Underwood, Ted, *The Work of the Sun: Literature, Science, and Political Economy, 1760–1860*, New York: Palgrave Macmillan, 2005.

Wallen, Martin, *City of Health, Fields of Disease: Revolutions in the Poetry, Medicine, and Philosophy of Romanticism*, Aldershot: Ashgate, 2004.

Narrative and the Novel

Romantic novels were a prominent and popular literary genre of the late eighteenth and early nineteenth centuries, reflecting the desire of authors to reach and influence a quickly expanding and diversifying readership. Yet against the achievement of great realist writers of the later nineteenth century (Dickens, Eliot, etc.), with few exceptions (Austen, *Frankenstein*) the Romantic novel was, if not marginalized in the same way that drama or Gothic fiction had been, at least institutionalized as culturally and philosophically somewhat inferior to Victorian fiction or to Romantic and Victorian poetry in general. In many ways the reclamation of Romantic fiction over the past decades has been as profound as that of women writers, and in fact the two resurgences, following in the wake of Gilbert and Gubar's *Madwoman in the Attic*, are intimately connected (see Armstrong). Watt, Lukács and Bakhtin are also key theoretical influences here. Watt ties the rise (and triumph) of the novel to eighteenth-century philosophy, the emergence of the middle class and individualism, and the re-negotiation of women's roles in the public sphere. Lukács's study, written in 1914–15, critiques the novel's relationship to and reflection of an essentially bourgeois ideology, thus exposing the agon of the genre's historical consciousness. For Bahktin the novel is less genre than a cultural force expressed by the text's sedimented and shifting historical voices. This radicalization of the form in theory meets more recent poststructuralist, historicist, and cultural materialist approaches to literature to produce a rich body of subsequent criticism on the Romantic novel. This work examines the Romantic novel's reflection and critique of nationalist (Duncan, Ferris, Trumpener) and political (Kelley) ideas and ideals, in the process subtending the spectres of colonialism and empire. Others read narrative as an expressive mode that both diagnoses and is symptomatic of the body politic (Logan) or as a radical hermeneutic power challenging Romantic historical, cultural and political presuppositions (Rajan). Still others take up the significance of Gothic fiction (Kilgour) and the rise of detective or forensic fiction (Rzepka, Thomas) in the Romantic period. Simpkins' special issue of *Studies in the Novel* crystallizes the emergence of the Romantic novel at a particularly crucial moment in the criticism. The essays collected by Heydt-Stevenson and Sussman offer a current, if brief, survey of the field.

See also: General Introductions; Class, Economics, Politics; Gothic; Nationalism, Race, Colonialism, Empire; Poetry; Print Culture and Readership

Armstrong, Nancy, *Desire and Domestic Fiction: A Political History of the Novel*, New York: Oxford University Press, 1987.
—— *How Novels Think: The Limits of British Individualism from 1719–1900*, New York: Columbia University Press, 2005.
Duncan, Ian, *Scott's Shadow: The Novel in Romantic Edinburgh*, Princeton: Princeton University Press, 2007.
Ferris, Ina, *The Romantic National Tale and the Question of Ireland*, Cambridge: Cambridge University Press, 2002.
Heydt-Stevenson Jillian and Charlotte Sussman (eds), *Recognizing the Romantic Novel: The New Histories of British Fiction, 1780–1830*, Liverpool: Liverpool University Press, 2008.
Kelley, Gary, *English Fiction of the Romantic Period*, London: Longman, 1989.
Kilgour, Maggie, *The Rise of the Gothic Novel*, London: Routledge, 1995.
Logan, Peter Melville, *Nerves and Narrative: A Cultural History of Hysteria in Nineteenth-Century British Prose*, Berkeley: University of California Press, 1992.

Lukács, Gyorgy, *The Historical Novel*, Hannah and Stanley Mitchell, trans., London: Merlin Press, 1962.

Rajan, Tilottama, *Romantic Narrative: Shelley, Hays, Godwin, Wollstonecraft*, Baltimore: Johns Hopkins University Press, 2011.

Rzepka, Charles J., *Detective Fiction*, New York: Polity, 2003.

Simpkins, Scott (ed.), 'The Romantic Novel', special issue of *Studies in the Novel*: 26.2 (Summer 1994), pp. 1–197.

Thomas, Ronald R., *Detective Fiction and the Rise of Forensic Science*, Cambridge: Cambridge University Press, 1999.

Trumpener, Katie, *Bardic Nationalism: The Romantic Novel and the British Empire*, Princeton: Princeton University Press, 1997.

Watt, Ian, *The Rise of the Novel: Studies in Defoe, Richardson, and Fielding*, Berkeley: University of California Press, 1957.

Nationalism, Race, Colonialism, Empire

Closely related to (and as capacious as) the above category on Class, Economics, and Politics is writing on issues of Nationalism, Race, Colonialism and Empire in Romantic literature. Three central theoretical orientations here, if not always confronted directly, are Bhabha, Said, and Spivak, who explore national and international literary projects for the identities they efface as well as represent in order to implement and enforce their cultural power. The works cited below examine the relationship between 'domestic' British identity and 'global' ambition in the East and West, although this 'colonialism' also becomes the template for exploring the multiple national personalities of British writing closer to home, especially via the negotiation between British, Irish, and Scottish writings.

See also: Class, Economics, Politics; Drama and Theatre; Gender and Sexuality; Narrative and the Novel; Poetry

Bhabha, Homi K., *The Location of Culture*, New York: Routledge, 1994.

Bolton, Carol. *Writing the Empire: Robert Southey and Romantic Colonialism*. London: Pickering and Chatto, 2007.

Colley, Linda, *Britons: Forging the Nation, 1707–1837*, New Haven: Yale University Press, 1992.

Davis, Leith, Ian Duncan, and Janet Sorensen (eds), *Scotland and The Borders of Romanticism*, Cambridge: Cambridge University Press, 2004.

Fulford, Tim and Peter J. Kitson, *Romanticism and Colonialism: Writing and Empire, 1780–1830*, Cambridge: Cambridge University Press, 1998.

Kitson, Peter J., *Romantic Literature, Race, and Colonial Encounter*, New York: Palgrave Macmillan, 2007.

Leask, Nigel, *British Romantic Writers and the East: Anxieties of Empire*, Cambridge: Cambridge University Press, 1992.

Lloyd, David, *Anomalous States: Irish Writing and the Post-colonial Moment*, Durham: Duke University Press, 1993.

Makdisi, Saree, *Romantic Imperialism: Universal Empire and the Culture of Modernity*, Cambridge: Cambridge University Press, 1998.

Porter, Roy and Mikuláš Teich, *Romanticism in National Context*, Cambridge: Cambridge University Press, 1988.

Richardson, Alan and Sonia Hofkosh, (eds.), *Romanticism, Race, and Imperial Culture, 1780–1834*, Bloomington: Indiana University Press, 1996.

Said, Edward, *Culture and Imperialism*, New York: Knopf, 1993.

Spivak, Gayatri Chakravorty, *In Other Worlds: Essays in Cultural Politics*, New York: Methuen, 1987.

Thomas, Helen, *Romanticism and Slave Narratives: Transatlantic Testimonies*, Cambridge: Cambridge University Press, 2000.

Wright, Julia M., *Ireland, India, and Nationalism in Nineteenth-Century Literature*, Cambridge: Cambridge University Press, 2007

Philosophy

The study of Romantic philosophy needs to be separated from, if ultimately linked back to, that of Romantic theory and criticism, primarily because of the vexed relationship between British and German thought. British thought, and subsequently literary criticism, has tended to view with some suspicion the influence of German Romantic, idealist and transcendentalist philosophy brought to English soil (and often plagarized) by Coleridge (see McFarland), despite its profound influence on later Victorian cultural mores (as in Arnold or Carlyle). That so much of this German 'theory' was not yet read in translation at the time and so existed as part of the 'ideology' through which we have read Romanticim (see McGann above) has, the argument goes, occluded our appreciation of the profound influence of British empiricist thought on Romantic literature. Such recent historicist turns also react against the influence of continental philosophy and theory in Romantic criticism (Krell, Rajan and Plotnitsky, Redfield), without recognizing the extent to which these works are in profound dialogue with the British tradition itself. Of particular relevance here is the productive revisitation of the Scottish Enlightenment (Broadie) and Scottish Common Sense (Budge), although productively complicating this narrative is Caruth, who reads the anxiety of British empiricism forward to Kant and eventually to psychoanalysis. A number of studies put aesthetics, politics and philosophy, both British and German, in productive dialogue (Caruth, Esterhammer, Ferris, and again Redfield). For a detailed sense of the achievement of German Romantic thought, see Beiser as well as others on the list.

See also: General Introductions; Romantic Theory and Criticism

Beiser, Frederick, *Enlightenment, Revolution, and Romanticism: The Genesis of Modern German Political Thought, 1790–1800*, Cambridge, MA: Harvard University Press, 2003.

—— *The Romantic Imperative: The Concept of Early German Romanticism*, Cambridge, MA: Harvard University Press, 2000.

Broadie, Alexander (ed.), *The Cambridge Companion to the Scottish Enlightenment*, Cambridge: Cambridge University Press, 2003.

Budge, Gavin (ed.), *Romantic Empiricism: Poetics and the Philosophy of Common Sense, 1780–1830*, Lewisburg: Bucknell University Press, 2007.

Caruth, Cathy, *Empirical Truths and Critical Fictions: Locke, Wordsworth, Kant, Freud*, Baltimore: Johns Hopkins University Press, 1991.

Esterhammer, Angela, *The Romantic Performative: Language and Action in British and German Romanticism*, Stanford: Stanford University Press, 2002.

Ferris, David, *Silent Urns: Romanticism, Hellenism, Modernity*, Stanford: Stanford University Press, 2000.

Krell, David Farrell, *Contagion: Sexuality, Disease, and Death in German Idealism and Romanticism*, Bloomington: Indianapolis University Press, 1998.

Lacoue-Labarthe, Philippe and Jean-Luc Nancy, *The Literary Absolute: The Theory of Literature in German Romanticism*, Philip Barnard and Cheryl Lester, trans., Albany: State University of New York Press, 1988.

McFarland, Thomas, *Coleridge and the Pantheist Tradition*. Oxford: Oxford University Press, 1969.

Rajan, Tilottama and Arkady Plotnitsky (eds), *Idealism without Absolutes: Philosophy and Romantic Culture*, Albany: State University of New York Press, 2004.

Redfield, Marc, *Phantom Formations: Aesthetic Ideology and the Bildungsroman*, Ithaca: Cornell University Press, 1996.

Poetry

If the Romantics were anxious about the status of poetry and the role of the poet, especially in the face of the rise of the novel and the rise of a mass readership for prose, by the mid-twentieth century their poetry (at least that of Big Five or Six, depending on Byron's inclusion) ended up, rather paradoxically, at the centre of the British literary canon as a sign of literature's civilizing function in the classroom. By the later twentieth century all that had changed. The various influences of poststructuralism, deconstruction, New Historicism, and cultural materialism started to chart in Romantic poetry and contemporary responses to poetry the forces of irony (Cooper, Simpson), history (Roe, Zimmerman), and/or politics (Cox, Cronin, Janowitz, Keach), or read poetry's anxiety about its future influence (Bennett). Slightly preceding this body of work is the examination of Romantic poetic form as a mode of historical thought, a concerted response to history (Curran, McFarland, Wolfson) rather than repression of it (Levinson), and in the wake of it are readings of Romantic poetry as a mode of cultural regulation (McLane, Mee). Chaviva/Hosek and Kroeber/Ruoff are excellent collections that reflect the state of Romantic poetry criticism at particularly crucial historical moments, though all their contributions remain relevant. The Chandler/McLane Companion brings that comprehensive overview to the present. Either directly or indirectly all of the above expand the previously narrow consideration of 'legitimate' or classical poetic genre (epic, elegy, etc.) to entail the study of popular forms such as ballads, working-class poetry, and satirical and political verse by both canonical and non-canonical writers.

Bennett, Andrew, *Romantic Poets and the Culture of Posterity*, Cambridge: Cambridge University Press, 1999.

Chander, James and Maureen McLane (eds), *The Cambridge Companion to British Romantic Poetry*, Cambridge: Cambridge University Press, 2008.

Cooper, Andrew, *Doubt and Identity in Romantic Poetry*, New Haven: Yale University Press, 1988.

Cox, Jeffrey N. *Poetry and Politics in the Cockney School: Keats, Shelley, Hunt and Their Circle*, Cambridge: Cambridge University Press, 1998.

Cronin, Richard, *The Politics of Romantic Poetry: In Search of the Pure Commonwealth*, New York: St. Martin's Press, 2000.

Curran, Stuart, *Poetic Form and British Romanticism*, Oxford: Oxford University Press, 1986.

Hošek, Chaviva and Patricia Parker (eds), *Lyric Poetry: Beyond New Criticism*, Ithaca: Cornell University Press, 1985.

Janowitz, Anne, *Lyric and Labour in the Romantic Tradition*, Cambridge: Cambridge University Press, 1998.

Keach, William, *Arbitrary Power: Romanticism, Language, Politics*, Princeton: Princeton University Press, 2004.

Kroeber, Karl and Gene Ruoff (eds), *Romantic Poetry: Recent Revisionary Criticism*, New Brunswick: Rutgers University Press, 1993.

Levinson, Marjorie, *The Romantic Fragment Poem: A Critique of a Form*. Chapel Hill: University of North Carolina Press, 1986.

McFarland, Thomas, *Romanticism and the Forms of Ruin: Wordsworth, Coleridge, and the Modalities of Fragmentation*, Princeton: Princeton University Press, 1981.

McLane, Maureen, *Romanticism and the Human Sciences: Poetry, Population, and the Discourse of the Species*, Cambridge: Cambridge University Press, 2000.

Mee, Jon, *Romanticism, Enthusiasm, and Regulation: Poetics and the Policing of Culture in the Romantic Period*, Oxford: Oxford University Press, 2003.

Simpson, David, *Irony and Authority in Romantic Poetry*, Totowa: Rowman and Littlefield, 1979.

Wolfson, Susan, *Formal Charges: The Shaping of Poetry in British Romanticism*, Stanford: Stanford University Press, 1997.

Zimmerman, Sarah M., *Romanticism, Lyricism, History*, Albany: State University of New York Press, 1999.

Psychology, Subjectivity, Identity

Like the keyword Imagination, Psychology, Subjectivity or Identity suggest notions of Romantic individuality, progress and self-fulfilment, traditionally associated with Romantic literature and thought. Such notions are expressed in many of the studies listed under General Introductions or Imagination,

Prophecy, and the Sublime. In one way or another the studies below all complicate or contest these notions. The Bloom collection indicates this darkening of our critical vision of Romantic consciousness, a complicating of the Romantic turn inward taken up later by Beer and Wilner. Others explore the history of madness in the Romantic period (Burwick, Porter). The psychological disciplines were not yet defined in the Romantic period; nonetheless one can trace the affinity between psychoanalysis and Romanticism (Faflak, Punter) or use a psychoanalytical methodology to re-think the Romantic cultural psyche (Pfau). Richardson explores psychology in relationship to an incipient Romantic cognitive science, while Henderson explores how, instead of a singular Romantic identity, various discourses – literature, science, philosophy, political economy – produced competing models of the mind and thus a diverse number of Romantic subjectivities.

See also: General Introductions; Gender and Sexuality; Imagination, Prophecy, the Sublime; Medicine, Science, Technology; Narrative and the Novel; Poetry; Print Culture and Readership

Beer, John, *Romantic Consciousness: Blake to Mary Shelley*, New York: Palgrave Macmillan, 2004.

Bloom, Harold (ed.), *Romanticism and Consciousness: Essays in Criticism*, New York: W. W. Norton and Company, 1970.

Burwick, Frederick, *Poetic Madness and the Romantic Imagination*, University Park, PA: Pennsylvania State University Press, 1996.

Faflak, Joel, *Romantic Psychoanalysis: The Burden of the Mystery*. Albany: State University of New York, 2008.

Henderson, Andrea, *Romantic Identities: Varieties of Subjectivity, 1774–1830*. Cambridge: Cambridge University Press, 1996.

Pfau, Thomas, *Romantic Moods: Paranoia, Trauma, and Melancholy, 1790–1840*, Baltimore: Johns Hopkins University Press, 2005.

Porter, Roy, *Mind-Forg'd Manacles: A History of Madness in England from the Restoration to the Regency*, London: Athlone Press, 1987.

Punter, David, *The Romantic Unconscious: A Study in Narcissism and Patriarchy*, New York: New York University Press, 1989.

Richardson, Alan, *The Neural Sublime: Cognitive Theories and Romantic Texts*, Baltimore: Johns Hopkins University Press, 2010.

Wilner, Josh, *Feeding on Infinity: Readings in the Romantic Rhetoric of Internalization*, Baltimore: Johns Hopkins University Press, 2000.

Print Culture and Readership

Guided by the tutelary spirits of post-Marxist critics like Thompson and Williams, there has been a surge in interest in Romantic print culture as a broader designation that takes in literature as only one mode for the dissemination and communication of ideas in the Romantic public sphere. A central theoretical influence on this material has been the work of German philosopher and sociologist Jürgen Habermas, who articulates the rise of an independent sphere for the formation and reformation of public opinion between the private or domestic sphere and the official interests of the state. Closely related to the political empowerment entailed by print culture is the issue of readers, both as they are formed by print's various media and genres and as these readerships influence shifts in public tastes in turn. Klancher is the key text here for reading Altick's pioneering work on the explosion of print and reading in the Victorian era back to its origins in the later eighteenth century. See also Franta, Jackson, Magnuson and, most recently, St Clair's exhaustive study of England as a reading nation. Other works explore the radical politics of alternative print cultures (Gilmartin, McAlman), anxieties about the status of literature and the public control of readerships (Keen, Mazzeo, Newlyn), the professional status of literature and literary writers (Siskin), or the psychological complexities of the hermeneutics of Romantic reading (Rajan). A more recent development has been work on book history and the cultural status of the book (Viscomi, Ferris and Keen).

See also: Nationalism, Race, Colonialism, Empire; Class, Economics, Politics

Altick, Richard, *The English Common Reader: A Social History of the Mass Reading Public, 1800–1900*, Chicago: University of Chicago Press, 1957.

Ferris, Ina, and Paul Keen (eds), *Bookish Histories: Books, History, and Commercial Modernity, 1700–1900*, Basingstoke: Palgrave Macmillan, 2009.

Franta, Andrew, *Romanticism and the Rise of the Mass Public*, Cambridge: Cambridge University Press, 2007.

Gilmartin, Kevin, *Print Politics: The Press and Radical Opposition in Early Nineteenth-Century England*, Cambridge: Cambridge University Press, 1997.

Jackson, Heather J., *Romantic Readers: The Evidence of Marginalia*, New Haven: Yale University Press, 2005.

Keen, Paul, *The Crisis of Literature in the 1790s: Print Culture and the Public Sphere*, Cambridge: Cambridge University Press, 1999.

Klancher, Jon, *The Making of English Reading Audiences, 1790–1832*, Madison: University of Wisconsin Press, 1987.

Magnuson, Paul, *Reading Public Romanticism*, Princeton: Princeton University Press, 1998.

Mazzeo, Tillar J., *Plagiarism and Literary Property in the Romantic Period*, Philadelphia: University of Pennsylvania Press, 2007.

McCalman, Iain, *Radical Underworld: Prophets, Revolutionaries, and Pornographers in London, 1795–1840*, Cambridge: Cambridge University Press, 1988.

Newlyn, Lucy, *Reading, Writing, and Romanticism: The Anxiety of Reception*, Oxford: Oxford University Press, 2000.

Rajan, Tilottama, *The Supplement of Reading: Figures of Understanding in Romantic Theory and Practice*, Ithaca: Cornell University Press, 1990.

Siskin, Clifford, *The Work of Literature: Literature and Social Change in Britain, 1700–1830*, Baltimore: Johns Hopkins University Press, 1998.

St Clair, William, *The Reading Nation in the Romantic Period*, Cambridge: Cambridge University Press, 2007.

Viscomi, Joseph, *Blake and the Idea of the Book*, Princeton: Princeton University Press, 1993.

Popular and Visual Culture

The recent cultural turn in Romantic studies has opened the field to the possibilities of interdisciplinarity, especially as the Romantics not only anticipate but formulate this approach. Two key areas of this development are the study of popular and visual culture. Galperin traces the emergence of the visual in Romantic literature, while Sha and Fay extend the verbal to visual media. Both working with Blake, Eaves and Viscomi explore visual print media as conduits of aesthetic and political expression and resistance, a political technology of aesthetic production also taken up by Broglio. Thomas and Gidal examine the public culture of exhibition and visual spectacle, which Wood reads in terms of the traumatic impact of an impending modern visuality on Romantic sensibilities. Others write this spectacle large in terms of the city (Chandler and Gilmartin) or the popular culture of improvisation (Esterhammer). McGavran's is one of the few earlier studies on the genre of popular children's literature in the Romantic period. The collection by Connell and Leask offers the most recent overview of the study of Romantic popular culture.

Broglio, Ron, *Technologies of the Picturesque: British Art, Poetry, and Instruments, 1750–1830*, Lewisburg: Bucknell University Press, 2008.

Chandler, James and Kevin Gilmartin (eds.), *Romantic Metropolis: The Urban Scene of British Culture, 1780–1840*, Cambridge: Cambridge University Press, 2005.

Connell, Phillip and Nigel Leask (eds), *Romanticism and Popular Culture in Britain and Ireland*, Cambridge: Cambridge University Press, 2009.

Eaves, Morris, *The Counter-Arts Conspiracy: Art and Industry in the Age of Blake*, Ithaca: Cornell University Press, 1992.

Esterhammer, Angela, *Romanticism and Improvisation, 1750–1850*, Cambridge: Cambridge University Press, 2009.

Fay, Elizabeth A., *Fashioning Faces: The Portraitive Mode in British Romanticism*, Durham: University of New Hampshire Press, 2010.

Galperin, William H., *The Return of the Visible in British Romanticism*, Baltimore: Johns Hopkins University Press, 1993.

Gidal, Eric, *Poetic Exhibitions: Romantic Aesthetics and the Pleasures of the British Museum*, Lewisburg: Bucknell University Press, 2001.

McGavran, James Holt (ed.), *Romanticism and Children's Literature in the Nineteenth Century*, Athens: University of Georgia Press, 1991.

Sha, Richard C., *The Visual and Verbal Sketch in British Romanticism*, Philadelphia: University of Pennsylvania Press, 1998.

Thomas, Sophie, *Romanticism and Visuality: Fragments, History, Spectacle*, New York: Routledge, 2008.

Wood, Gillen D'Arcy, *The Shock of the Real: Romanticism and Visual Culture, 1760–1860*, New York: Palgrave, 2001.

Religion

More recent work on Romantic religion has revised an earlier philosophical sense of a singular Romantic 'religion' of the imagination (see Abrams, *Natural Supernaturalism*) to take up the rather more vexed historical and political situation of religious fervour and movements in the Romantic period (Canuel, Fulford, White), to read how a specific Romantic 'religion' influenced later Victorian thinkers (Prickett), or to explore religious identities previously effaced in the criticism (Spector).

Canuel, Mark, *Religion, Toleration, and British Writing, 1790–1830*, Cambridge: Cambridge University Press, 2002.
Fulford, Tim (ed.), *Romanticism and Millenarianism*, New York: Palgrave, 2002.
Prickett, Stephen, *Romanticism and Religion: the Tradition of Coleridge and Wordsworth in the Victorian Church*, Cambridge: Cambridge University Press, 1976.
Spector, Sheila (ed.), *The Jews and British Romanticism: Politics, Religion, Culture*, New York: Palgrave Macmillan, 2005.
White, Daniel E., *Early Romanticism and Religious Dissent*, Cambridge: Cambridge University Press, 2006.

Romantic Theory and Criticism

The impact of critical theory on Romantic studies from the 1970s and 1980s onwards produced a return to Romanticism as the ground for the emergence of our modern notions of theory and criticism, as a mode of expression concerned to historicize its own place within a history *of* thought. Abrams's text is the classic exploration of Romanticism's reaction to classicism as a shift from the rational to the expressive in theories of literature and aesthetics. The advent of deconstruction (de Man, Bloom) took aim at this expressive model's assumption of organic totality in Romantic literature and identity. Studies or collections by Clark and Goellnicht, Rajan, Wang and Wheeler follow in the wake of this critique. Somewhat later critics explore affinities between Romanticism and postmodernism (Larissy) or re-examine the place of feeling in theory apparently eschewed by a poststructuralist paradigm (Terada). Simpson reads a more recent revolt against the excesses of theory, back to a nationalist divide between an authentic English literary criticism and an overly rational and inhuman theory associated with French and German thought: between empiricism and theory. Behler offers a comprehensive examination of German literary theory, and Swift reads contemporary theory in relationship to a trajectory from French, German, to British Romantic thought.

See also: General Introductions; Philosophy; Sensibility, Sentiment, Sympathy

225

The best recent companion to the study of Romantic Theory and Criticism is Brown.

Abrams, M. H., *The Mirror and the Lamp: Romantic Theory and the Critical Tradition*, New York: Oxford University Press, 1953.

Behler, Ernest, *German Romantic Literary Theory*, Cambridge: Cambridge University Press, 1993.

Bloom, Harold et al., *Deconstruction and Criticism*, New York: Continuum, 1979.

Brown, Marshall (ed.), *The Cambridge History of Literary Criticism, Vol. 5*, Cambridge: Cambridge University Press, 2008.

Clark, David L. and Donald Goellnicht C. (eds), *New Romanticisms: Theory and Critical Practice*, Toronto: University of Toronto Press, 1994.

De Man, Paul, *Romanticism and Contemporary Criticism: The Gauss Seminar and Other Papers*, E. S. Burt, Kevin Newmark, and Andrzej Warminski, eds, Baltimore: Johns Hopkins University Press, 1993.

Larrissy, Edward (ed.), *Romanticism and Postmodernism*, Cambridge: Cambridge University Press, 1999.

Simpson, David, *Romanticism, Nationalism, and the Revolt Against Theory*, Chicago: Chicago University Press, 1993.

Swift, Simon, *Romanticism, Literature and Philosophy: Expressive Rationality in Rousseau, Kant, Wollstonecraft and Contemporary Theory*, London: Continuum, 2006.

Terada, Rei, *Feeling in Theory: Emotion after the Death of the Subject*, Cambridge, MA: Harvard University Press, 2001.

Wang, Orrin, *Fantastic Modernity: Dialectical Readings in Romanticism and Theory*, Baltimore: Johns Hopkins University Press, 1996.

Wheeler, Kathleen M., *Romanticism, Pragmatism, and Deconstruction*, Oxford: Blackwell, 1994.

Sensibility, Sentiment, Sympathy

Concurrent with the reclamation of women writers and the exploration of gender and sexuality in Romantic studies is a revisitation of Romantic literature's concern with modes of feeling associated more with the body than with the intellect. Such feeling was previously marginalized in Romanticism and later in Romantic criticism because of its association with women, radicalism or troubling forms of political or religious enthusiasm. Todd's text is foundational here, followed by the work of Barker-Benfield, Ellis, Johnson, McGann and Pinch. More recent work takes up the politics of sensibility in relationship to abolitionism (Carey), ethics (Bell), and radical culture (Jones). Related to these texts is the study of how sentiment and sensibility are connected to eighteenth-century notions of sympathy as they influence a later Romantic politics of community and justice – how sympathy orchestrates the state (Mitchell) and its social networks (Tuite and Russell's anthology). Marshall explores sympathy's darker internal mechanism, whereas Khalip deploys this critique of sympathy to explore a more radical sense of Romantic community as a mode of dispossession rather than social binding.

Barker-Benfield, G. J., *The Culture of Sensibility: Sex and Society in Eighteenth-Century England*, Chicago: Chicago University Press, 1992.

Bell, Michael, *Sentimentalism, Ethics, and the Culture of Feeling*, Basingstoke: Palgrave, 2000.

Carey, Brycchan, *British Abolitionism and the Rhetoric of Sensibility: Writing, Sentiment, and Slavery, 1760–1807*, Basingstoke: Palgrave Macmillan, 2005.

Ellis, Markman, *The Politics of Sensibility: Race, Gender and Commerce in the Sentimental Novel*, Cambridge: Cambridge University Press, 1996.

Johnson, Claudia L., *Equivocal Beings: Politics, Gender, and Sentimentality in the 1790s: Wollstonecraft, Radcliffe, Burney, Austen*, Chicago: University of Chicago Press, 1995.

Jones, Chris, *Radical Sensibility: Literature and Ideas in the 1790s*, New York: Routledge, 1993.

Khalip, Jacques, *Anonymous Life: Romanticism and Dispossession*, Stanford: Stanford University Press, 2009.

Marshall, David, *The Surprising Effects of Sympathy: Marivaux, Diderot, Rousseau, and Mary Shelley*, Chicago: Chicago University Press, 1988.

McGann, Jerome, *The Poetics of Sensibility: A Revolution in Literary Style*, Oxford: Clarendon Press, 1996.

Mitchell, Robert, *Sympathy and the State in the Romantic Era: Systems, State Finance, and the Shadows of Futurity*, New York: Routledge, 2007.

Pinch, Adela, *Strange Fits of Passion: Epistemologies of Emotion, Hume to Austen*, Stanford: Stanford University Press, 1996.

Todd, Janet, *Sensibility: An Introduction*, London: Methuen, 1986.

Tuite, Clara and Russell, Gillian (eds), *Romantic Sociability: Social Networks and Literary Culture in Britain, 1770–1840*, Cambridge: Cambridge University Press, 2002.

Appendix: A Survey of Romantic Literature Curricula

Sue Chaplin

Chapter Overview

This Chapter is available online at
www.continuumbooks.com/resources/9781441190024

Notes on Contributors

Carol Bolton is a Lecturer in English at Loughborough University. She has published several articles and books on Romantic-period literature and colonialism, the most recent being *Writing the Empire: Robert Southey and Romantic Colonialism* (2007). She is currently working as an editor on *The Collected Letters of Robert Southey*, an eight-part electronic edition of his correspondence, as well as researching British exploration of West Africa in the 1820s.

Sue Chaplin is a senior lecturer at Leeds Metropolitan University and specializes in Romanticism and Gothic Studies. She is the author of *Law, Sensibility and the Sublime in Eighteenth-Century Women's Writing* (2004) and *The Gothic and the Rule of Law* (2007), as well as a number of articles on Romanticism and Gothic fiction. She is executive officer of the International Gothic Association.

Joel Faflak is Associate Professor in English at the University of Western Ontario. He has a special interest in psychoanalysis and Romanticism, and his publications include *Nervous Reactions: Victorian Recollections of Romanticism* (2004), *Cultural Subjects: A Popular Culture Reader* (2005), and *Sanity, Madness, Transformation: The Psyche in Romanticism* (2005). He is currently editing a Broadview edition of Thomas De Quincey's *Confessions of an English Opium Eater*.

Elizabeth Fay is Professor and Director of The Research Center for Urban Cultural History at the university of Massachusetts, Boston. She specialises in literature and society, women's writing and feminist criticism, and is the author of *A Feminist Introduction to Romanticism*, as well as *Romantic Medievalism: History and the Romantic Literary Ideal* (2002) and *The Siege of Valencia: A Parallel Text Edition* (2002).

Adeline Johns-Putra is Senior Lecturer in English at the University of Exeter. She is author of *Heroes and Housewives: Women's Epic Poetry and Domestic Ideology in the Romantic Age, 1770–1830* (2001) and *The History of the Epic* (2006), and editor, with Catherine Brace, of *Process: Landscape and Text* (2010). She is currently co-writing a monograph, with Adam Trexler, on literary representations of climate change.

Peter Kitson holds a Chair in English at the University of Dundee and has published widely in Romanticism studies. His recent publications include *Romantic Literature, Race, and Colonial Encounter* (2007) and *Slavery and the Cultures of Abolition: Essays Marking the British Abolition Act of 1807*, edited with Brycchan Carey. He is currently working on a monograph, *China and the Far East in the Romantic imagination*.

Simon Kövesi is Senior Lecturer in Romantic Literature at Oxford Brookes University. He is editor of the *John Clare Society Journal*, and has been involved in editing work on Clare and other labouring-class poets. His book *James Kelman* (Manchester University Press, 2007) is a study of the contemporary Scottish novelist, and his next monograph on John Clare and Ecopolitics will be published by Palgrave.

Rhian Williams is a lecturer in nineteenth-century literature at the University of Glasgow. She has particular research interests in nineteenth-century poetry, especially focused on form and genre, and eco-criticism and has published several articles in these areas. She also has an particular interest in poetry and pedagogy and is the author of *The Poetry Toolkit: The Essential Guide to Studying Poetry* (Continuum, 2009).

Index

Appendix: A Survey of Romantic Literature Curricula

Sue Chaplin

Chapter Overview	

A Note on the Survey

This survey is based upon information provided by universities that is either in the public domain, or that was provided in response to specific queries regarding specialist modules. Thirty-five institutions were considered: 20 in the UK, 12 in the USA and 3 in Canada. What follows is an overview of prevailing trends within and dominant features of Romanticism curricula in terms of periodization, authors, texts, themes, contexts and genres. The material presented here is representative of general pedagogic practices across the curriculum, though consideration is also given to modules that diverge in interesting ways from common practices in terms of content, delivery and methods of assessment.

Where a module is stated to give coverage of a certain author, this signifies that the module includes at least one work (or, at least, an extract from a long poem, essay or novel) as required reading in relation to at least one session. Where an author's work constitutes background or supplemental reading, the module will not be said to give coverage of that author. It is possible that as a result certain writers might appear to be less represented than they are, since lectures invariably cover more than the required reading most of the time. Since it was difficult to assess the content of the curriculum in such detail on the basis of the information provided for this survey, however, the decision was taken to limit 'coverage' to instances where it was clear on the basis of the reading lists and class plans that an author was considered in reasonable detail.

Periodisation, Themes and Contexts

The vast majority (over eighty per cent) of modules focus on the period between 1780 and 1830, with a small number within this percentage narrowing down the time-line to 1785–1820. The remainder extend the period to 1770–1830/40 or some permutation thereof. Around half of modules nevertheless offer introductory coverage of influential pre-Romantic, mid-eighteenth-century writings and contexts such as the Literature of Sensibility, the Graveyard Poets and the work of Jean Jacques Rousseau.

The majority of modules (over 60 per cent) organize the curriculum with reference to themes and contexts rather than the work of individual authors, and the most popular thematic and contextual headings for lectures and seminars include: Revolution; the Sublime; Imagination; Nature; Religion; Gender; the Self; and Empire, Colonialism, or Abolition. Some other less common but still relatively recurrent themes include: Childhood; Eco-Romanticism (or Green Romanticism) and Print Culture. Even those modules that do predominantly organize material according to the work of individual Romantic writers tend to include at least two lectures of a broadly thematic and contextual nature: usually positioned at the beginning and/or the end of the programme, these sessions function as introductions and/or conclusions to the module. None of the modules considered organized the curriculum *purely* in terms of the work of individual writers, which no doubt reflects recent shifts in the conceptualization of 'Romanticism' and, especially, sustained critical interrogations of the traditional Romantic canon.

A significant minority of modules (just under twenty five per cent) offer two or more sessions that address specific theoretical approaches to Romanticism, the most popular of which are Psychoanalysis, Feminism, Eco-Criticism and New Historicism. The dominant pedagogic practice here is to link the theoretical approach under consideration with a key primary source. Understandably, *Frankenstein* serves frequently to open up psychoanalytical readings not only of that text, but of its Romantic and Gothic contexts. Anne Mellor's *Gender and Romanticism* remains a key critical work in terms of addressing primary sources by female and male writers in terms of 'feminine' and 'masculine' Romanticism. The growing influence of Eco-Criticism is also evident even in instances where the module overall does not have an especially theoretical orientation and it is interesting to note that the most common critical approaches to which a session, or part of a session is devoted are Eco-Criticism, New Historicism and Feminism. It is probably safe to say that the inclusion of Eco-Criticism in the undergraduate curriculum is very much a twenty-first-century development.

Poetry

Unsurprisingly, poetry still dominates the undergraduate Romanticism curriculum and all institutions surveyed offer coverage of at least four from Wordsworth, Coleridge, Blake, Keats, Shelley and Byron. All modules considered include at least one work by Wordsworth and the majority of modules give extensive coverage of Wordsworth, Coleridge and Shelley, with at least one session devoted to one or more works by at least one of these poets. A minority of modules (around fifteen per cent) omit coverage of at least one of the 'Big Six', most usually Byron and/or Keats. There was quite considerable diversity in the works chosen, though a certain pattern does emerge: poems from Blake's *Songs of Innocence and Experience* (Blake's longer poems, by contrast, are not that widely represented on the curriculum); poems from *Lyrical Ballads*; one or more of Shelley's longer poems (*Alastor* and *Prometheus Unbound* are most common); extracts from *The Prelude*; Keats shorter poems of 1819; Byron's *Childe Harold's Pilgrimage*. What is evident is that certain works have significant pedagogic value in introducing students to key Romantic themes and contexts (the Sublime, Imagination, the Self, Nature, Revolution, Religion) and poetic genres (the Romantic ode, sonnet, elegy and so on) and, as has been observed, most modules organize the material thematically and contextually to at least some degree. Poetry is rarely separated from its historical contexts and the majority of modules set literary works alongside a range of other non-literary materials; sometimes these are the prose works of the Romantic poets (Coleridge's *Biographia Literaria*, Wordsworth's Preface to the *Lyrical Ballads* and Shelley's *Defence of Poetry* are frequently taught), or essays on aesthetics, politics and literary criticism (Burke on the Sublime; Burke, Wollstonecraft and Paine on the French Revolution; magazine and periodical reviews of Romantic poetry), or autobiographical writings of specific relevance to a key theme (de Quincey's *Confessions of an English Opium Eater*, the journals of Dorothy Wordsworth, the travel writings of Mary Wollstonecraft and Helen Maria Williams, and the proto-Romantic *Confessions* of Rousseau are quite well represented, in different contexts, on various modules).

Over ninety per cent of modules, moreover, have opened up the curriculum to include poetry by writers other than the 'Big Six' and this is especially evident in the growing coverage of poetry by women and the labouring classes. Around three-quarters of modules offer some coverage of the poetry of Charlotte Smith (at least one poem, or extract from a longer poem) and about a fifth of modules devote a session to Smith. The vast majority of modules also include at least one poem by at least one of the following: Anna Laetitia Barbauld; Hannah More; Ann Yearsley; Felicia Hemans; Letitia Elizabeth Landon. Just over half of modules include coverage of the work of John Clare, with many of these modules devoting a session to Clare. A slightly smaller percentage (just under one-third) cover the work of Robert Burns and around fifteen percent include one or more poems by John Thelwall. There is also quite extensive coverage of the role of poetry in the Abolitionist movement and this again has opened up the syllabus to include, for instance, the work of William Cowper, Anna Laetitia Barbauld, Hannah More, Robert Southey, Ann Yearsley and Phyllis Wheatley.

Romantic-Era Fiction

One implication of the broadening of the romantic curriculum has been the increasingly prominent place afforded to fiction of the period. Indeed, this appears to be the area of the curriculum that is developing most rapidly; texts that were almost universally neglected ten years ago (Morgan's *The Wild Irish Girl* and Wollstonecraft's *Maria; or, the Wrongs of Woman*, for instance) now have some presence on undergraduate modules in Romanticism. Over eighty per cent of modules surveyed include a least one work of fiction and it perhaps comes as little surprise to find that Jane Austen is the most well-represented novelist overall. Three-quarters of modules surveyed included at least one of Austen's works, the most popular being *Pride and Prejudice* and *Sense and Sensibility*, with *Mansfield Park* also a common favourite. The coverage given to Austen can hardly be taken for granted, however; the inclusion of her fiction specifically within a *Romanticism* curriculum (as opposed to modules on the long eighteenth century, for instance) represents a fairly recent development, and it undoubtedly offers tutors the opportunity to interrogate traditional constructions of the Romantic canon by alerting students to the problematic relation of Jane Austen to Romanticism until relatively recently. Even students who have not studied Austen previously will be aware of her privileged status with regard to the English literary canon as a whole, and they can be asked to consider why her work might have been for so long excluded from the defining literary movement of her time.

A variety of other fiction is included on Romanticism modules, often presented under diverse headings such as: the Gothic Romance; the Jacobin Novel; the Historical Novel; Irish Writing; the Novel of Manners. The diversity of texts makes it difficult to generalize, but a significant proportion of modules include one or more of the following: a novel by Anne Radcliffe;

Godwin's *Caleb Williams*; a novel by Walter Scott; James Hogg's *Confessions of a Justified Sinner* and – the most popular overall – Mary Shelley's *Frankenstein*. Indeed, where *Frankenstein* is present, it is now often posited as a major text of British Romanticism and it has clear pedagogic value in allowing tutors to re-frame in various ways some of the key themes and contexts of the period. This text can also function to introduce students in an accessible manner to different theoretical approaches to literary texts, especially given the productive Psychoanalytic, Feminist, Marxist and New Historicist readings of the novel that are now widely available in critical anthologies and case books. Along with other Gothic fiction that occupies an increasingly significant place within the curriculum, *Frankenstein* also allows students to engage with the complex interface between Romanticism and the Gothic; it is noteworthy in this regard that around one-fifth of modules include sessions specifically devoted to 'Romantic-era Gothic' and that this is a popular topic for specialist undergraduate modules at level three.

It is fair to say on the basis of this survey, though, that the fiction of the late-romantic period is less well represented than fiction published between 1780 and 1820, though this undoubtedly reflects to some extent the timeline preferred by most tutors in terms of periodizing Romanticism at undergraduate level (see above). What it also suggests, perhaps, is the wider problem of periodization pertaining to late-Romanticism and early Victorianism, particularly with regard to the fiction of the 1820s and 1830s. In terms of the history of the British novel, these decades are often regarded as a rather ambivalent and unproductive period between, to put it broadly, the work of Austen and Scott and the emergence of Victorian Realism. There is evidence that this is changing, however; the emerging critical interest in the 'Silver Fork Novel' (exemplified by the return to print of several significant examples of the genre) is slowly making its way into the undergraduate curriculum especially through specialist option modules at level three; five option modules in the survey gave some coverage to this genre. Texts such as Disraeli's *Vivian Grey* and R. P. Ward's *Tremaine* offer tutors fresh contexts within which to consider questions of genre, class and gender, the production and reception of texts (these works were, of course, mass-produced and exceptionally popular literary commodities), Romantic-era satire, and the cultural and aesthetic significance of 'Dandyism'.

Romantic-Era Drama

Drama is not well represented on undergraduate curricula with around one half of modules teaching no drama whatsoever. Where the genre is taught, it is often positioned in relation to a major canonical author: the most commonly taught example is Byron's 'closet drama' *Manfred*, followed by

Wordsworth's *The Borderers* and Shelley's *The Cenci*. The writer who does receive some attention as a dramatist is Joanna Baillie; she was one of the most highly regarded playwrights of the period, of course, and her inclusion on a significant minority of modules (around twenty per cent) is a welcome acknowledgement of her literary status, as well as a clear indication of the critical re-appraisal of the Romantic canon.

A minority of specialist modules give space to Gothic drama of the Romantic era and to the adaptation of Gothic novels for the stage. This is indeed a small minority (just under five per cent), but it does represent increasing critical interest in previously marginalized genres and in the broader, diverse cultures of the Romantic period. Given the wider shifts in critical conceptualizations of 'Romanticism', and the extent to which these shifts are increasingly influencing the content of the curriculum, it is to be expected that drama, in its various forms, will form an increasingly important component of Romantic-era undergraduate modules in future years.

Specialist Modules

A large number (over seventy per cent) of the universities surveyed across the United Kingdom and North America offer advanced specialist option modules in the Romantic period and these modules are extremely diverse in their content and focus. A significant minority of specialist modules (just over one-third) offer advanced coverage of a single author; in the majority of cases the author is a canonical poet, with Wordsworth, Blake and Shelley emerging as popular choices for specialist study. Other writers who are well represented in this regard, however, include Jane Austen, Charlotte Smith and John Clare. Frequently, specialist modules mediate the work of a single author through a specific theme or context: popular combinations of author, theme and context include Wordsworth and the British landscape; John Clare and 'Green Romanticism'; Blake and Religion; Shelley and Revolutionary Romanticism.

Other specialist modules are organised according to a theme or context that students are likely to have encountered earlier in their studies; indeed, module information in almost all instances stresses the extent to which the specialist module builds upon and expands students' existing understanding of a given topic. Around half of modules are organized around one or two key themes: the Romantic Imagination, the Romantic Sublime, Revolution, Nature and the Self, for instance, and most of these modules to some degree prioritize the poetry of the period, though by no means only the poetry of the traditional canon. On the contrary, many advanced modules are clearly concerned to challenge traditional notions of canonicity and the work of previously neglected writers features noticeably at advanced level. Several modules study exclusively the work of women poets, or, more broadly, women writers of the Romantic period. The trend towards broadening out the Romantic curriculum is thus reflected more strongly at this level, as one would perhaps expect given some of the limitations that inevitably constrain tutors teaching large undergraduate survey courses at lower levels.

Specialist modules are also more diverse in terms of their treatment of genre. A number of modules take as their subject various forms of Romantic-era fiction, most commonly Gothic fiction and fiction by women. Here one observes a certain elasticity of historical boundaries with modules on the Gothic novel often beginning in the 1760s (with Walpole, of course) and stretching into the 1820s, 30s and 40s (*Wuthering Heights* is a common choice of Gothic-Romantic text and several modules that consider women's fiction include Mary Shelley's *The Last Man* as well as or instead of *Frankenstein*, which will probably have been considered at an earlier point on the curriculum). Several modules devote space to autobiographical and travel writing, and common themes across many courses at advanced level include print cultures, processes of literary production and reception, and the complex politics of authorship and authority in this period. It is within these sorts of contexts that previously marginalized genres come to assume priority, with around ten per cent of advanced modules offering some coverage of, for example, Gothic chapbooks, Gothic drama, the fictions of the Minerva Press and the late-Romantic 'silver fork' novel.

Another broad feature of specialist modules across both continents is their willingness to introduce students to (or deepen students' understanding of) different theoretical, critical and historical approaches to Romanticism. The colonial contexts of the period are often emphasized and the increasing avail-ability of slave narratives and writings by Black authors of the late-eighteenth and early-nineteenth centuries is opening up the curriculum to new content and perspectives. Modules at this level, moreover, are more likely to include on the syllabus quite challenging theoretical and critical works, with these works often deployed specifically to challenge mid-twentieth-century critical approaches to Romanticism. It is not unusual, for instance, to find the work of Paul de Man, Geoffrey Hartman or Mary Jacobus included as *required* (as opposed to recommended) secondary reading; around 60 per cent of modules include a significant element of theoretical reading, and many cite as an assessed learning outcome the acquisition by students of advanced under-standing of theoretical approaches to Romanticism.

Assessment and Teaching

The dominant teaching method across both continents is by way of lecture and seminar with students receiving 2–3 contact hours per week, plus, in many cases, added consultation time related to the submission of assignments at various points during the semester. All modules carry fairly detailed reading lists of primary and secondary sources divided into required and recommended reading, though the quantity and difficulty of the reading of course depends upon the level at which the module is being offered. Most modules on Romanticism are offered in the second year of a degree where one would expect students to be able to read several short poems, say, and two or three secondary sources (depending on length and level of difficulty) for each session. Where modules are offered in the first year of a degree (around 25 per cent of cases), students are generally encouraged to develop skills of close reading and critical analysis through exposure to a smaller range of material: a seminar might focus upon one or two extracts from a longer poem and one relevant secondary source, for example, though detailed supplemental reading will invariably offer the opportunity for a wider engagement with the topic on a week-by-week basis, and students will be required to engage with such reading in order to pass an assignment on a given topic.

In terms of sources used, most modules make use of an anthology of primary materials and the two most popular are *Romanticism: an Anthology*, edited by Duncan Wu and *The Norton Anthology of the Romantic Era*, edited by Stephen Greenblatt and M. R. Abrams. Where novels are studied, critical editions published by Oxford University Press and Norton are very popular. With regard to secondary sources, many modules continue to introduce students to key works of mid-twentieth-century criticism, of course, including Abrams' *The Mirror and the Lamp* and Northrop Frye's *Fearful Symmetry*. In terms of expanding and contesting the boundaries of Romanticism, Jerome McGann's *The Romantic Ideology*, Anne K. Mellor's *Romanticism and Gender*, Mary Jacobus' *Romanticism, Writing and Sexual Difference*, Duncan Wu's *Romanticism: a Critical Reader*, Gary Kelly's *English Fiction of the Romantic Period*, Mary Poovey's *The Proper Lady and the Woman Writer*, Jonathon Bate's *The Song of the Earth* and Marilyn Butler's *Romantics, Rebels and Reactionaries* are some of the diverse secondary materials that have a key place on the undergraduate curriculum in the UK and North America.

There is a trend within academic institutions, and this is especially apparent in the UK, for student materials to specify in detail the learning outcomes and assessment criteria associated with the module, and students are increasingly encouraged actively to reflect upon the process of their learning. In this respect, tutors are making innovative use of web-based technology to promote debate and reflection among students and the tutors themselves. A number of modules are set up to allow students to make use of blogs and online discussion boards in order to discuss their responses to the primary and secondary materials before seminars (for discussion in the seminars), or to reflect upon debates that have taken place in class. In the main, it appears that these blogs and discussion boards are used informally to promote wider discussion throughout the module and to supplement regular sessions, but in some instances web-based learning is used as a component of assessment, with students asked to participate in detailed online discussion as part of a particular class project. Online resources are also frequently utilized in the delivery of modules, with one module at a US institution using only online primary sources which students are to locate themselves, from reputable electronic archives, of course, and present in class. When managed effectively, this form of delivery no doubt has potential in encouraging students to become independent, reflective learners.

Assessment across the romantic curriculum still favours the long essay (2–3000 words, up to 5000 words on advanced modules) and/or an examination at the end of the semester, though increasingly these core assessments are coupled with one shorter assignment, such as a class presentation or a critical analysis of a given primary text, or texts. The North American model favours on the whole more diverse components of assessment throughout the term and, of course, the structure of undergraduate degrees in North America has some impact here; students do not specialize in their core subject until a later stage in their degree programme, whereas British survey modules will invariably be taught to a cohort studying English Literature as their chosen programme of study at levels one and two. There is some evidence, though, that the UK model of assessment is switching towards a more North American model, with shorter and more diverse forms of assessment taking place at various points throughout the semester on around a quarter of modules. Short research exercises, mid-semester class tests, annotated bibliographies and literature reviews are forms of assignment that increasingly complement the more familiar combination of essay and examination.

Conclusion

It is clear that the literature of the Romantic period continues to occupy a central place in the English Literature curriculum and that it continues to be contextualized and theorized in terms of 'Romanticism', even though this term is becoming an increasingly contested category even at undergraduate level. This no doubt reflects key critical and theoretical developments in the discipline over the last thirty years, and it is interesting and encouraging to note the extent to which often complex and intellectually challenging scholarly debates concerning the limits and stability of 'Romanticism' are reflected in the undergraduate curriculum. It remains to be seen how recent moves towards the conceptualization of the 'long nineteenth century' might impact upon the teaching of the Romantic period; one might expect the historical and conceptual borders of 'Romanticism' to be stretched and inter-rogated further in the future.

What is evident also is the diversity that characterizes approaches to teaching Romanticism in the United Kingdom and North America. While, as this survey demonstrates, curricula remain committed broadly to offering coverage of the Romantic canon and its familiar contexts, the majority of modules afford students significant opportunities to encounter litera-tures that would not have been studied at undergraduate level until fairly recently. The inclusion of very varied Romantic-era writings, even at level one, indicates also the extent to which the research interests of staff have a direct bearing upon the formulation of Romanticism curricula across the two continents.

Those interested in exploring further the content and delivery of Romanticism curricula across various institutions might find the following websites useful:

www.bars.ac.uk (the web site of the British Association for Romanticism Studies)

www.rc.umd.edu/pedagogies (offers detailed information regarding current pedagogic practice within the discipline and the range of courses offered in North America and the United Kingdom)

Notes

1 See Wallace and Tayebi on Charlotte Smith. Vardy explores Clare's alternative perspective in detail; recently Adams has considered how Clare's labouring identity shapes his depiction of rural leisure. White's essay demands attention be paid to the material differences in the landscapes Clare inhabited in order to develop a more sophisticated and grounded sense of his psychological engage-ments with the natural world.

2 I would like to thank Alex Benchimol, Tom Bristow and Jeffrey Robinson for their generous conversation and correspondence about these issues during my prepa-ration of this chapter.

3 I wish here deliberately to echo the deep ecology of Devall and Sessions' view of 'Nature as a constant flux or flow of energy transformations' (p. 88).

4 See Bate (1991).

5 See Bate (1997), in which he states, 'Empson is Modernism's Einstein among literary critics. His "both/and" is the twentieth century's most powerful contri-bution to the understanding of Shakespeare because it is both a microscopic and a macroscopic way of seeing. It begins with ambiguous words and syntaxes [...] but it can be extended to the world as a whole' (p. 316).

6 The lines might be interestingly considered in the light of the Acts of Enclosure that were introduced from the middle of the eighteenth century. However, such comparison needs also to take into account Cowper's aesthetic and moral attachment to modestly enclosed spaces, as seen in his enthusiasm for gardens,

expressed variously across *The Task* and in other short lyrics such as *The Pineapple and the Bee* and *The Winter Nosegay* (both 1782).

7 I have chosen a student-accessible edition from Wu (2006, pp. 624–628); this is the earliest version of the poem, which went through subsequent revisions.

8 I use the edition included in Bate (2003, pp. 168–171).

9 Clare's approach here might be likened to that which Pite identifies in Cowper: 'the self does not experience a sublime, self-extinguishing identification with the forms of nature; instead, it seeks to establish with natural things a relation "founded on the affections"' (2002, p. 150).

10 Quotations are from Wu (2006, pp. 1395–1397).

11 Keats and Clare were both published at various points by John Taylor (1781–1864).

CPSIA information can be obtained
at www.ICGtesting.com
Printed in the USA
LVHW080513311020
670295LV00008B/57